# WASHINGTON AND BALTIMORE ART DECO

# WASHINGTON
## AND BALTIMORE
# ART DECO

A DESIGN HISTORY OF NEIGHBORING CITIES

**RICHARD STRINER AND MELISSA BLAIR**

JOHNS HOPKINS UNIVERSITY PRESS ☆ BALTIMORE

Johns Hopkins University Press
2715 North Charles Street
Baltimore, Maryland 21218-4363
www.press.jhu.edu

Library of Congress Cataloging-in-Publication Data
Striner, Richard, 1950–, author.
Washington and Baltimore Art Deco : a design history of
neighboring cities / Richard Striner and Melissa Blair.
        p. cm.
Includes bibliographical references and index.
ISBN 978-1-4214-1162-0 (hardcover : alk. paper)
ISBN 1-4214-1162-8 (hardcover : alk. paper)
1. Architecture—Washington (D.C.)—History—20th
century.  2. Architecture—Maryland—Baltimore—
History—20th century.  3.  Art deco (Architecture)—
Washington (D.C.) 4.  Art deco (Architecture)—Mary-
land—Baltimore.  5. Washington (D.C.)—Buildings,
structures, etc.  6. Baltimore (Md.)—Buildings,
structures, etc.  I. Blair, Melissa, 1975–, author.  II. Title.
NA735.W3S75 2014
720.9753'0904—dc23        2013019365

A catalog record for this book is available from the
British Library.

Special discounts are available for bulk purchases of this
book. For more information, please contact Special Sales
at 410-516-6936 or specialsales@press.jhu.edu.

Johns Hopkins University Press uses environmentally
friendly book materials, including recycled text paper
that is composed of at least 30 percent post-consumer
waste, whenever possible.

Designed and typeset in Scala, Avenir, and Cassannet
by Amy Ruth Buchanan/3rd sister design.

TO OUR SPOUSES, SARA AND STEVE

# ☆ CONTENTS

We, Richard Striner and Melissa Blair—hereafter to be named in the third person—have written this study for as broad a readership as possible. Striner, a native of Washington, DC, and the founding president of its Art Deco Society, wrote the Washington sections. Blair, a trained architectural historian and resident of Baltimore, wrote on the design of that neighboring city.

The book revisits and builds on two earlier works, *Washington Deco: Art Deco in the Nation's Capital* (1984), coauthored by Striner and Hans Wirz, and *Baltimore Deco: An Architectural Survey of Art Deco in Baltimore*, by Sherry Cucchiella (1984). From the beginning we planned a book that would treat both cities in a single new volume. Washington/Baltimore comprises a single metropolitan statistical area, and it claims its own television market, one of the largest in the country. Each morning, many families disperse to both places for work or school, and on weekends and holidays residents can easily travel the forty-five or so miles between city centers for concerts, ball games, and other events. The cities have their own baseball and football teams but nonetheless share a region that the telephone company once took as its name, the Chesapeake and Potomac.

More importantly, the two cities—in the 1930s and 1940s the one a white-collar, New Deal nerve center and the other a gritty port

city—lend themselves to comparative study. Their contrasts prove instructive. Their commonalities and affinities, among them the regional work of Baltimore's John Jacob Zink, who designed fine Art Deco cinemas in both cities, deserve exploration.

Since the two books of 1984, new research, much of it pursuant to preservation campaigns, has added greatly to our knowledge of buildings in both cities. The 1984 studies, in part preservation manifestos, aimed to provide a prima facie case for historic preservation, that is, a literature that preservation activists could use in their efforts to save Art Deco buildings from destruction. The Art Deco Society of Washington emerged as the Washington book neared completion, and Sherry Cucchiella helped to found the Baltimore Deco Society while working on her own book. Neither volume pretended to supply the last or even the best word on the subject.

The campaigns to save Washington and Baltimore Art Deco buildings led to waves of new scholarship that make an updated study appropriate, and of course the preservation challenge remains. More threats to important Art Deco buildings will doubtless develop in both cities. We offer occasional commentary here on successes and failures of preservation campaigns to date. Complete files for the preservation casework of the Art Deco Society of Washington may be found in the Richard Striner Historic Preservation Papers, on deposit with the Historical Society of Washington, DC. These files contain correspondence, internal memoranda, the records of legal proceedings, and illustrations.

Throughout the book we endeavor to place the buildings in interpretive contexts: the evolution of building types, the developmental patterns of the various developers and builders, the careers of architects, and the impact of the buildings on localities and broader urban patterns. In the final analysis, however, this book focuses on a design movement and its presence in the built environment.

Our method was to update the coverage of buildings in both of the 1984 studies by assimilating all the newer scholarship. The endnotes reflect our vast debt to the work of other historians, work that led not only to journal articles but also to National Register and local landmark nominations. We did substantial "windshield surveys" to assess the condition of the buildings today. We pursued new research in archival repositories to uncover as many historical images of the buildings as possible in order to depict them in all of their original glory, as the architects designed them.

Architectural historians approach their work in different ways. Some devote attention to undisputed masterworks or clear and unambiguous examples of "style." We seek to be as comprehensive as possible, especially in light of our view that Art Deco spans a range of overlapping tendencies. Other students of architectural history look away from stylistic exemplars, seeking ever-wider arcs of association, arcs that link architecture with national and local trends, with economics and sociology, and with other interdisciplinary issues of wide interest. We approve of such work and have sought to provide

as much context as possible without straying far from our subject. But we must also note that clear-cut generalizations about builders, architects, patrons, and users of these buildings do not come easily. The builders of 1930s garden apartments, for instance, were often small-scale entrepreneurs for whom biographical data is in many cases scarce and in some cases nonexistent. We combine analysis and presentation throughout, while deferring most generalizations until the conclusion.

Above all, we hope that this book will help the residents of Washington and Baltimore to appreciate what they have. The types of buildings we present—though some may be less glamorous than the Art Deco masterworks of New York City and many do not rise to the flamboyancy of South Miami Beach—illustrate what many other American cities possess. We intend here to show how an international design movement found its way into ordinary places. For this reason the book may be interesting and useful to audiences beyond Washington, DC, Baltimore, and the Mid-Atlantic region.

We thank the following people who assisted us with this book: Joanne Allen, Christopher Ames, Anne Bruder, Robert Brugger, Yvonne Carignan, Carol Chatham, Sherry Cucchiella, Eben Dennis, Zach Dixon, Catherine Scott Dunkes, Carol Ebright, Richard Ervin, Elizabeth Evitts Dickinson, William Evitts, April Fehr, Andria Field, Stephanie Foell, Bill Fort, James Goode, Jennifer Goold, George Gurney, Nancy Hadley, Jacques Kelly, Eric Kohler, Jeff Korman, Richard Longstreth, Linda Lyons, Jerry McCoy, Brian Palmer, Vince Peraino, Alex Sabotka, Julie Schablitsky, Leah Schroeder, Fred Shoken, James Singewald, Kerry Skarda, Richard Wagner, Hans Wirz, and Joe Yates.

# WASHINGTON AND BALTIMORE ART DECO

It emerged from the 1925 Paris Exposition of the Decorative and Industrial Arts. Unfettered by an orthodox creed, Art Deco was a link between the avant-garde, the industrial designers, and the mass-consumption culture of the 1920s and 1930s. It represented the daydreams of an age: the Chrysler Building, with its gleaming pinnacle of stainless steel terraces; the future metropolis envisioned by the filmmaker Fritz Lang and by the artist Hugh Ferriss; swanky apartments full of stylish objects of onyx and blue-tinted glass. Art Deco was the streamlined locomotive designs of Raymond Loewy, the huge clipper planes, and the ocean-liner designs of Norman Bel Geddes. It was the World's Fairs of 1933 and 1939—and the Emerald City of Oz.

The sources of Art Deco can be traced to the early twentieth century: Art Nouveau, the Vienna Secession, and the work of individual designers such as (in Europe) Josef Hoffmann, whose Palais Stoclet in Brussels displayed prototypical Art Deco massing as early as 1905; Erich Mendelsohn, who did pioneering work in the streamline idiom; Eliel Saarinen; and (in America) Bertram Grosvenor Goodhue, whose Nebraska State Capitol building (1922–32) was a prototypical Art Deco skyscraper. These and other early inspirations were fused at the 1925 Exposition Internationale des Arts Décoratifs et Industriels Modernes, a rather lengthy title

that led at the time to abbreviated terms like *Moderne*.

*Art Deco*, a much newer term for the 1925 show and the design movement that it represented, emerged in the 1960s. In 1966 the term was used at a retrospective exhibition at the Musée des Arts Décoratifs in Paris. Then two years later the British art historian Bevis Hillier used *Art Deco* as the title of the first book on the subject.[1]

Scholars disagreed about Art Deco's range. In 1970 the architectural historian David Gebhard argued that the "popular modernism" introduced at the 1925 Paris Exposition had been supplanted in the 1930s by a streamlined style inspired by industrial design.[2] But the influence of the Paris exposition continued long after the twenties, and it frequently combined with the streamlined aesthetics of the thirties. As Hillier emphasized in 1971, "The art of the twenties was not suddenly snuffed out in 1930 with a magician's 'Now you see it, now you don't. . . .' There was a strong continuity."[3]

Proliferating studies of 1930s design revealed a wealth of architectural hybrids, buildings in which the so-called streamline style and the design language of the 1925 Paris Exposition were combined. Even Gebhard viewed them as related subdivisions of an overall movement that he called "the Moderne." For the sake of convenience, we shall use the term *Art Deco*, which is now quite pervasive and for practical purposes canonical.[4]

A more important issue in the task of defining Art Deco is the challenge of assessing its role within the broader crosscurrents of design, and design ideology, between the world wars. A ferocious war of words was taking place among architects, designers, and theorists; it was a polemical war between the advocates of radical modernism and the defenders of design tradition. The traditionalists were increasingly inclined to espouse the principles of Greco-Roman classicism. Many of the radicals invoked what they advertised as "functionalism." They scorned the inherited traditions and instead embraced the future, that is, the future as they envisioned or imagined it: a future whose designs would be bold, abstract, and coolly "rational."

Much of the intensity suffusing this war of words can be linked to World War I (the "Great War" to people living at the time). Its horrendous destructiveness instilled in the 1920s and 1930s a haunted mood among artists and intellectuals. Many believed that Western civilization was approaching decline and fall. Others believed that a new rebirth was approaching. As the intellectual historian Roland Stromberg has observed, for many the war triggered "a sort of apocalyptic, Nietzschean mood which saw in this catastrophe both an awful judgment on a doomed civilization and a necessary prelude to a complete rebirth."[5] This mood became the basis for many of the literary works of the twenties, from Oswald Spengler's *Decline of the West* to T. S. Eliot's *Waste Land* to the cyclical theory presented in Arnold Toynbee's books and essays.

This was also, of course, the milieu in which designers and commentators such as Lewis Mumford, Frank Lloyd Wright, and Le Corbusier developed their diverse sociocultural (and ideological) prescriptions. "The war shattered all continuity afforded by feeling," wrote the commentator Fritz Schumacher in the April 1931 issue of *Architectural Forum*. Consequently,

architects were under "pressure to express [their] time completely. . . . Out of the darkness grows slowly the rose hour of dawn."[6]

The radical modernists sought to make a clean break with the past. Through "machine aesthetics," they argued (and hoped), a new *rational* spirit would arise to redeem the world. "Society is filled with a violent desire for something which it may achieve or may not," proclaimed Le Corbusier in 1923. "Everything lies in that," he continued: "everything depends upon the effort made and the attention paid to these alarming symptoms. Architecture or Revolution. Revolution can be avoided." The way to avoid it was through the "mass production spirit. The spirit of constructing mass production houses. The spirit of living in mass production houses." "The styles are a lie," he insisted.[7] Many others took up the battle cry. In 1929 the social commentator Waldo Frank decried the "architectural lies that our ambitious architects smear over our steel structures." He condemned the ornamental flourishes from previous ages that were "pilfered and stuck about our buildings."[8]

Traditionalists, especially those trained in the École des Beaux Arts tradition, returned the fire. In 1927 Milton B. Medary, president of the American Institute of Architects (AIA), condemned the insistence on abstract form that the radical modernists were foisting upon the profession. With pointed but genteel sarcasm, he tried to poke fun at them: "Let us have an entirely new written language, as well as the physical one; let us stop using the words used by Shakespeare and express our thoughts by sounds never heard before."[9]

Three years later, at a subsequent AIA convention, the traditionalist C. Howard Walker was more severe. He declared that "it has been reserved for the so-called Modernists to be irritated at any resemblance to anything that has calm, and to adore excess in every direction, to be shapeless, crude, eliminated in detail to nothingness, explosive in detail to chaos."[10] Chaos, of course, was the last thing society needed in the aftermath of war, and so impassioned conservatives insisted that the best *design traditions*—the *inspirational* traditions—should be upheld.

This "architecture war" between conservatives and radicals would rage throughout the twenties and thirties. But between the warring camps a kind of "mediation" occurred. And this is where the emergence of Art Deco becomes clear as intellectual history. For in many ways Art Deco was a *middle range* of interwar design between the polarized extremes. The rich eclecticism of its repertoire was in some respects an intellectual signifier.[11]

In 1928 the architectural historian and critic Henry-Russell Hitchcock wrote about the key architectural tendencies of the times. They were essentially past-related, future-related, and mediational. In one camp were the "Traditionalists," those whose "controlling idea" demanded the "adaptation of the various architectural manners of the past to the needs of the moment." At the other extreme were the "New Pioneers," who sought "purity" and "austere beauty" through "ascetic avoidance of ornament." In the middle were the "New Traditionalists," those who were "retrospective in their tendency to borrow freely from the past" yet "modern in that they feel free to use and combine . . . the elements thus borrowed [with] new materials developed by science, controlling them so that they shall not shock the eye." Hitchcock wrote that the 1925 exposition was a prime example of this latter tendency.[12]

Many architects were receptive to design mediation, and they said so. In 1930 an editorial in the *Federal Architect* declared that "modern architecture can be good" so long as it entailed not only a "breaking away from the old architecture" but also a "loyalty to it," in other words, "the Moderne traditionalized, the Traditional Modernized."[13] By the same token, Charles R. Richards, director of New York's Museum of Science and Industry, condemned "the two sets of ideas that divide the architects, viz., dependence upon tradition as the sole source of inspiration and

the conviction that design should be thoroughly adapted to modern requirements." He continued: "In each camp one or the other of these ideas is held with such tenacity and intolerance of the other that real progress is severely handicapped." The antidote: "We need to relinquish our extreme attitudes and bring the two opposing camps together."[14]

One obvious result was the movement in design that is now called "modernized classicism," a ubiquitous presence in Washington and Baltimore between the world wars. A prototype was the Folger Shakespeare Library (1929–32), designed by Paul Philippe Cret. Cret's formula: Greco-Roman foundations—both in compositional principles (symmetry, hierarchy, containment) and in ornamentation (fluted pilasters and bas-relief sculpted panels)—combined with a modernist simplification of form and even a touch of the curvilinear streamlining that would soon become a signature of the thirties.

Modernized classicism was an obvious gesture of reconciliation in the war between conservatives and radicals. So was Art Deco, and the movements would often overlap. It bears noting that an unmistakable synthesis of classical and modernist form had been present at the 1925 Paris Exposition. And the ornamental language of the show was perceived to be a form of architectural compromise right away. In February 1928, for example, the editors of *Architectural Forum* provided close-up views of floral ornamentation in the manner of Edgar Brandt (a key designer whose work had been featured at the Paris Exposition) in an Art Deco commercial building in New York City. The editors observed that "the architects have struck a new note in this example of *conservative modern* decoration."[15]

Many Art Deco designers went beyond the Greco-Roman tradition in their use of ancient iconography. What they sought was the ancient—and the exotic. An extremely important presence in the repertoire of Art Deco was the imagery of ancient Egypt, which was all the rage in the twenties after the sensational discovery (and "opening") of King Tut's tomb. The rampant Egyptology of Art Deco combined with Meso-American Aztec and Mayan motifs.[16] To top it all off, the ancient imagery was juxtaposed with futuristic visions—Buck Rogers and Flash Gordon whimsy.

Now consider these trends in relation to the period's literary output. In *Manhattan Transfer* (1925) John Dos Passos described the Manhattan of the future in relation to the storied world of the ancients: "There were Babylon and Nineveh; they were built of brick. Athens was gold marble columns. Rome was held up on broad arches of rubble. . . . Steel, glass, tile, concrete will be the material of the skyscrapers. Crammed on the narrow island the millionwindowed buildings will jut glittering, pyramid on pyramid like the white cloudhead above a thunderstorm."[17] A few years later the novelist and critic Rebecca West observed that on New York's Lexington Avenue "there is a vast apartment house which rears its dark masses like the Pyramids and which like them is an example of mystery-making in stone."[18]

Through such imagery—imagery that pointedly reached back and forth from the ancient past to the Buck Rogers future to the Jazz Age themes of the twenties—Art Deco offered commentary, through its symbols. It sought to "locate" the culture of the twentieth century in broader patterns of meaning. As the writers of the period obsessed about historical cycles, Art Deco through its very iconography posed the great question that haunted so many intellectuals, Who—and where—are we, in this bewildering age of "the Machine"?

The ancient past and the distant future were temporal points of comparison. Symbols of nature and machine were another form of polarity—and of synthesis. Zigzag forms suggested the force of electrical power, both chained and free, the thunderbolt as well as the harnessed power of the dynamo. Plant, sun, and cloud motifs were among the other nature symbols

adapted by Art Deco. At the spire of the Chrysler Building (1928–30) triangular windows gestured up toward the heavens in a manner that suggested sunrays—but also the interlocking of gears.

The movement that catalyzed at the Paris exposition diffused with astonishing speed around the world. In the same year—1925—an Art Deco commercial building broke ground in New York City: the Barclay-Vesey Building, designed by Ralph T. Walker, of Voorhees, Gmelin & Walker, which was completed in 1927. In 1928 an Art Deco building designed by Walker appeared in Washington: the Chesapeake and Potomac Telephone Company building, at 730 12th Street NW. Walker was one of the American Deco designers who were able to articulate the meaning of their work. In 1928 he proclaimed that designers had come to "a bend in the road, a place in which to pause, where we can look backward over the past and see its contributions and at the same time look forward over the future and glimpse its possibilities."[19]

Few Americans in 1928 could glimpse the future that was hurtling toward them, one of bleak hard times that would afflict the American people on a scale they had never experienced before (notwithstanding the severity of earlier depressions and recessions). The Great Depression, which began in the United States in 1929, was part of a huge global crisis that would give new meaning to the apocalyptic fears of the age. In America, of course, it resulted in the New Deal of Franklin Delano Roosevelt. This began in 1933, the very same year in which Hitler took over in Germany.

Totalitarian movements and regimes were in place around the world already. Italian Fascism and the Soviet tyranny of Joseph Stalin had been part of the political and global picture in the 1920s. But with the rise of Nazi Germany during the thirties, American democracy was under increasing pressure to solve its social problems—especially so as another world war began to loom—lest the "wave of the future," as Anne Morrow Lindbergh would call it,[20] prove to be totalitarian in nature.

American moods in the thirties spanned the full emotional range. The bitterness of the Hoover years would recur and even intensify as the depression lingered. But the upbeat moods of the New Deal era were unmistakable. For some, the dynamic burst of federal action, with its powerful emphasis on public works, gave a whole new dimension to the futuristic state of mind. Some enthusiasts invoked the *opportunity* provided by the Great Depression, the opportunity to clear away outmoded and dysfunctional arrangements and build anew in the manner of twentieth-century pioneers—to "design this day," as Walter Dorwin Teague would express it.[21] It was this state of mind that infused the design vogue for streamlining.

Streamlining became an obvious symbol of progress—progress through speed. But it could also suggest a kind of comfort through stability; it implied a new *control* of unruly events through the "smooth" coordination of planning. A new breed of industrial designers—men like Raymond Loewy, Donald Deskey, Norman Bel Geddes, and Walter Dorwin Teague—imbued the decorative arts with a worship of sleek lines. As early as 1930 Frank Lloyd Wright had proclaimed that "today, it seems to me, we hear this cry 'Be Clean' from the depths of our own need. It is almost as if the Machine had, by force, issued edict similar to Shinto—'Be Clean.' Clean lines . . . clean purposes."[22]

The influence of streamlining in the thirties was comprehensive. At first nothing more than a device for vehicular design (to increase fuel efficiency and speed by reducing wind resistance), it became a pervasive mode of "packaging" applied to a remarkable range of objects. It had customer appeal—it had *sex appeal*—and Americans embraced it in the thirties. It was quickly applied to the building arts, and it even had a musical counterpart: the jazz of the twen-

ties gave way to the *smoother* dynamics of swing in the 1930s.

Streamlining was a powerful presence in American commercial design. But the movement that triumphed in the realm of *governmental* architecture was modernized classicism. By the thirties this mode of design was the preeminent architectural language for public buildings. And it could serve almost any ideology. Both Hitler and Stalin used it, and FDR endorsed it. In Hitler's Berlin it was put to the use of expressing the grandeur of the Nazi Reich. In FDR's Washington it signified what all the different iterations of classicism have conveyed in the American capital down the years: the majesty of free institutions.

Harold Ickes, FDR's secretary of the interior and also his chief of the Public Works Administration (PWA), was delighted by the modernized classical lines of the new Interior Department building, designed by Waddy B. Wood and completed in 1936.[23] Latter-day observers who regard the modernized classicism of the thirties as "fascist architecture" would benefit from pondering the example of Ickes, a fervent anti-Fascist and civil rights advocate who worked with First Lady Eleanor Roosevelt to sponsor the 1939 concert of Marian Anderson, the African American contralto, at the Lincoln Memorial.

Streamlining and modernized classicism were among the distinctive design movements of the thirties. Indeed, they were so distinctive that the people who study (as a matter of preference) the *cohesive* tendencies in architecture regard them as separate "styles." For those who prefer the side of architectural history that yields unambiguous results—as opposed to the study of *eclecticism*, the freewheeling tendency that people who disdain ambiguity in general tend to ignore—a definite range of self-conscious and to some extent mutually hostile design movements can be seen in the 1930s. Regardless of whether we tag them as "styles," they existed, and they had great power.

At one extreme, as we have already noted, were the Beaux-Arts conservatives, who hated "modern design." At the other extreme were the High Art modernists, who prided themselves on the abstract "functionalism" of their work. (Henry-Russell Hitchcock and Philip Johnson began to call the movement for abstract modernism in architecture "the International Style"; they helped to organize a special exhibition in 1932 at the Museum of Modern Art.)[24] Between these poles were the middle-range movements represented by modernized classicism and the work of the 1925 Paris Exposition. And of course by the thirties there was streamlining. But should these movements be defined as separate "styles"? Among the grounds for answering yes is the fact that every one of these movements appealed to an aggressive contingent of critics who proceeded to attack all or most of the others. The architecture war of the interwar decades could be fought on a multitude of fronts.

Parisian Art Deco had its partisans and its defenders. The art critic Helen Appleton Read, for example, declared that the 1925 show was in overall terms an exaltation of machine aesthetics; both the "credo of modern art" and the "glorification of the machine" were "determining factors in the development of this new décor," she declared in 1925.[25] But myriad critics were deriding Art Deco for *not* adopting a consistent "machine-age aesthetic."

Consequently, some defenders of Art Deco took a different tack. The muralist and sculptress Hildreth Meière, whose work was featured in Rockefeller Center and also in the Baltimore Trust Company building, attacked the "Left Wing Modernists" and proclaimed that "human nature demands interest and relief from barrenness by some sort of enrichment."[26] Ralph T. Walker concurred: "The fundamental, spiritual, and intellectual needs of man can never be satisfied with the thin, austere design of the engineer-architect," he wrote.[27]

None of this reasoning could fend off the scorn of the radicals. In addition to their vilification of Beaux-Arts classicism, they ridiculed Art Deco at every opportunity—gently at times but at other times with devastating scorn. In 1934 Alfred H. Barr Jr. and Philip Johnson lamented that the problem in getting Americans used to "machine aesthetics" was not "the conflict against a strong handicraft tradition but rather against a 'modernistic' French machine-age aesthetic."[28]

In the March 1932 issue of *Architectural Review* the British architect Michael Dugdale ridiculed Art Deco through satirical verse in the manner of Alexander Pope:

Lo! Rectilinear the Cupboard climbs
(Always politely moving with the Times).
Step upon step ascending to its Climax,
Within its sheath of Aluminum Plymax.
So too the Lights, that skillfully combine
The rival claims of Function and Design,
Before thy Shrine, Uncertainty, are lit,
To shed their Radiance o'er us as we sit
Discreetly on the Architectural Fence,
Too hard for Sentiment, too soft for Sense.[29]

A more ferocious attack upon Art Deco from the standpoint of "functionalism" was a tirade written by a critic named Ellow H. Hostache that appeared in *Architectural Forum* as the Paris Exposition was winding down:

October is waning—and so is this Exposition. This Exposition! What of it? . . . A few million cubic feet of concrete and plaster, shedding their varnishes and now ready for the *masse* of the demolisher. . . . And what of the Decorative Arts? *Les Arts Decoratifs* are no more! . . . This bastard offspring of anaemic artisanship and efficient salesmanship was not fit to live. . . . But what was it all about? About ornament! The dictatorship of ornament! . . . The modern world is in full formation, and drags with it too many elements of the past lacking any further reason for remaining.[30]

The plaintive tone of this polemic was echoed by a truly remarkable outburst in 1929 by the famous Le Corbusier, an outburst that momentarily swept aside the aspirations (or pretensions) of the modernists to scientific exactitude and expressed a kind of metaphysical mysticism instead: "This century has officially opened to us gates yawning on the infinite, on majesty, silence and mystery. . . . Never was there an epoch so powerfully, so unanimously inspired." And yet "the past has ensnared us. . . . We are cowardly and timorous, lazy and without imagination. . . . As yet we have seen nothing new, done nothing new."[31]

Other radicals adhered to the theme of rationality. They consistently invoked the utilitarian maxim "Form follows function." And according to the standards of no-nonsense functionalism, such critics declared that the streamlining fad of the thirties was just as ridiculous a lapse from the logic of functional design as the jazzy embroidery of Art Deco in its Parisian version. Philip Johnson disdainfully remarked that "principles such as 'streamlining' often receive homage out of all proportion to their applicability."[32] John McAndrew, who succeeded Johnson in the Museum of Modern Art's Department of Architecture and Industrial Art, pointed out sarcastically that "streamlined paper cups, if dropped, would fall with less wind-resistance" but were clearly no better "than the old ones for the purpose for which they were actually intended, namely drinking."[33]

The enthusiasts of streamlining defended their version of "machine aesthetics" energetically. One of the most vocal propagandists for streamlining was the critic Sheldon Cheney, whose 1936 book *Art and the Machine*, coauthored with his wife, Martha, matched the rhetoric of Le Corbusier in its oracular qualities. According to the Cheneys, the use of rounded contours for stationary objects (as opposed to their use in moving vehicles) went beyond the pragmatic: it served a spiritual function (or at least a "cosmic" function) as well. The Cheneys hailed streamlining as a "valid symbol of the contemporary life flow . . . when it emerges as

form expressiveness." The vagueness of this formulation was just the beginning for the Cheneys: "When we see a functionally-formed useful product, smoothly encased in some bright machine-age material, corners rounded off, projections sheared away . . . the machine-conscious mind begins to relate all such products of scientist-artist design back to the most conspicuous symbol and inspiration of the age, as the reverent medieval mind related everything to the symbol of the cross."[34]

Whether writing with his wife or on his own, Cheney would brook no abuse from the functionalists regarding the justifications for streamlining. On the other hand, he was quick to cite the standards of functionalism to denounce the influence of Art Deco, Parisian style. In 1930 he declared that five years earlier Paris had

> spread out the buildings of the Exposition of the Decorative Arts, avowedly to bring to focus contemporary French effort outside of the traditional styles—and to bring world Modernism into agreement with the graceful French talent. But that affair, and the sporadic outcroppings here and there . . . have only gone to show that outside of a few inspired engineers and one or two imported radical architects, the impotent Beaux Arts men still control France.[35]

Sometimes Art Deco was damned with very faint praise. In 1938 the critic Talbot Hamlin, a great admirer of modernized classicism, wrote ambivalently about the Paris Exposition and its influence: "Dislike as we may the overwrought eccentricities of much of the work at that show, it is, I think, indisputable that, without the flood of 'modernism' which followed that exposition [the current] readiness to consider and adopt new forms (slight as that may be) would have been impossible."[36] But while Hamlin disparaged some particular foibles of the Paris Exposition, he defended the eclecticism that the show brought together and exemplified. He attacked the radical modernists for their unmitigated humorlessness:

It is not quantitative functionalism that is at the root of great architecture. It is not abstruse intellectual content of any kind. . . . It is not conformity to any theory. . . . It is never a denial of joy in life. . . . To be beautiful, gracious, enticing—to take the bare limbs of building and make them flower like cherry trees in spring—is this not the engendering power of great architecture? . . . The root of great architecture is like the root of any created beauty, deep in the matrix of human consciousness. It is spontaneity, delight in form. . . . Can it be that the International Style has never learned how to play?[37]

The architecture war got worse as the thirties played out, and its effects were especially severe in the nation's capital. A sweeping revival of classical design was transforming the city. What resulted in the twenties and thirties was a series of buildings that contribute to the "postcard city" of today: the Lincoln Memorial, the National Archives (part of the Federal Triangle project), the Supreme Court building, the Jefferson Memorial, and the National Gallery of Art. All of these buildings were constructed or under construction in the years between the world wars. And most of them were denounced by radical modernists, at times in savage terms.[38] According to David Gebhard, "The intensity of the struggle between the High Art Modernists and the Traditionalists came close to being a religious war" in the 1930s.[39]

In light of the spectacular enmity that flared between the partisans of radical modernism in architecture (the International Style), the vigorous Beaux-Arts tradition of Greco-Roman classicism, the compromise movement for modernized classicism, the movement resulting from the 1925 Paris Exposition, and the captivating movement for streamlining, would it not be appropriate for us to call these movements different "styles"? How else can we keep track of all the many different things that these architects were doing? How else can we really understand the disagreements that were dividing them?

Wasn't Art Deco just one "style" among others in the twenties and thirties?

Yes and no. The era encompassed a very broad range of architectural movements. What matters most, in our opinion, is the fact that *among* these movements—in the broad middle range of design in the interwar decades—a reconciliation was occurring. It was a pattern of reconciliation that the Paris Exposition both exemplified and inspired. And it continued throughout the thirties.

A rich array of design making use of Parisian-style Art Deco, the methods of modernized classicism, and the fad for curvilinear streamlining surged in the thirties. And we can demonstrate that this was occurring. Hundreds of designers felt the impulse to scan the full range of ideas that were in play and then blend the different things they were seeing. We will call the resulting pattern *Art Deco* since the Paris Exposition helped create it. Without that event, as Talbot Hamlin observed, the great synthesis of middle-range design would have been less vibrant and less enduring.

And it was more than just expedient kitsch. It was a tacit declaration of freedom by some excellent designers, a freedom to explore the full range of inspirations that were giving this age its "personality."

Frank Lloyd Wright caught the flavor of the process when he stated in 1930 that neither the "sentimentality of the 'ornamental'" nor the newer "sterility of 'ornaphobia'" could satisfy the needs of the twentieth century. His preference? "I believe that Romance—this quality of the *heart*, the essential joy that we have in living—by human imagination of the right sort can be brought to life again. . . . Architecture, without it, could inspire nothing."[40]

What Wright would achieve as an idiosyncratic master had its counterpart in everyday buildings that expressed the sheer "romance" of modern times—through Art Deco. This book is the story of the movement in Washington and Baltimore.

## WASHINGTON

In 1901—when the nation's capital had reached the year of its centennial—some reform-minded congressmen took action to improve the appearance of the city. They wished it to be everything that their fellow Americans (and future generations) deserved. Led by Senator James McMillan of Michigan, chair of the Senate Committee on the District of Columbia, they created a special Senate Park Commission to revive—and extend—L'Enfant's original plan for the city. Among the members of the commission were distinguished architects such as Daniel H. Burnham and Charles McKim and the landscape architect Frederick Law Olmsted Jr.

Washington was in many ways an urban and civic backwater at the turn of the twentieth century. Local industries, except for the real-estate industry, were small in comparison with those of other major cities in America. With all due respect for the indigenous strengths of the city's intellectual and artistic institutions, much of the city's elite came from elsewhere, descending on Washington for the social season that accompanied sessions of Congress and the Supreme Court. As the twentieth century dawned, there were very good reasons to augment the stature of Washington. Public architecture was a handy and symbolic way to start.

Hence the so-called McMillan Plan of 1901–2, a revival of the classical vision from the era of Pierre Charles L'Enfant, the original designer of the urban plan for Washington, DC. After a six-week visit to European cities, the commission recommended the extension and clarification of Washington's monumental core, the construction of new memorials, and the creation of new parklands.[1] The recommendations of the Senate Park Commission, also known as the McMillan Commission, were institutionalized, albeit in a gradual manner and with results that fell short of the commission's recommendations.

Congress's creation of the Commission of Fine Arts in 1910 was the first in a series of actions in support of the McMillan Plan. The first of the projected new classical McMillan-style monuments for Washington was the Lincoln Memorial, designed by Henry Bacon and dedicated in 1922. But the lackluster politics of Harding- or Coolidge-style Republicanism in the 1920s seemed to threaten the long-term prospects for McMillan-type planning. So in 1923, some concerned Washingtonians founded the Committee of 100 on the Federal City. The committee, together with the Washington Board of Trade, drafted important legislation to extend the "park and forest preserves" of greater Washington under the oversight of a new park and planning agency. The result was Congress's creation in 1924 of the National Capital Park Commission, renamed the National Capital Park and Planning Commission two years later.[2] Much later it took on its current institutional identity: the National Capital Planning Commission (NCPC).

The fear of a Coolidge-era backlash against the McMillan program was ill-grounded. In 1917 another new federal commission, the Public Buildings Commission, had recommended the creation within a triangular precinct between Constitution and Pennsylvania Avenues of a cluster of buildings that would house the administrative offices of federal departments and agencies. Congress adopted this recommendation in a series of public-building acts passed from 1926 to 1928. From this legislation came the Federal Triangle, the classical, colonnaded enclave containing, among other great Washington landmarks, the National Archives building, designed by John Russell Pope.[3]

Indeed, in the years between the world wars the McMillan Plan would be the overall blueprint for classical buildings that make up much of what the public knows as the "postcard city" Washington: the Lincoln Memorial; the Supreme Court building, designed by Cass Gilbert and completed in 1935; and the Jefferson Memorial, designed by John Russell Pope and completed in 1943.

Back to the 1920s. The politics of Presidents Harding and Coolidge proved disappointing to political reformers, both Republicans and Democrats. Several scandals occurred under Warren G. Harding, most of them the work of his cronies, though he himself was untainted. Then his successor, Calvin Coolidge, came as close to a do-nothing president as the United States has ever had.

But the next president, Herbert Hoover, would be very different. In the 1920s Hoover was regarded as a "whiz kid" engineer. A businessman, he had entered public service in the Wilson era, heading the Committee for the Relief of Belgium in 1914. During World War I he

served as the wartime food administrator—the wizard of rationing. After the war, he headed the American Relief Administration, set up to send food and other vital supplies to the devastated regions of Europe. He won international fame as a humanitarian who fed the hungry, and he played a leading role in the American Red Cross.

Hoover served as secretary of commerce under both Harding and Coolidge. He was an activist. A moderate progressive, he urged regulation of the aviation industry. The 1926 Air Commerce Act gave his department some regulatory authority. Throughout the twenties Hoover urged the federal Reclamation Bureau to build a multipurpose dam in the Boulder Canyon of the Colorado River, what became the Hoover Dam.[4] In 1927 he participated in relief efforts when a devastating flood hit the Mississippi River valley. In 1928 he was elected president. He proclaimed a "new era" in which abundance would eliminate poverty. Americans looked to him as a humanitarian and master organizer who would bring prosperity to all.

Of course the 1929 stock-market crash soon belied such faith, but the most serious effects of the crash took some time to materialize.[5] Thus, in 1930 Washingtonians could sense that the coarser aspects of the twenties were yielding to a serious-minded and elegant new society.

The elegance seemed to be reflected in buildings like the Shoreham Hotel, designed by Joseph Abel and completed in 1930: the building had an Art Deco lounge. A Deco lounge would also be added to the older Carlton Hotel in 1934. The earliest traces of Art Deco had been filtering into Washington, where they steadily infiltrated the classicism of the McMillan Commission legacy.

To be sure, there was already a definite classical component within the eclectic mixture of design that had been presented at the Paris Exposition of 1925. But as the blend of American modernized classicism and Art Deco began to germinate, especially in the work of architects such as Bertram Grosvenor Goodhue, who designed the National Academy of Sciences Building (1924), and Paul Philippe Cret, designer of the influential Folger Shakespeare Library building (1928–32), both in Washington, something distinctive resulted. Washington would serve as an architectural proving ground for significant cutting-edge movements in eclectic design, as well as for some revolutionary building types, in the years between the world wars.

Construction of the Federal Triangle project began in the Hoover years. The Public Buildings Commission was in charge, with the final decision-making authority vested in the secretary of the treasury, Andrew Mellon, and the supervising architect of the Treasury Department, Louis A. Simon. Under plans proposed by the president of the American Institute of Architects, Milton B. Medary, Secretary Mellon selected a board of architectural consultants to plan the development, with each member of the board to be responsible for designing a particular building, to avoid monotony. The chairman, Edward H. Bennett, had previously served as an assistant to Daniel Burnham in the development of the Burnham Plan for Chicago.[6]

The cohesive group of architects and planners of federal buildings in 1927 formed the Association of Federal Architects. In 1930 they began to publish a magazine, the *Federal Architect*, which served as a forum on various issues, not least of which were issues of architectural taste. They rejected radical modernism but welcomed variations on classical design that could energize it. In 1930 an editorial in the *Federal Architect* condemned the "germ of Modern Architecture," with its "thumb-nosing at the past," but reserved the right to embrace any new approaches to design that could synthesize past, present, and future. "Believe it or not," the editorial admitted, "modern architecture can be good," but this meant both a "breaking away from the old architecture" and "a loyalty to it."[7]

Shortly before the construction of the Federal Triangle, the nation's capital received its first major airport, the privately owned Hoover Field,

just down the Potomac River from Washington, on the Virginia side. Representing a major advance over earlier local flying fields at Fort Myer, Virginia, and College Park, Maryland, Hoover Field, named in honor of the commerce secretary who championed commercial aviation, opened in 1926. In 1930 it was renamed Washington-Hoover Airport, and it received a new Art Deco terminal designed by the architectural firm Holden, Scott, & Hutchinson. From the start, however, the airport was plagued with problems: the runways were short and constructed of sod; the field was close to some dangerous obstacles, such as a busy highway, power lines, smokestacks, and fuel tanks; and the field was in truth too small.[8]

The 1930 improvements at Washington-Hoover Airport, however, created private-sector jobs. Simultaneously, the emergence of the Federal Triangle buildings just north of the Mall and the construction out west of the massive Hoover Dam both constituted job-creation projects. In New York City the workers who were building the Empire State Building pushed the great tower to completion. But increasingly— all over America—farms were failing, factories were closing their doors, banks were defaulting, and the worst economic depression in American history fell upon the land.

Humanitarian, coordinator of food relief, and master engineer, Hoover appeared to be the ideal chief executive to confront this crisis. But instead of rolling up his sleeves, he issued bromides on self-reliance. He uttered optimistic predictions that proved to be groundless. And then he became increasingly remote. In 1930, as a devastating drought hit Arkansas and Oklahoma, Hoover denied that starvation conditions existed, when the ugly truth was very different, and he opposed legislation to provide direct food relief to families.

What had happened? Perhaps Hoover was averting his eyes for a simple and in this case tragically needless reason: a sense of shame. He had predicted that prosperity was just around the corner, that the crisis would quickly blow over, but it didn't. Perhaps he went into denial for fear of being humiliated, revealed to the world as a windbag who didn't know what he was talking about. A quiet, introverted man, he was not a politician. He had entered public service through administrative work; the first federal office into which he had been voted was the presidency.

Whatever the cause of Hoover's strange isolation and remoteness, he was one of the first US presidents to try to reverse an economic contraction through federal effort, in his case the Reconstruction Finance Corporation.[9] But the action was too little and too late. By the end of his term, from about one-fourth to one-third of the American workforce was unemployed.

When Hoover faced the American electorate in 1932, a horde of unemployed veterans staged a march on Washington. Calling themselves the "Bonus Expeditionary Force," they came from as far away as California, requesting Congress to pay them a retirement bonus for their service in World War I many years before it was due. Popularly known as the "Bonus Army," they paraded through the streets of American cities and towns on their way to Washington. As they marched, they stretched out a large American flag into which many people threw coins to help them finance the trip. Hoover quietly ordered the army to help the marchers when they reached Washington. At Hoover's order, tents and field kitchens for the marchers were set up across the Anacostia River, at "Anacostia flats." But Hoover opposed the bonus bill, saying that it would unbalance the budget. Congress voted it down, then adjourned.

The marchers refused to leave town. They stoned the cars of recalcitrant congressmen. They camped out on Capitol Hill in abandoned buildings. Hoover ordered the army to move the marchers from Capitol Hill to their camp across the Anacostia. Exceeding Hoover's orders, Army Chief of Staff Douglas MacArthur ordered troops to force the bonus marchers out of town.

Using tear gas, sabers, and small whippet tanks, the troops carried out their orders, with MacArthur on hand to supervise. The newsreel cameras recorded the action, and the American voters were disgusted. The heroes of the Great War had been treated like bums.

Hoover could and arguably should have done what Truman would do to MacArthur many years later: relieve him of command. But Hoover was sunk too deep in depression. He never told the American people that MacArthur had exceeded his authority, and so Americans blamed Hoover. They threw him out of office and elected the Democratic Roosevelt.

Handsome, elegant, and charismatic, FDR had served during World War I as assistant secretary of the navy. Stricken with polio in 1921, he had sunk into his own depression. But he gradually recovered his natural high spirits. He perfected a method, using upper-body strength and leg braces, of appearing to walk with a cane, holding the arm of a companion who strolled by his side. The effect was electrifying—almost a miracle cure to those who saw it—and the voters of New York made Franklin Delano Roosevelt their governor in 1928.

Now he was president. And the man who had recovered, or at least seemed to have recovered, from paralysis would lead a paralyzed nation back to health. What followed his inauguration in March 1933 can hardly be imagined by those who have never experienced a major social crisis. Though historians have pointed out for years that the rhetoric of Roosevelt's inspiring first inaugural address was followed by contradictory policies, what the president pledged was precisely the "bold, persistent experimentation" that arguably was needed in a time of unprecedented problems. This was, after all, the greatest national crisis to hit the United States since the Civil War.

In an instant, Washington became the "nerve center" of the country. Young idealists flocked to the capital in multitudes. They came from colleges, from graduate schools, and from law firms. They brought with them energy, theories of reform both old and new, and divergent forms of expertise.[10] But not everyone in Washington was impressed. A pungent view was presented by George Peek, FDR's first administrator of the Agricultural Adjustment Administration (AAA), in his recollection of "the plague of young lawyers" who "settled on Washington," claiming to be "friends of somebody or other and mostly of Felix Frankfurter and Jerome Frank. They floated airily into offices, took desks, asked for papers and found no end of things to be busy about. I never found out why they came, what they did or why they left."[11]

This was the Washington of Thomas Corcoran and Benjamin Cohen, of Harry Hopkins and Harold Ickes, and of Senator Huey Long. From the desks of the "brain trusters" came a welter of "alphabet agencies" chartered to administer relief and promote rebuilding—the CCC (Civilian Conservation Corps) and the AAA, the NRA (National Recovery Administration) and the TVA (Tennessee Valley Authority), and perhaps most important of all for American architecture, the PWA (Public Works Administration), headed by Harold Ickes, who also served as FDR's interior secretary.

The New Deal era was characterized by a sense of both retrenchment and pioneering, regulation and expansion. It was an attempt to conserve America's broader continuities by keeping pace with the times. Against the chaos bred by conservative laissez faire was to be fashioned a *conserving* new *liberal* order. "Reform if you would preserve," declared FDR in 1936, paraphrasing Thomas Babington Macaulay; "I am that kind of conservative because I am that kind of liberal."[12]

The "common man" all over America looked for help to the country squire, the humanitarian aristocrat, who occupied the White House. In his radio "fireside chats" FDR talked to the American people like a friend. He sought to promote the twin goals of safety and decency in a rejuvenated, almost reborn United States.

The nerve center for the redevelopment was Washington. Eagles and thunderbolts symbolized its role. The paraphernalia of mobilization was everywhere apparent, especially in terminology. Young men went forth to reforest America's desolate regions in a new Civilian Conservation Corps, a joint project of the War and Interior Departments. In the *Architectural Forum* were schematic charts showing "Washington's Building Battalion," some twenty-eight different federal agencies and programs affecting construction and building. Some of these were housed in temporary buildings left over from World War I on Washington's Mall.

Others were quartered in vacant mansions in Georgetown or in the neighborhood of Dupont Circle, mansions the rich were abandoning in favor of homes being built farther out in the new developments of Wesley Heights and Spring Valley. In one such mansion Rexford Guy Tugwell and planners from the new Resettlement Administration (created in 1935 and replaced by the Farm Security Administration, or FSA, in Roosevelt's second term) conceived the program of "greenbelt towns"—model towns to absorb the flow of impoverished migrants and to demonstrate how the virtues of city and country life could be combined through benevolent planning—which they hoped would be a model for America's suburbanization.

In all, Washington's population grew by 36 percent in the thirties owing to the influx of workers to staff the New Deal.[13] In 1939 Edwin Rosskam spoke of the city's "nameless horde with civil service rating," a horde he believed accounted for half the city's residents. "The Federal Government is the destiny of Washington, D.C.," he wrote. "Here almost everybody either works for the government, depends on somebody who works for the government, works for somebody who works for the government, or is trying to sell something to somebody who works for the government." Rosskam believed that the majority of the new arrivals had small-town antecedents, "which accounts for some of the provincial aspects of our cosmopolitan capital," along with its transience: "Washington has more boarding houses and bath-sharing apartments than any other city of comparable size."[14] The great population influx would feed the local real-estate industry. The result was significant experimentation in architecture to accommodate the expanding middle class: new garden-apartment complexes and "park-and-shop" shopping centers.[15]

The youthful spirit of New Deal Washington was represented in the Hollywood capers of bashful Jimmy Stewart and insouciant Jean Arthur in Frank Capra's film classic of 1939, *Mr. Smith Goes to Washington*, with its tough-guy reporters won over in the end to the freshness and idealistic fervor of provincials like "Jefferson Smith." One can almost hear swing music when gazing at surviving pictures of 1930s Washingtonians—women in calf-length dresses and sloping hats, men in white linen suits or Norfolk-style jackets with half-belts and pleats in the back, departing from federal offices in taxis or in streetcars bound, perhaps, for a newsreel showing of a speech by President Roosevelt at the Trans-Lux theater or for the elegant new high-rise apartments of Connecticut Avenue or 16th Street with their stylish glass-bricked entranceways and Deco ornamentation.

Years later, a Washingtonian recalled what it was like to be young and on the town in those days: it was a matter of "listening to Stuff Smith at the Blue Mirror; laying into the ribs at Arbaugh's; getting drunk at John Macropolis's Silver Fox; snuggling with your date at the Birdcage Lounge at the Shoreham; sitting in the parking lot at the Hot Shoppe; listening to Hal Thornton sing 'Caviar Comes from Virgin Sturgeon' at Olivia Davis's Merry-Land; or grabbing a fast lunch at Whitlow's."[16] All of these places exuded the spirit of "moderne," as people used to call it.

For black Washingtonians, most of these realities were different. Washington was still a very "southern town," as people said in those days, and the African American community subsisted

as a world apart, even as its influence in culture and the arts kept emanating outward in the age of jazz and swing. The extent of segregation and racial prejudice in Washington was overwhelming during these years. At the same time, Washington's black community could boast of a large middle class and a talented leadership elite. At the Lincoln theater, at 1215 U Street NW, near Howard University, black entertainment greats such as Duke Ellington, Billie Holiday, and Paul Robeson appeared. Later, in the forties, the Carver theater, on Nichols Avenue SE, brought Art Deco theater architecture to black Washingtonians.[17]

Art Deco began to influence the Federal Triangle as the project neared its completion in the mid-thirties. The Justice Department and Federal Trade Commission buildings abounded with Deco features, as did the Library of Congress Annex, completed in 1939.[18] New Deal values permeated the public art in these buildings. Though much of the federal art in the thirties is popularly referred to as "WPA art" (for the Works Progress Administration, instituted in 1935), a great deal of it was actually channeled through the Treasury Department's Public Works of Art Project (PWAP), succeeded by the department's Fine Arts Section, headed by Edward Bruce. Through programs such as these, the murals of Harold Weston, William Gropper, and painters of the Social Realist school became part of the New Deal legacy. In contemporaneous scenes that were juxtaposed with visions of covered-wagon days and the exertions of early pioneers, they depicted common men of the thirties as the builders of a bold new society. Other murals, especially those adorning the Justice Department building, contained scenes of social protest that sometimes approached surrealism.

The spirit of the murals (and sculpture) coexisted with the voguish appeal of the Art Deco ornamentation that adorned the buildings. The interplay between the Social Realist art and the glitzier aspects of Art Deco was a commentary on a land diverse enough to encompass both the ritziness of Fred Astaire and the homely direct-ness of Woody Guthrie.

The *pièce de résistance* of federal Art Deco in New Deal Washington was Greenbelt, the model town in the Maryland suburbs designed by the architects Douglas Ellington and Reginald D. Wadsworth and built by the Resettlement Administration in 1936 and 1937.[19] From an original list of one hundred cities that seemed to merit the development of greenbelt satellite towns, or "green towns," only three cities—Washington, Milwaukee, and Cincinnati—were selected. Budget restrictions limited the project, as did challenges to its constitutionality. Green-belt, Maryland, Greendale, Wisconsin, and Greenhills, Ohio, were pushed to completion, while the Greenbrook, New Jersey, project was canceled due to local opposition.

The spirit of Greenbelt's original residents may be sensed from the dedication address—"We Pioneers," by Mary E. Van Cleave—which was published in the *Greenbelt Cooperator*, the town's first newspaper, in 1937:

> Let us keep ourselves, our community, our city government, our ideals, as clean as our new, windswept roofs. Let us conduct ourselves and the management of our Greenbelt in such a way as to deserve the pride with which all America will be looking on. We who have been endowed with the greatest living heritage on earth by our ancestors still have that hardiness and determi-nation underneath. Greenbelt will be a success, with the cooperation of her citizens and with the help of God.[20]

Greenbelt followed the curves of a crescent-shaped ridge. The housing blocks were clustered according to the lay of the land, and a network of bicycle pathways and courtyards unified the plan. The town center was designed with a pe-destrian mall and underpasses for pedestrians and bicycles that permitted the residents to pass below the central ridge road—Crescent Road—without encountering cars. The sweeping lines of the theater and the shopping center reflected the streamlining trend, as did the more flamboy-ant lines of the school, which also served as a civic center and library. The style of the housing blocks was an expressive mixture of the Inter-national Style and Art Deco. The school, with its streamlined entrance, its facade with a colon-nade of fluted "struts"—the outermost edges of the overhead "ribs" that form the load-bearing structure of the building—and its bas-relief sculpted panels depicting common men, was di-rectly inspired by the composition of the Folger Shakespeare Library on Capitol Hill.

Other approaches to low-cost housing in Washington were based upon the new authority of the Federal Housing Administration (FHA) to insure loans, an authority that several astute developers, notably Gustave Ring, the developer of Arlington's "Colonial Village," took advan-tage of to create the myriad garden-apartment complexes that were built throughout greater Washington. More serious housing problems were addressed by Washington's Alley Dwelling Authority, created by Congress in 1934 to help the District of Columbia rid itself of thousands of slums and replace them with public housing. While Washington remained a Jim-Crow city in the 1930s, such projects were a slight contri-bution to improving race relations, as was the symbolic intercession of Eleanor Roosevelt and Harold Ickes to help the black contralto Marion Anderson perform at the Lincoln Memorial in 1939 after the Daughters of the American Revo-lution refused to let her perform at Constitution Hall.

The modernization of New Deal Washing-ton continued in Roosevelt's second term. FDR played a principal role in designing and locating a new naval hospital. Inspired by a glimpse of Nebraska's skyscraper capitol building, designed by Bertram Grosvenor Goodhue, during a visit in 1936, Roosevelt decided that a tower design would be appropriate for the naval hospital in Washington, DC. He drew a sketch on a piece of White House stationery.[21] The hospital was built in Bethesda, Maryland, a Washington suburb, because the building-height limitation in the District of Columbia would have prevented such a project within the city limits. Built in the years 1939–42, it was dedicated by FDR. F. W. Southworth, in consultation with Paul Philippe Cret, designed the hospital in overall accord with Roosevelt's conceptions.

In 1938 construction began on a state-of-the-art airport to replace Washington-Hoover. Once again President Roosevelt played a key role. He selected the site for the airport, at Gravelly Point, Virginia, on the shore of the Potomac. A landfill operation by the Army Corps of Engineers created space for the construction of long, paved runways. In overall charge of the project was the Civil Aeronautics Administration (CAA), created by Congress in 1938. Funding was channeled through the CAA and the two largest New Deal public-works agencies, the PWA and the WPA.

Washington National Airport opened on June 16, 1941. By 1942 it boasted more hangar space than any other airport in the world. By the standards of the time, it was an ultramodern facility, a sparkling "aerodrome."[22] The architect Charles M. Goodman designed the airport, with the help—some would say the interference—of President Roosevelt. FDR, who found the airport's aesthetics too radical, prevailed upon Goodman to classicize the facade in a manner that suggested the portico of nearby Mount Vernon.

A year before the airport opened, Washington received another state-of-the-art transportation portal, a modern bus terminal that some called the "Grand Central of the motor bus world." The Greyhound "super terminal," which opened on March 25, 1940, on New York Avenue NW, between 11th and 12th Streets, in downtown Washington, was designed by William S. Arrasmith, of the Louisville, Kentucky, firm Wischmeyer, Arrasmith, and Elswick. More than twenty-five thousand sightseers thronged the building when it opened, and the *Washington Post* ran a special section that day to cover the event.[23]

Greyhound Lines had been consolidated dur-ing the 1920s by an entrepreneur named Carl Eric Wickman. Offering comfortable low-cost travel to people on a very tight budget—people who could not afford cars in the depths of the Depression—the company flourished.[24] By 1940 Greyhound operated twenty-two hundred buses, whose annual mileage exceeded 165 million miles.

First listed in city directories in 1930, Greyhound established an ever-growing presence in Washington. Its first terminal, at 1336 New York Avenue NW, required extensive parking of interstate buses along the curb of a congested thoroughfare. This was unsatisfactory to Washingtonians, so in 1931 the city's Public Utilities Commission ordered Greyhound and other bus companies to establish off-street parking and loading. By 1933 Greyhound was in compliance, with a new terminal at 1407 New York Avenue NW. This terminal, however, also proved inadequate,[25] and work began on the much larger, state-of-the-art "super terminal" in 1938. When it was dedicated in 1940, it made the nation's capital accessible to thousands of communities that lacked any railroad connection. During World War II it became a little "Ellis Island" for thousands of blacks who were leaving the South for a better life in northern cities.

While Washingtonians were proud of these new transportation facilities, some other exciting new architectural projects never got off the drawing boards owing to opposition by aesthetic traditionalists. As the new National Gallery of Art, designed by John Russell Pope, took shape on Constitution Avenue NW—it was built to house the opulent art collection donated by Andrew Mellon, who personally commissioned and paid for the design by Pope—a "Smithsonian Gallery of Art" was planned for the opposite side of the Mall. An architectural competition was approved by Congress in 1938, but the winning entry, a modern design from the firm Saarinen, Saarinen, & Swanson, would never be built; the traditionalistic Commission of Fine Arts was stalwartly opposed.[26]

A comparable defeat for avant-garde modernists was the rejection by planning and civic authorities of a massive complex that Frank Lloyd Wright, at the behest of the developer Roy S. Thurman, proposed to build in 1940 on the site of the present Washington Hilton. Wright's multiuse project, which he called "Crystal Heights"—the press called it "Crystal City," a designation that should not be confused with the later Crystal City complex in northern Virginia—would have featured twenty-one futuristic towers clad in bronze, white marble, and glass. Planned for construction on Temple Heights, the buildings would have epitomized Wright's aspiration to create "organic" architecture. He insisted that the buildings would be "fused with the landscape rather than imposed upon it." But the District of Columbia Zoning Commission refused to grant a height variance, and the three District commissioners, who governed the local affairs of the city, opposed it as well.[27]

No doubt Wright's vituperative remarks about local architects, whom he dismissed as clods and dullards, and his snide denigration of the federal enclave's classicism, which he called banal, did little to endear him to Washington authorities. The defeat of this proposal was nothing less than a major artistic and civic tragedy. Perhaps someday an audacious and well-financed visionary will acquire this site and create as much of Wright's design as his surviving drawings permit.

Roosevelt's second term was disappointing. After a landslide reelection victory in 1936, the popular president became overconfident and committed some blunders. In 1937 he attempted to "pack" the Supreme Court, which had been toppling New Deal agencies, declaring them unconstitutional. Congress stunningly rejected FDR's attempt, and this setback damaged both the credibility and the morale of the president. Then, to balance the budget, FDR decided to reduce relief spending, believing that the private-sector economy was strong enough to bring America back to prosperity on its own.

He was wrong. The economy plunged as the so-called Roosevelt recession began in 1937 and continued into 1939. Defeatism spread among the president's advisers. Harry Hopkins, the social worker in charge of the WPA, predicted that depression conditions might now be a permanent feature of American life. It might be "reasonable," he wrote, "to expect a possible minimum of 4,000,000 to 5,000,000 unemployed men even in future prosperity periods."[28] To make matters worse, another war was raging: Hitler launched the European phase of the war with his invasion of Poland in 1939.

The war would be the central point of controversy in election year 1940, when FDR sought an unprecedented third term. France had surrendered to Hitler, and the Battle of Britain was under way. Americans were deeply divided: isolationists fought interventionists. But almost everyone agreed that year that the United States had to re-arm for the purpose of national defense. The resulting new mobilization, followed by the production imperatives of total war, brought the long-sought economic recovery. During World War II the American unemployment problem vanished.

The building boom of the 1930s continued in wartime Washington. The preparations for war led to even more alphabet agencies: the War Production Board (WPB), the National War Labor Board (NWLB), the War Manpower Commission (WMC), the Office of War Mobilization (OWM), the Office of Price Administration (OPA), and the Office of Scientific Research and Development (OSRD). The War Department, housed in multiple buildings, was physically unified within the rapidly constructed Pentagon, near National Airport. The building was the brainchild of General Brehon B. Somervell, chief of the Construction Division of the Quartermaster Corps. In the summer of 1941 he challenged George E. Bergstrom, president of the American Institute of Architects, and Lieutenant Hugh J. Casey with the task of designing a building that would house the entire War Department. The result was a massive horizontal fortress containing fully twice the floor space of the Empire State Building.[29]

The population surge of the 1930s continued in wartime Washington. To accommodate the ever-growing workforce, garden-apartment complexes like Park Fairfax in Virginia continued to proliferate. The federal presence spread beyond the Pentagon and beyond the federal enclave in downtown Washington. Out in Silver Spring, Maryland, for instance, an automobile showroom was converted to house the new Johns Hopkins Applied Physics Laboratory, where military contracts for classified weapons research were carried out. This lab would help develop the radio proximity fuse. The site was probably chosen for its location midway between the Johns Hopkins University in Baltimore and the Pentagon in northern Virginia. Classified briefings were held in the nearby Silver Theater.[30] Another new garden-apartment complex, Montgomery Arms, was built down the street.

In another close-in Maryland suburb—Carderock, below the Great Falls of the Potomac—the David Taylor Model Basin was built. Its purpose was to test ship designs. The Army Map Service moved to Brookmont, in Montgomery County. In 1942 Andrews Air Force Base was constructed at Camp Springs, in Prince George's County, to help protect the nation's capital from air attack.

Such were the additions to wartime Washington in the forties. Again the city was a nerve center—this time for fighting global war. FDR devoted what remained of his life to the task of defeating the Axis. Working steadily with innumerable advisers, associates, and cabinet members—Secretary of War Henry Stimson, Army Chief of Staff George Marshall, and his new friend British Prime Minister Winston Churchill, who traveled to Washington for meetings with FDR and who actually lived in the White House for a month—Roosevelt carried on.[31] He did not live to see the end of the war. Like another great war captain, Lincoln, he died

in the dawn of his victory. But surely both men died in the knowledge that victory was theirs.

## BALTIMORE

In 1940 H. L. Mencken set forth his many memories of Baltimore. "The city into which I had been born," he wrote, "had a reputation all over for what the English, in their real estate advertising, are fond of calling the amenities." After summarizing the qualities for which his city had been praised, Mencken tried to be dispassionate. "There was some truth in all of these articles," he admitted, "but not . . . too much." With one exception: the food. "Baltimore lay very near the immense protein factory of Chesapeake Bay," Mencken wrote, "and out of the bay it ate divinely."[32]

The port city of Baltimore contrasted dramatically with nearby Washington. With the major exception of the Civil War years, the nation's capital remained a sleepy metropolis in the nineteenth century, at least by the standards of many northern urbanites. But Baltimore boomed. Its commercial and manufacturing operations, its shipping lines and its "smokestack" industries, gave it economic vitality.

From the 1920s through the 1940s, as Washington at last grew into the role of a national nerve center, Baltimore kept pace. Its industrial operations increased. In the 1920s the city rose to third place among American exporting cities, and more than a hundred new factories appeared there.[33] The city itself grew quickly in the 1920s, tripling in geographic size after the Maryland state legislature passed an annexation act in 1918. From thirty square miles the city's size jumped to ninety-two square miles.[34] Civic boosters were exultant—and visionary. They publicized visions of a futuristic city whose skyscrapers reached to the heavens.[35]

The scope of Baltimore's physical development during the twenties was impressive. Companies such as Esskay Meats (1919) in east

Baltimore and Domino Sugars (1922) in Locust Point built looming, utilitarian, steel-framed, and reinforced-concrete structures of a type that inspired the leaders of European modernism. Lever Brothers, Proctor & Gamble, Coca-Cola, McCormick Spice, and Western Electric built large plants as well. Baltimore also became a center for the commercial aviation industry. Beginning in 1929 the Glenn L. Martin Company built a huge industrial complex at Middle River. On the Chesapeake Bay the Martin Company tested the famous "flying boats," or "clipper planes," one of the firm's specialties.[36] One of the plant's earliest buildings, the Administration building (1929), showed the influence of Art Deco.[37]

New jobs led to a demand for more homes. By the mid-1920s, six thousand houses were being constructed each year, twice the level of previous decades. This housing boom resulted in new neighborhoods of single-family homes, from the modest cottage developments along the city's arterial roads radiating out from the urban core to the expansion of the city's elite northern suburbs. Row-house developers kept pace, making innovations to the city's tried-and-true residential form, building English-style and "daylight" rows, so named because each main room had a window, throughout the city.[38]

Along with the surge in industrial and population growth came the characteristic problems: labor-management conflicts, air and water pollution, urban congestion. As early as 1923 Mencken posed the question, "In what way, precisely, has the average Baltimorean benefitted by the great growth of the city. . . ?" "So far as I can make out," he continued, "in no way at all. . . . Every time they bring in another glue factory, with another trainload of slaves to work it, they fill the newspapers with hosannas. Well, what is the good of another glue factory? What is the good of bringing in another trainload of slaves?"[39] Mencken, for one, wanted Baltimore to stop competing with larger cities like New York. What was the use of skyscrapers? he

asked. "There was never any need of them here. . . . Wasting millions on such follies is a kind of confession that Baltimore is inferior to New York, and should hump itself to catch up." But the true Baltimorean "lives in Baltimore because he prefers Baltimore. One of its greatest charms, in his eyes, is that it is not New York."[40]

Baltimore was famous in the 1920s as a "wet" town, a place where people got away with resistance to the prohibition of alcoholic beverages. The governor of Maryland, Albert Ritchie, was defiant toward federal authority. State and local police did nothing to assist the Prohibition agents sent out from Washington. Baltimore was a center of illicit alcohol consumption. Rumrunners from Cuba and elsewhere steamed up the bay under cover of darkness, and Baltimoreans cruised out to meet them.[41]

Following the repeal of the Eighteenth Amendment, Baltimore's love of drink manifested itself in the opening and in many cases reopening of numerous corner bars in the older neighborhoods around the harbor. Many of these establishments modernized their street-level facades with Deco materials, including multicolored bricks, glass block, shiny steel doors, and D-shaped windows.

The demographics of Baltimore shifted in the 1920s; blacks entered the city in increasing numbers, while continued immigration from Europe declined because of postwar quotas. Overall, the black population of the city grew by 50 percent from 1920 to 1940, while the white population grew by only 25 percent.[42] Just as the Lincoln theater in Washington served as an entertainment Mecca for blacks, the new Royal theater in Baltimore served the same purpose. Fats Waller did the honors in the Royal's opening-night ceremonies. Down the years the Royal featured performances by Chick Webb, Ella Fitzgerald, Ethel Waters, Pearl Bailey, and Earl "Fatha" Hines.[43]

Baltimore architecture in the twenties and thirties was largely in line with most national patterns. Fueled by a robust manufacturing sector, the city became fertile ground for a wide-ranging architecture that mixed freely with the prevailing design trends of the day—albeit leaning toward the traditional—an important representative of America's major industrial cities in the interwar years. Like Washington, Baltimore was influenced by the turn-of-the-century City Beautiful ideal of civic uplift through classicism. The McMillan Plan for the nation's capital had its counterpart in the plans put forth by Baltimore's Municipal Arts Society, founded in 1899.[44]

Among the new classical monuments created in Baltimore during the twenties and thirties were the War Memorial and War Memorial Plaza (1925–27), designed by Laurence Hall Fowler; the Abel Wolman Municipal Building (1928), designed by William H. Emory Jr.; the new Baltimore Museum of Art building (1929), designed by John Russell Pope; and the new home for the Central Branch of the Enoch Pratt Free Library (1933), designed by Clyde N. Friz. Civic leaders and the designers they hired employed classical compositions, yet these were buildings designed for contemporary needs—products of their time—and some were enlivened with Deco features.

Art Deco began filtering into Baltimore during the twenties. The Baltimore Trust Company building (1924–29), designed by the firms Taylor & Fisher and Smith & May, was a thirty-four-story skyscraper with setback terraces. The elegant Hutzler Brothers department store building (1931), designed by James R. Edmunds Jr., featured a tower with superb entrance-level ornamentation. Such overt, large-scale expressions of Art Deco were far fewer in number than the hundreds of modest Deco-inspired buildings, most evident in commercial structures throughout the city.

Baltimore suffered just as much as other American cities of comparable size in the Great Depression. Banks failed, and a number of financial leaders committed suicide. By 1931 the unemployment level in Baltimore was nearly 20 percent, and the city's charitable organizations took action. Institutions such as the Community Fund, the Red Cross, the Family Welfare Association, the Bureau of Catholic Charities, the Jewish Social Service Bureau, and the Salvation Army did everything they could. But as 1931 dawned, one in every eight Baltimore workers was out of a job. Soup kitchens opened at nineteen locations around the city, and police offered food at several police stations. At the end of 1931 a spokesman for the Family Welfare Association would assess the situation as follows: "Never in the experience of the organization have we seen so much suffering and such dire conditions of want as exist now."[45] Anger and despair found destructive outlets: deaths due to alcoholism soared, as did divorces, domestic abuse, illegitimate births, and infant abandonment.[46] At last even Maryland's states'-rights governor, Albert Ritchie, was willing to ask the federal government for relief.

The New Deal brought a significant amount of economic relief to the city, especially through job-creation projects such as the PWA and WPA, together with the Civil Works Administration (CWA), a short-term agency active in the winter of 1933–34. Abel Wolman, a civil engineer, led the PWA in Maryland, and the agency spent $100 million in the state from 1934 to 1937. With PWA funding, Baltimore's Bureau of Water Supply accelerated a ten-year construction program and completed it in four years. The bureau's massive steel-tank reservoir on Melvin Avenue in Catonsville embodied the bold optimism of PWA architecture. The school board used PWA funds to build the Eastern High School campus and additions at five other schools. Other PWA projects included the Baltimore Municipal Airport, an addition to the Baltimore Museum of Art, facilities at the Baltimore City Hospitals, sewage-disposal plants, bridges and viaducts, and road widening and extensions.[47]

But Baltimore's mayor, Howard Jackson,

was intermittently hostile to the New Deal. He resisted the efforts of the PWA to build public housing, which he viewed as a threat to the private-sector real-estate and construction industries. It was only on the eve of World War II that federally supported public housing arrived in Baltimore.[48]

Created after the demise of the PWA's Housing Division, the Baltimore Housing Authority initiated the site selection, design, construction, and management of Baltimore's earliest public housing, completing twelve projects in the years 1939–44.[49] Working within guidelines and budgetary restraints set by the newly founded US Housing Authority, local architectural firms designed multifamily, low-scale residential buildings with flat roofs and minimal exterior ornamentation organized around open spaces and courts. Many of the complexes replaced older neighborhoods of dense row houses occupied by low-income residents, some of whom could not afford the rents of the new government-built housing. Thus the new complexes altered the city in social as well as visual terms.

As in Washington, the influence of Art Deco continued to proliferate during the thirties. Among the notable Deco commercial buildings downtown were the streamlined Kresge store (1937) and the streamlined Greyhound Terminal (1941), designed by William Arrasmith, which opened just a year after the dedication of Washington's "super terminal," which Arrasmith also designed. And industrial growth continued, though on a lesser scale than during the twenties. Light manufacturers constructed modest factories that incorporated the clean lines of American industrial architecture and Deco flourishes, such as the cluster of industrial buildings in the vicinity of Kirk Avenue and 25th Street in northeastern Baltimore.

Baltimoreans enjoyed life as best they could during the Depression. Many found a pleasant if vicarious gratification in the love affair of Baltimore's Bessie Wallis Simpson (née War-

field) with Britain's Prince of Wales. After a very brief reign as King Edward VIII, he abdicated in order to marry the American divorcée. A real-life version of the Cinderella fairy tale—a pervasive Hollywood theme in the 1930s, for example, in films such as *Mr. Deeds Goes to Town* (in which the title character is New York's "Cinderella Man") and the Deanna Durbin musical *First Love*—the story dominated tabloid news on both sides of the Atlantic.

Other forms of diversion were available closer to home, at the Hippodrome, for instance, or the Baltimore Symphony, or at plays performed by the Vagabond Players, who specialized in Broadway revivals, or the Hopkins Players, who preferred a mixture of the classics and avant-garde drama.[50] Movies were more popular than ever. The Baltimore cinema architect John Jacob Zink designed scores of Deco movie theaters in both Baltimore and Washington.

The black migration to Baltimore continued throughout the thirties, even though many of these migrants, who were clearly hoping to find a better life, found little more than misery in Baltimore's slums. Some of them were driven by fear. A series of horrific lynchings on Maryland's Eastern Shore (across the Chesapeake Bay) made life in the hinterland frightening for many blacks at the time. The Baltimore-born jazz star Billie Holiday sang a song entitled "Strange Fruit," the "fruit" being lynched black bodies swinging from trees. But many Baltimore blacks achieved success in the 1930s. In 1935 Thurgood Marshall, on behalf of the Baltimore chapter of the NAACP, convinced the Maryland Court of Appeals that the University of Maryland's law school had to admit qualified blacks.

Even more opportunities for blacks would come along during World War II. The war would open up a vast new array of possibilities for blacks in military service. Indeed, the war would generate much of the momentum that propelled the civil rights movement in the 1940s and 1950s. Many blacks were well aware of what the war could mean for civil rights. In 1942 the *Baltimore Afro-American* urged potential draftees to "get all the training you can [because] when the reverses get big enough Army, Navy and Defense will be open to all citizens."[51]

World War II would put the people of Baltimore to work as never before. As FDR set his unprecedented goals for wartime production of ships and airplanes, Baltimore factories produced them. The Martin Company adapted its famous "clipper" seaplane and turned it into the versatile PBM patrol bomber used by the navy. The company built the world's largest aircraft assembly floor. Martin quickly adapted techniques derived from the automobile assembly line, techniques that would soon prove their worth in the production of ships as well as aircraft. Albert Kahn's Detroit firm designed the complex's monumental buildings, including the streamlined airport terminal (1938–40).[52] Bethlehem Steel and its Fairfield shipbuilding division built five hundred Liberty ships and victory ships in Baltimore, launching two every week by April 1942.[53]

The homefront mobilization led to hundreds of thousands of new jobs for Baltimoreans. Forty thousand who remained unemployed throughout the 1930s (notwithstanding the significant impact of the New Deal) found jobs during World War II.[54] An influx of defense workers led to a housing shortage. The Federal Works Agency commandeered the Baltimore Housing Authority's Armistead Gardens, a seven-hundred-unit, modernistic housing project initially proposed as public housing, to provide shelter for Martin Company and Bethlehem Steel workers and their families.[55]

Twenty thousand Baltimore women entered the workforce. They drove Baltimore buses for the first time, operated blast furnaces and made aircraft, and worked at oil refineries.[56] And Baltimore men, together with their fellow soldiers and sailors from Washington and cities all over the country, gave their lives in the hope that their leaders would redeem all the suffering through victory.

Different in so many respects, these Mid-Atlantic cities—the nation's capital with its grand monumental core and its predominantly white-collar workforce and the great industrial port city just to the north—grew closer during this generation. Today's Baltimore-Washington corridor was coming into being.

## WASHINGTON

Art Deco's earliest influence on residential architecture in Washington appeared in the larger building types, the tall apartment buildings and hotels. In the 1930s, Deco design began to permeate low-rise garden-apartment complexes. Simultaneously, but to a lesser extent, it appeared in some single-family houses.

### LARGE APARTMENT BUILDINGS AND HOTELS

Art Deco infiltrated apartment design in Washington just a few years after the Paris Exposition of 1925. As early as 1927, the Moorings (1901–1909 Q Street NW), designed by Horace Peaslee, showed the unmistakable influence of Art Deco. Relatively small at five stories, the building was one of an ensemble of "smart flats" commissioned by a Washington socialite, Mrs. John R. Williams. Two were built at the intersection of Connecticut Avenue and Q Street NW, just north of Dupont Circle: the Moorings and the Anchorage.

For the Moorings, Peaslee created an essentially stripped classical block with a rusticated ground floor, a three-story central section, and a top floor defined by a stringcourse—all clad in limestone. The ground floor was leased for commercial use. The nautical theme in this building possessed such appealing whimsy that it caught the eye of the editors of *Architectural Record*. In March 1928 they described the theme: "Bathrooms and 'galleys' are ventilated by 'portholes.' The roof is developed as a promenade pier, with penthouse camouflaged as a lighthouse; smokestacks and vents are also handled in a maritime manner. As a result, the exterior has achieved a definite character all its own, perhaps suggesting some of the modern Continental architecture."[1] Additional nautical touches in the ornamentation of the building include the rope and shell motifs in the limestone surrounds for the main entrances, placed at either end of the ground floor. The promotional floor plans for the building referred to the rooms in the apartments as "cabins," "bunkrooms," and "galleys." The apartments at the ends of the building were vertically stacked upon two floors and connected by a stairway. The topmost apartments had working fireplaces.[2]

After 1927 the influence of Art Deco in apartment-building design appeared in more than half a dozen buildings in northwest Washington and on Capitol Hill.[3] The Westchester apartment complex (1930), designed by Harvey Warwick Sr. (4000 Cathedral Avenue NW), shows significant Deco tendencies in the massing of its four buildings, though it does not have Deco ornamentation.

On the southern edge of Dupont Circle a large residential building arose in 1931. Based upon an unexecuted design for a medical building, it opened its doors as an apartment building in 1932. A decade later it was converted into an office building. The Dupont Circle Building (1332–1366 Connecticut Avenue NW) was the work of the architect Mihran Mesrobian. It remains a prominent Washington landmark, not least because the narrow site upon which it was built (between radial arteries converging at Dupont Circle) led to a flatiron-style composition. Mesrobian had to incorporate an earlier one-story building that the owner of the site, Joseph J. Moebs, constructed in 1926. For the Dupont Circle Building, the architect was able to salvage and adapt his design for a medical building commissioned, but never built, by the developer Harry Wardman.[4]

As designed in 1930–31, the Dupont Circle Building was a block-long display of Art Deco. A thirteen-story building clad in buff brick and limestone, it features an interplay of vertical and horizontal elements. The middle floors are punctuated with vertical and colonnaded limestone sections with three window bays apiece. The two floors above feature horizontal lines, but the vertical rhythm resumes in the upper floors, which have setbacks. A pyramid-roofed penthouse sheathed in an ornamental grillwork of vertical piers crowns the building. Ornamental limestone panels include bas-reliefs of goddesses, horses, and birds. Mesrobian's design suggests the influence of Deco buildings built in New York City in the twenties, especially the 1925–27 Barclay-Vesey Building and the 1928–30 Western Union Building, both designed by Voorhees, Gmelin & Walker.

It is interesting that a contemporaneous Deco apartment building had a multiuse history approximating that of the Dupont Circle Building: the twelve-story Keystone apartments (1931), at 2150 Pennsylvania Avenue NW (near Washington Circle in Foggy Bottom), designed by Robert O. Scholz, was later converted into a medical office building.

Farther up Connecticut Avenue, across Rock Creek, at the intersection with Calvert Street, the large Shoreham Hotel (2500 Calvert Street NW) arose in 1930. The original developers (the investment firm Swartzell, Rheem, & Hensey) went bankrupt in the middle of the year, and then Harry M. Bralove, an attorney and developer who had built four large apartment buildings already, took over. The building was originally an apartment-hotel, a building type to serve both permanent residents and "transient" guests, as they were called in the trade.

Joseph Abel gave the hotel a symmetrical plan that can be visualized in overhead view as two cross-shaped wings joined by a central section comprising the lobby, ballrooms, dining rooms, nightclubs, and amenities. The principal exterior cladding material was buff brick. The hotel boasted a two-hundred-car garage, an indoor-outdoor playground, and a beautiful, spacious site on a rolling hillside overlooking Rock Creek Park. The most luxurious apartments had three bedrooms, two bathrooms, a kitchen, a living room, a dining room, and a working fireplace. Most of the apartments had balconies.

Abel's design for the building was eclectic; the Shoreham reflected the influence of several design trends, both traditional and modern. The influence of Art Deco is apparent in many parts of the building, not only in the ornamental details of various public rooms, apartments, and hallways but also in the massing of architectural features, especially the penthouses.

When the hotel opened, the owners got nerve-wracking publicity. They had booked Rudy Vallee, the popular crooner, radio personality, and bandleader, with his "Connecticut Yankees" to provide entertainment. Vallee's band flew down from New York in a trimotored plane, but they were caught in a thunderstorm and the rumor spread that the famous singer was missing. Anxious guests milled around until

The **Shoreham Hotel** from the other side of Calvert
Street NW, 1930s.

Photograph by Theodor Horydczak, Theodor Horydczak Collection,
Prints and Photographs Division, Library of Congress.

4:15 a.m., when a weary Vallee arrived, played for fifteen minutes, and departed.[5] The Shoreham is a prominent landmark whose guests over the years have included presidents and movie stars (among them Clark Gable, Marlene Dietrich, and Marilyn Monroe), as well as foreign dignitaries.

Even farther uptown in the Connecticut Avenue corridor, two large and sumptuous Art Deco apartment buildings opened in the Hoover era: the Kennedy-Warren and Sedgwick Gardens. The larger of the two, the Kennedy-Warren (3133 Connecticut Avenue NW), opened in October 1931.[6] As with the Shoreham Hotel, the original builders went bankrupt, in this case a few months after the building opened. And their architect committed suicide a year later.

Edgar S. Kennedy and Monroe Warren Sr. commissioned architect Joseph Younger to design an enormous apartment building on a site overlooking Rock Creek, just north of the National Zoo. The building was originally conceived as an apartment-hotel. Unlike the Shoreham, which overlooks Rock Creek Park atop a magnificent and rolling lawn, the Kennedy-Warren overlooks the park at the edge of a wooded precipice. By constructing the building athwart the cliff, it was possible to build six stories to the rear below street level. The building is nine stories tall in the front.

Younger's design, like that of the Shoreham, had a central section containing the great public rooms. Two massive wings—configured very differently—were designed, but only the north wing was completed in the 1930s. This north wing crosses the central section at a right angle. Each end of the wing is crossed by a lateral section that projects out into pavilions. Because of the Depression, the construction of the H-shaped south wing was delayed and would not be built until 1996. An extraordinary project completed in 2002, this latter-day completion of the building followed Younger's original blueprints for the exterior.[7]

The north wing extended all the way to Connecticut Avenue, while the central section was recessed, with a porte-cochere entrance. The entrance appears at the base of a tower that suggests a skyscraper, with "Aztec" terraces near the top. Above these terraces is a pyramid-shaped roof clad in copper. The window bays within the outermost sections of the tower and the north wing's facade have aluminum spandrels with geometric Deco motifs. Alcoa Aluminum produced these spandrels. Aluminum combined with burnished bronze also appears in the entrance marquee and much of the interior Deco ornamentation. Most of this metal ornamentation came from the A. F. Jorss ironworks in Washington.

The cladding of the Kennedy-Warren is blonde brick and limestone. Carved bas-relief ornamentation is featured at both the base and the top of the tower. To the sides of the entrance are windows surmounted by sculpted birds. At the top of the tower, sculpted griffins appear at the outer edges. The sculpted panels came from the Edmonds Art Stone Company of Washington.

Designed in the grand manner, the Kennedy-Warren features a large and elegant two-level lobby with an exposed-beam ceiling, a public dining room, a ballroom, a garage, and stores, including a "news stand, beauty salon, gift and gown shops, laundry service, valet service," according to a promotional brochure.[8] Art Deco detailing is pervasive in the public spaces, from the plasterwork and the aluminum mezzanine railings in the lobby to the ornamentation of the ballroom to the black-and-copper elevator doors to the aluminum knockers on the apartment doors.

The two-story foyer of the Kennedy-Warren takes the form of a projecting glazed bay; five vertical stained glass windows are located above the doors. On entering the lobby, one immediately beholds the mezzanine, supported by reeded and marble-clad piers treated as pilasters. The mezzanine railings feature twisted-cross motifs that alternate with floral motifs. The walls of the lobby were originally clad with

The **Kennedy-Warren** apartment building from
Connecticut Avenue NW soon after its construction.

Photograph by Theodor Horydczak, Theodor Horydczak Collection,
Prints and Photographs Division, Library of Congress.

The lobby of the **Kennedy-Warren** in its original state.

Photograph by Theodor Horydczak, Theodor Horydczak Collection,
Prints and Photographs Division, Library of Congress.

matte-finish Prima Vera synthetic wood veneer. The beamed ceiling was painted with stenciled geometric motifs and sunbursts.

Below the mezzanine is a staircase leading to the lower lobby, which contains two banks of elevators. Black elevator doors contain inset triangular and fountain motifs that have a Meso-American character. North and south step-down lounges stand adjacent to the lobby, and a dining room and a ballroom are located in the north wing. In the ballroom are rectangular piers containing bas-relief panels of classical figures; a beamed ceiling; large reeded columns; a raised balcony to accommodate table seating; and a raised bandstand with streamlined trim.[9]

Though heavily composed of small rental units, the Kennedy-Warren also had luxurious larger apartment suites. The building was the first in the nation to feature a so-called air-conditioning system—actually a forced-air circulation system—which used large fans in the subbasement to pull cool air from the Rock Creek valley and circulate it.

After Kennedy and Warren went bankrupt, ownership passed to the mortgage holder, the B. F. Saul Company, which completed the north wing of the building in 1935. Among the famous Depression-era tenants were Harry Hopkins, FDR's adviser and administrator of the WPA, and a young Texas congressman, Lyndon Johnson, and his wife, Lady Bird. The Kennedy-Warren remains one of the great Art Deco landmarks of Washington. It is a designated historic landmark in the District of Columbia.

Slightly north, at the intersection of Connecticut Avenue and Sedgwick Street, the 1931–32 Sedgwick Gardens (3726 Connecticut Avenue NW) has been called the *pièce de résistance* of Mihran Mesrobian.[10] The plan of the five-story building comprises two U-shaped sections that are tilted diagonally away from each other and "hinged" to form the shape of an inverted V at the corner of the intersection. Within this V is a single-story entrance and lobby pavilion, with an Art Deco porte-cochere. The entrance doors

are surmounted by a glazed arch, at the sides of which are two high-relief sculpted figures grasping scepters. At the top of the building, in the middle of the V, is a pyramid-roofed elevator penthouse with a rose window.

An eclectic building, Sedgwick Gardens fuses Deco ornamentation (and a measure of Art Deco massing) with Byzantine, medieval, and Moorish inspirations. Its red brick facades are enlivened by bands of white brick in the middle section and white-brick belt courses at the top and bottom. Less grand than the Kennedy-Warren (which, after all, was designed as an apartment-*hotel*), Sedgwick Gardens had no great public rooms besides the spectacular Moorish lobby. The apartments, enhanced by projecting bays that housed porches, featured small dinettes, Murphy beds, and other economizing features for Depression-era renters. The builder was Max Gorin.

Another large Deco apartment building was completed near the end of the Hoover era: Rhode Island Gardens (1931), designed by Harvey P. Baxter and constructed at 230 Rhode Island Avenue NE. This imposing H-shaped building of red brick is built on a slope; it is six stories high at the top of the slope and seven stories high at the bottom. Its ornamentation—except for some Deco limestone panels that surround individual windows on the sixth and second floors—consists of brick courses running vertically beside window bays. The ornamentation at the entrance consists exclusively of intricate brickwork. The developers were Monroe and Hugh Warren.

As the New Deal commenced, construction of apartment buildings proliferated throughout the city. Many larger apartments were the work of the developer Morris Cafritz and designed by his capable architects Alvin Aubinoe Sr. and Harry L. Edwards. Cafritz built most of his apartments in the major northwest corridors, especially 16th Street and Connecticut Avenue— and in Foggy Bottom. Cafritz had built two Deco apartments in the Foggy Bottom area before the

The **Majestic** apartment building soon after its completion.

New Deal: the Park Central and the Parklane, both built in 1928 and both designed by Harvey Warwick. By 1937 all the major Cafritz apartment buildings were the work of Aubinoe and Edwards until Aubinoe left to start his own development company in 1938. Edwards carried on in the employ of Cafritz until he joined the Aubinoe firm after World War II.

The New Deal apartments created by Cafritz employed many earlier Deco conventions, while adding newer flourishes such as streamlining and the use of glass block. Many regard the splendid 1937 Majestic apartment building (3200 16th Street NW) as the supreme architectural achievement of the Cafritz team. The Majestic is located several blocks north of Meridian Hill Park and on the other side of the street.

A U-shaped building, the Majestic is slightly asymmetrical because of the space constraints of its site, which led Aubinoe and Edwards to make the south wing longer than the north. As with previous Washington Deco apartments, the ornamental use of vertical piers, in this case capped by zigzag finials, conveys a sense of "skyscraper" aesthetics.

The entrance of the blonde brick Majestic features stainless steel doors. Each door has a semicircular window, giving the effect of a large circular window where they meet. Immediately above the doors is a curving stainless steel marquee. Above the marquee and to the sides of the doors is a glass block wall, and to the sides of the wall are black decorative piers. Cafritz and his architects would use this particular entrance treatment in other buildings.

Perhaps the most striking feature of the Majestic—and also an apt demonstration of the way in which the streamlining fad became superimposed upon earlier Deco conventions—is the pair of rounded, towerlike window bays on the front facades of the building's wings. These bays feature ribbon windows. Most likely Aubinoe and Edwards were inspired by the very same feature on the 1936 Rockefeller Apartments in New York City, designed by J. André Fouil-

houx and Wallace K. Harrison. An eight-story building, the Majestic offered small efficiency apartments.[11]

Aubinoe and Edwards designed the Cafritz apartment building at 2000 Connecticut Avenue NW (1936) in association with Harvey Warwick. Then, in addition to the Majestic (1937), they designed another four apartment buildings for Cafritz: Ogden Gardens (1937), at 1445 Ogden Street NW; Otis Gardens (1937), at 1445 Otis Place NW; Park Crescent (1937), at 2901 18th Street NW; and High Towers (1938), at 1530 16th Street NW. After Aubinoe's departure, Edwards single-handedly designed the Gwenwood (1938), at 1020 19th Street NW (demolished); the Empire (1939), at 2000 F Street NW; and 1660 Lanier Place NW (1940). And Aubinoe designed and built several Deco apartment buildings, including the Congressional Apartments on Capitol Hill (1939), at 215 Constitution Avenue NE; and Winthrop House (1940), at 1727 Massachusetts Avenue NW.

As Aubinoe and Edwards designed their large apartment buildings, other Washington architects were working on comparable buildings. One of the most accomplished of these architects was Robert O. Scholz, who, like Aubinoe, became a developer as well.

Scholz's best-known Deco apartment building is the General Scott (1940), at 1 Scott Circle NW. Rectangular in plan, the building sports streamlining at a prominent corner: a rounded window bay with curved wrap-around windows at the intersection of Scott Circle and 16th Street. The nine-story building blends symmetry and asymmetry. Its blonde brick facade is set off by black stone panels functioning as spandrels within the pavilions projecting to the left and right. The entrance featured an aluminum marquee surmounted by an expanse of glass block and surrounded by black stone panels with setbacks at the top. The step-down lobby was developed with streamlined features: soft cove lighting in the ceiling, a curved front desk, a linoleum floor, and aluminum elevator doors with black geometric forms. The apartments were efficiencies. But the building had central air-conditioning, and the small apartments were designed with pleasant solariums.[12]

A few blocks away is another Scholz apartment building, completed in 1940: the Bay State, at 1701 Massachusetts Avenue NW. In this building one can see (in embryonic form) some of the ideas that Scholz would use in the General Scott.

Across town, in Foggy Bottom, two contemporaneous Deco apartment buildings designed by Scholz were very different in spirit. Munson Hall and Milton Hall, at, respectively, 2212 and 2222 I Street NW, were built in 1938. These rectangular, blonde brick apartment buildings were less streamlined than the other Scholz projects and used more ornamentation derived from the 1925 Paris Exposition. Both of these buildings eventually became dormitories for George Washington University, as did a third apartment building constructed a block to the south and back to back with Munson and Milton Halls: the Everglades (1939), at 2223 H Street NW. The design of the Everglades, by Joseph Abel, was clearly contrived to exist harmoniously with Scholz's work; it was an act of gallantry, especially since Abel's work had been moving in a different direction.

In the aftermath of the Shoreham Hotel project, Abel moved away from eclectic traditionalism toward increasingly interesting combinations of radical modernism (International Style) and streamlining. After Abel established a partnership with Charles Dillon in 1935, the firm employed the designer William Henry Shoemaker (1908–1976). Shoemaker's conceptual drawings suggest that he helped design many of the firm's most celebrated buildings.[13] Several apartment buildings designed by Abel show the influence of Shoemaker's work: 2929 Connecticut Avenue NW (1936); 4801 Connecticut Avenue NW (1938), a building attributed by its developer to the architect David L. Stern; and the

Governor Shepherd (1938, demolished), at 2121 Virginia Avenue NW.

The design of 2929 Connecticut Avenue NW is particularly brilliant. A U-shaped composition—from the street it appears to be a simple rectangular block, since the courtyard is placed along the side, by the alley—this nine-story building just south of the National Zoo in Woodley Park combines asymmetry with horizontality. A projecting left pavilion, enclosed with the exception of some short balconies extending on the right-hand side, is counterbalanced on the other side of the building by a nonprojecting tier of long balconies thrusting to the right. The result is a horizontal rightward impetus that flows from the north to the south across the facade. The dynamism here is remarkable, since the building materials are understated. Power and serenity are held in energetic equipoise, with a sophisticated effect. A decade later, in 1947, Abel observed that "the skillful placing and arrangement of balconies and porches give opportunity for many interesting effects, which contribute to making a good facade as well as being in themselves useful."[14]

The building is clad in red brick with concrete trim, which runs in long stringcourses, most of which are horizontal. There are ribbed "speed lines" of brickwork on the front walls of the balconies. The entrance is contained in a wall of glass block with a short rectangular marquee projecting across it. Flanking the entrance are rectangular limestone pillars. At the inner edge of each pillar is an ornamental latticework pattern. Within each hollowed-out block of the lattice—at the upper left corner—is a low-relief pattern of concentric squares; at the bottom are rectangular shapes.

The step-down lobby uses streamlined elements with a vaguely nautical feel. It has thick, rounded columns linked by the very crisp lines of a mezzanine balcony, a wall of glass block that faces the street, and recessed cove lighting. Like the Kennedy-Warren, this building had a

**4801 Connecticut Avenue NW**, 1983.

Photograph by Herbert Striner.

forced-air cooling system. The developers were Gustave Ring and Henry Jawish.[15]

Comparable flourishes were employed at 4801 Connecticut Avenue NW, but with a vastly different result. This nine-story building has a very interesting plan; it is an X- or cross-shaped building with an extra wing extending from the corner of one of the main wings. Although the arms of the cross come together at a right angle, they meet off-center, so the wings that extend to the north and east are longer than the ones that extend south and west. These latter "short wings" form a V at the intersection of Connecticut Avenue and Davenport Street. The building is clad in blonde brick with a limestone base at the principal corners. Between the windows are spandrels of gray brick.

The entrance to the building is located within the V at Connecticut and Davenport. As with Sedgwick Gardens a few blocks away, a single-story entrance pavilion was inserted into the V. But in this case a circular stainless steel marquee surges forward. This cantilevered disc is an eye-catching feature, but the form of the entrance itself, at the back of the pavilion, is a notable feature as well. It is a glass-block cylinder or drum, a columnar expanse that surrounds the building's foyer. Perhaps the cylinder was inspired by the use of the very same feature, but on a vastly larger scale, in the entrance corner of the Hecht Company warehouse, completed the previous year. Within the foyer of 4801 Connecticut, the terrazzo floor has a sunray pattern. Above and below the ground-floor windows to the sides of the entrance pavilion at 4801 Connecticut are cast-concrete spandrels with a latticework pattern featuring low-relief ziggurats. They are similar to the panels used at 2929 Connecticut.

Although David L. Stern was credited as the architect in some of the promotional pamphlets for the building, Abel and his surviving partner, Jesse Weinstein, asserted in interviews conducted in the 1980s that Abel developed the de-

sign as some sort of a personal favor to Stern.[16] Conceptual drawings in the William Henry Shoemaker collection suggest that he developed some basic ideas for the building, especially the composition of the brilliant entrance and lobby. The developer of this project was Alvin Aubinoe.

In the same year, Abel, with apparent assistance from Shoemaker, designed the Governor Shepherd apartment building in Foggy Bottom. In 1940 the building appeared in the Museum of Modern Art's *Guide to Modern Architecture— Northeast States*.[17] Abel himself considered it significant enough to merit comment in a book that he coauthored a decade later.[18] This long, rectangular, nine-story building clad in blonde brick was symmetrical. Its long central section was flanked by pavilions. Four tiers of balconies within these pavilions (two tiers to each) formed a zigzag pattern, with one tier of balconies placed on the front of each pavilion and the other tier inserted (and thereby recessed) at the side. Above each balcony tier, a protective canopy flared to the front and the side of the building from the roof.

The exterior base of the Governor Shepherd was clad in black marble. The lobby presented yet another demonstration of the streamline aesthetic as employed by Dillon & Abel. Asymmetrical, the room featured mirrored side walls, a black terrazzo floor, and at the rear a rounded drop ceiling supported by columns sheathed in aluminum. The building also had a forced-air cooling system. The builder was John J. McInerney.

An attempt to preserve this building in the 1980s was defeated, in part because of "expert witnesses" who assisted the owners in persuading the DC Historic Preservation Review Board to deny protected status to the Governor Shepherd. The antipreservation testimony stands as an egregious example of bought-and-paid-for pedantry, procured by a law firm. Among their other contentions, these "experts" asserted that the Governor Shepherd's symmetrical composition made it less than a "pure" example of the International Style, an assertion that was not only preposterous (many buildings of Mies van der Rohe, for example, would flunk such a "purity" test) but also grounded in the sad presupposition of would-be connoisseurs that only "pure" examples of a "style" deserve to be protected.[19] The Governor Shepherd was demolished in 1985.

Another architect of large Deco apartments at the time was Francis L. Koenig, who designed (in collaboration with Harvey Warwick) the Marlyn (1938), at 3901 Cathedral Avenue NW, and Dorchester House (1941), at 2480 16th Street NW. The Marlyn, a six-story irregular U-shaped building, is distinctive for several reasons. Because of its sloping site, the architect figured out a way to place the lobby between the first and second floors. That is, the lobby sits farther up the hill than the first floor. Hence a stairway leading both up and down is a notable design element within the lobby. Another prominent feature of the lobby is its streamlined and fluted walls. The Marlyn was the very first apartment building in the nation to feature central air-conditioning properly so called. Clad in blonde brick, the facade of the Marlyn is enlivened by darker horizontal bands of brown brick, along with porcelain enamel spandrels and Art Deco medallions executed in polychrome concrete by John Joseph Earley. The developer was Gustave Ring.[20]

The scale of Dorchester House is vastly greater. Developed by a consortium of owners— Herbert Glassman, Morris Gewirz, Harry Viner, and Edward Ostrow—this building designed by Koenig had 394 rental units. Located slightly south of the Majestic apartments on 16th Street, Dorchester House is an irregular cross-shaped building clad in blonde brick. It is nine stories tall.

The arms of the cross that form the building are joined off-center, so that one of them has a "short end." The other ends of the arms are crisscrossed by short pavilions. The pavilion closest to 16th Street contains the entrance, which was placed off-center for the purpose of gaining a 16th Street address. As a result, the pedestrian flow is unconventional. Guests approach the building, pass under an aluminum marquee, walk through the doors and across a short foyer, ascend some stairs, turn left, and then walk down a very long "Peacock Alley" to the center of the building, where the desk and the elevators are located. This configuration was and is highly unusual.

The entrance pavilion features soaring verticality and bulky mass. Narrow window bays surge up the building. In a central section they extend all the way to the top. To the left and the right of this section, they extend up the first eight floors and then are intersected at the ninth by a wide band of black bricks. Small columnar tiers of rounded window bays were inserted at the intersections of the principal facades, affording the apartments at these locations more space and light. Dorchester House contained one- and two-bedroom apartments as well as efficiencies. The building included a roof deck and stores in the basement. Among the notable residents during World War II were the secretary of labor, Frances Perkins; a dozen members of Congress; and from October 1941 until January 1942 a young naval ensign, John F. Kennedy.[21]

One of the most prolific designers of Deco apartment buildings in Washington was George T. Santmyers. Most of his projects in the 1930s and 1940s were garden apartments, but he also designed a few notable large apartment buildings. In sequence, the most significant of these were the Metropolitan (1936), at 200–210 Rhode Island Avenue NE; Macomb Gardens (1937), at 3725 Macomb Street NW; the Normandie (1938), at 6817 Georgia Avenue NW; the Yorkshire (1941), at 3355 16th Street NW; and two other 1941 buildings constructed in Woodley Park: the Delano and 2800 Woodley Road NW.

The Delano is located at 2745 29th Street

NW. Built by the developer Sidney Brown, this H-shaped building is clad in blonde brick. Since 29th Street runs along a slope, the Delano is five stories tall at the north end and six stories tall at the south. The understated treatment of the exterior, including a simple but graceful marquee built of cast concrete, conceals a flamboyant Deco lobby featuring a domed ceiled with recessed cove lighting, a fancy plasterwork Deco cornice, blue-mirrored walls, wrought-iron balustrades with swags, and wainscoting upholstered in blue leather.[22]

A comparable Santmyers building, 2800 Woodley Road NW, was constructed immediately to the north of the Delano in the very same year. Much larger than the Delano, this five-story building has a fascinating overhead plan—from the street it looks almost symmetrical, but it isn't—a plan that was developed to fit the irregular site. This plan is complex, notwithstanding the uniform height of the building and the overall illusion of symmetry.

From Woodley Road, where the entrance to the building is placed, looking south in the direction of the Delano, the overhead plan of this building can be read as a crooked, asymmetrical E (the prongs facing down) with a lop-sided T projecting off-center to the right from the back of the E. When seen in elevation from the street, the design reads as follows: In the middle of the Woodley Road facade is a pavilion flanked by projecting wings at either end. Each of these wings contains smaller projecting pavilions. The left-hand wing flares diagonally away from the facade.

Along the west side of the building, on 29th Street NW, is a deep recessed courtyard framed by wings to the north and south. At the rear of the building (where the back wall faces the Delano across an alley) the elevation is flat. But what cannot be seen from the street is the east side of the building, which is wildly irregular: it features square and diagonal corners on much larger wings that frame a much larger inner courtyard. Muted Deco ornamentation is established on the blonde brick facades of this building through simple devices such as vertical piers and zigzag patterns of vertical brick courses within the spandrels.

As in the Delano, a spectacular Art Deco lobby is contained within the unassuming exterior of this building. The lobby's great size is counterbalanced by the warm tones of the wood veneer sheathing vertical supports treated as bundles of columns incorporating furniture—sofas and planters. A room of considerable scale was thus given great warmth. The entrance to 2800 Woodley Road was also flamboyant: graceful inward-curving walls are sheathed in blue Carrara glass, called "Vitrolite" in the trade. The floor of the porch is terrazzo with geometric patterns.

Santmyers's Normandie (1938), at 6817 Georgia Avenue NW, was built right across the street from the army's Walter Reed Hospital. The developer was Webster Construction Company. Quite possibly this building was planned to be a small apartment-hotel to serve military families. As with the previously mentioned Santmyers buildings, the exterior of this six-story, H-shaped building is subdued. Clad in red brick, the Normandie is a conservative composition. One interesting feature is the two square pavilions with tiers of screened porches tucked into the inner corners of the H at the front of the building. The only Deco ornamental feature on the exterior is the entrance. And yet the Normandie lobby is richly adorned with intricate Deco moldings, stainless steel balustrades, and a fountain sheathed in glazed tile.

When Deco apartments are considered from the strictly ornamental point of view, the work of many less prominent architects in Washington can be interesting. The Deco apartment at 1417 N Street NW is a good example. Originally built in 1930 but renovated in 1938 by the architect Frank Tomlinson, the entrance features sleek panels of Carrara glass, or Vitrolite, with stripes and medallions sandblasted into a black background. Placed within vertical panels of Vitrolite were light fixtures covered by aluminum grilles with a sunray pattern. The lobby of 1417 N Street featured Formica panels simulating different hues of wood veneer and arranged in geometric patterns.

Comparable treatment of an entrance can be found in Rock Creek Gardens West (1939), at 2511 Q Street NW (above Georgetown), designed by Joseph J. Maggenti. In this case the name of the building was sandblasted into the black Vitrolite transom bar above the door in Art Deco letters.

In the vicinity of some major Deco apartment buildings are lesser but interesting examples of Deco apartment-building design. For example, near the Majestic—the masterpiece of Cafritz and his architects—are the subdued but sophisticated Century apartments (1936), at 2651 16th Street NW, designed by Louis T. Rouleau, and the Yorkshire (1941), at 3355 16th Street, designed by Santmyers. The entrance of the Yorkshire features an elegant marquee consisting of a thick half-cylinder of polished gray stone. And the Yorkshire salutes the Majestic in the use of rounded towers at the front corners.

Perhaps the last of the large Art Deco apartment buildings to be built in Washington was the Capitol Plaza (1949), at 35 E Street NW, in the vicinity of Union Station. The front edge of the marquee contains concrete mosaic designs, and the building is clad in blonde brick. Mihran Mesrobian was the architect, and Harry Loveless was the developer.

One final, sad note on the subject of large residential buildings: In 1939, an older Washington hotel, the Roger Smith (earlier the Hotel Powhatan), a block from the White House at Pennsylvania Avenue and 18th Street NW, remodeled its lobby. The new lobby, designed by Laurence Emmons, was an elegantly understated fusion of Art Deco and classicism. Emmons used walnut paneling, torchères, and a Greek key pattern in the mezzanine railing, a pattern that was replicated in the carpet. The president of the New York–based Roger Smith chain reminisced about the work:

> Laurence Emmons spent several weeks at his draughting table in designing [the lobby] and perhaps several months out in the field trying to find just the right walnut paneling to carry out his design. Laurence Emmons was an outstanding decorator, and a very sensitive master of his profession. There never was a draughtsman quite as proficient, and quite as sure at his draughting table. He amazed all his fellows with the speed in which he executed complicated designs.[23]

In 1975 the Roger Smith Hotel in Washington was demolished.

## GARDEN APARTMENTS AND PUBLIC HOUSING

Garden apartments, both private-sector developments and public housing projects, emerged from the Garden City movement of the 1890s. The Garden City movement, like the kindred and contemporaneous City Beautiful movement, advanced new ideals for the planning of cities and suburbs, ideals that would mediate the dialectical forces of city and country, development and nature, formality and informality, progress and continuity, and thereby achieve a new harmony in the built environment.

Ebenezer Howard's *Garden Cities of To-Morrow* was a British manifesto that led to the creation in the early twentieth century of new model towns around London, Birmingham, and Liverpool.[24] American architects such as Clarence Stein (1883–1975) and Henry Wright (1878–1936) championed the idea and sought to put it into action: to build low-density, decentralized housing for people of modest means. Stein helped to found the Regional Planning Association of America (RPAA) in 1923. The RPAA, in turn, was instrumental in creating the City

The lobby of the **Roger Smith Hotel** soon after its 1939 renovation.

Richard Striner collection.

Housing Corporation, which constructed two demonstration communities: Sunnyside Gardens in the New York City borough of Queens (1924–28) and Radburn, New Jersey (1928–33).[25]

During the Great Depression new garden apartments were built at a furious pace across the greater Washington area. Two projects—Colonial Village (1935–37, 1940), in Arlington, Virginia, designed by Harvey H. Warwick Sr.; and the Falkland (1936–37), in Silver Spring, Maryland, designed by Louis Justement—set the standard. Both of these low-rise garden-apartment complexes were designed in the mode of Colonial Revival. Both offered low-cost rental housing in low-rise buildings that were sited together in parklike surroundings. Both created the sense of a villagelike community.[26]

Privately built garden apartments in Washington that bore the imprint of Art Deco design—most of them small-scale projects or even single buildings—were clustered in several neighborhoods or precincts within the city. The most compact of these districts is in Glover Park NW, between Georgetown and Wesley Heights. Another is extended along several commuting corridors. It begins in the neighborhood in and around Military Road and 14th Street NW (both north and south of Military Road) and radiates outward in several directions: along Missouri Avenue to North Capitol Street and also in a northeast direction toward noncontiguous clusters in Takoma Park and Silver Spring.

A more extensive and better-planned Deco garden-apartment project, Lee Gardens, was built across the Potomac River in Arlington, Virginia. Other Deco garden apartments were scattered in additional commuting corridors (such as Pennsylvania Avenue SE) or developing locales (such as Rosslyn, Virginia; Hyattsville, Maryland; and the Arlandria and Del-Ray section west of Alexandria, Virginia, on Mount Vernon Avenue).

The Glover Park "district" of Deco garden apartments is spread out upon a residential plateau bounded on the south by Calvert Street, on the east and north by the curving Tunlaw Road, and on the west by 42nd Street NW. To the north are the wealthy neighborhood of Wesley Heights and the campus of American University. Wending its way along the district's edge—to the west and north—is Glover-Archbold Park.

Two of the most substantial Deco garden-apartment projects in this district were designed by George T. Santmyers and developed by Maurice Korman: Park View Terrace (1939), at Davis Place, 42nd Street, and Edmund Street NW; and Park Crest Gardens (1941), at W Street, 42nd Street, and Benton Street NW. Park Crest Gardens is by far the larger of the projects, made up of five buildings arranged in a slightly irregular pattern on a steep slope. Two larger buildings at the top of the slope and three smaller buildings at the bottom are connected by an open hillside with terraces, footpaths, and stairways.

All the buildings in the project are four stories high and clad in blonde brick. The two buildings at the crest of the ridge are L-shaped. Placed side by side, with an alley in between, they form a long expanse that turns its back upon the street: all but two entrances, which are corner entrances at side streets, open to the hillside courtyard. The short sides of these L-shaped buildings face inward, back to back, toward the courtyard. Each of these buildings has five separate entrances, resulting in five separate street addresses. The entrances are placed upon and also in between pavilions. The three lower buildings are rectangular and E-shaped, with pavilions at the ends of each building and also in the center. Each pavilion has its own separate entrance and stair hall, and each has a different street address. They all face the street at the bottom and the side of the hill.

The entrances were built of concrete panels that were probably produced by the John Joseph Earley studio. Simple and handsome, they contain the name of the complex, the address of the entrance, and some Deco ornamentation using geometric and floral forms. Above the door is a short marquee. And over some of the entrances

The **Park Crest Gardens** apartment complex, Glover Park, 2011.

Photograph by Melissa Blair.

is a vertical expanse of glass block to illuminate the stair hall.

Park View Terrace, slightly to the north, comprises three rectangular E-shaped buildings that are almost identical in plan and ornamentation to the lower buildings of Park Crest Gardens.[27]

The district of Deco garden apartments clustered around 14th Street and Military Road NW is a concentrated sector of a broader sequence of development. The concentrated sector forms a most extraordinary streetscape: block after block of Deco garden apartments (interspersed, to be sure, with more traditional buildings) with some interesting Deco duplex houses. One finds a seemingly endless display in these contiguous blocks—14th Street NW (both above and below Military Road); 13th Place, Fort Stevens Drive, and Luzon Avenue NW (all north of Military Road); and Colorado Avenue NW (south of Military Road)—of the Deco ornamental repertoire in the hands of George T. Santmyers: geometric patterns and floral motifs, an abundance of glass block, and marquees of aluminum adorned with Vitrolite panels.

Unlike the entrances to Park View Terrace and Park Crest Gardens in Glover Park, which were obviously custom-designed, the ornamented limestone panels that Santmyers used in many of these buildings appear to have been mass-produced. It bears noting, however, that a highly distinctive form crowns the entrance to 1400 Somerset Place NW, designed by Bryan Connor: a limestone sculpture in the form of a gear.

Most of these buildings are clad in red brick, though some blonde brick buildings appear in the blocks toward the northern end of the district. These latter buildings combine Deco features such as streamlined corners and zigzag brick courses with decorative elements that anticipate 1950s modernism, such as large, rectilinear stainless steel marquees that tilt up at sharp angles.

The largest of the Santmyers Deco buildings in this district are the 1938 Luzon (6323 Luzon Avenue NW), and the 1939 Fort View Apartments (6000 and 6050 13th Place NW), which face Fort Stevens, where a Civil War battle took place on July 11, 1864. (The fort was partially restored in the 1930s by the Civilian Conservation Corps.)

Perhaps the handsomest of the Santmyers garden apartments in the district is the two-building complex that contains the street addresses 5915–5925 14th Street NW. Facing each other on a hillside—with stairs, sidewalks, and a courtyard plaza in between—the two buildings are different in plan. The upper building, containing the street addresses 5921–5925 14th Street NW, is L-shaped. The three entrances to this four-story building feature limestone door surrounds and lintels with curvilinear geometric forms, a vertical expanse of glass block above each entrance, and a limestone spandrel with Deco floral ornamentation in the middle of the glass block column. The lower building, containing the street addresses 5915–5919 14th Street, is U-shaped, its wings flaring diagonally out from the center. It too has three entrances. The back of this building runs along Military Road. Constructed in 1940, this complex was built by Louis Luria and Herman Shapiro.

From this highly concentrated sector, the development of Deco garden apartments spread eastward along Missouri Avenue NW all the way to North Capitol Street, and beyond, along Riggs Road. The most notable buildings there are Concord Manor, at 430 Missouri Avenue NW; the garden apartment at 5301 New Hampshire Avenue NW; and the garden apartment at 5210 North Capitol Street.

Concord Manor, designed by Santmyers and built in 1941, is especially interesting. A four-story, L-shaped building, its principal facades face north and west, along Missouri Avenue and 5th Street NW, respectively. The longer west facade contains four projecting pavilions. The Deco entrance, in the middle of the building, features limestone door surrounds with fluted pilasters, a lintel emblazoned with decorative chevrons, and two separate columns of setback terraces at the top. The shorter north facade features two projecting pavilions with the entrance off-center, to the left. This entrance is completely different from that on the west facade, with the setback terraces converging into a ziggurat. Perhaps the most interesting feature of the building is the decorative program at the roofline: inverted ziggurat inlays of limestone are embedded at the principal corners of the red brick facades. These corner motifs are joined by horizontal limestone bands containing chevrons. The developer was Harry Cohen.

The building at 5301 New Hampshire Avenue NW, whose longest elevation runs along Missouri Avenue, is also distinctive. Designed by Claude Norton and built in 1939, this L-shaped, four-story building features rear pavilions whose multiple facades are sculpted into intricately geometric sawtooth patterns. The resulting zigzag aesthetic is also expressed in the ziggurat finials that punctuate the roofline. This red brick building is ornamented with horizontal belt courses of darker brick. The front and back entrances are located at the corner of the L. The developer was J. Charles Shapiro.

Farther north, the same development wave produced the Whittier Gardens complex (1939), designed by Santmyers. This three-building cluster at the edge of Takoma Park (on the District of Columbia side of this suburb) comprises the following addresses: 301–305 Whittier Street NW, 300–304 Aspen Street NW, and 6718–6722 3rd Street NW. Each of the three-story, red brick buildings is essentially two attached buildings configured as a chunky Z—two adjacent cubes, one of which is shoved to the rear. Each section has its own entrance, around which are limestone door surrounds with geometric patterns on either side of the door, along with Deco light fixtures. Above the door is the name of the complex, surmounted by a Deco ornamental

panel. The door surrounds taper into setbacks. Above each door is a vertical column of glass block, at the base of which is a spandrel with a small octagonal window that mimics a longer octagonal window in the middle of the door.

The siting and placement of the buildings is graceful. All contained generously proportioned tiers of screened porches—the screens were subsequently replaced with glass when the buildings "went condo"—arranged upon pavilions placed in a zigzag or sawtooth pattern on the backs of the buildings. Ida Baylin was the developer.

Another farther-out Santmyers garden-apartment complex, Montgomery Arms, was built within the central business district of Silver Spring, Maryland, at 8700–8722 Colesville Road, in 1941. The complex consists of three five-story, rectangular buildings arranged around a landscaped courtyard. Each building has multiple projecting pavilions on the side that faces the courtyard. The central building has a very large entrance, spanning four window bays, with a cast-concrete marquee very similar to the one Santmyers used in the Delano, built the same year. In all likelihood, this development was built to serve as "war housing" for the workforce of the Johns Hopkins Applied Physics Laboratory, around the corner on Georgia Avenue. The Montgomery Arms apartments were given protection by Montgomery County in 1991.

Another Deco garden-apartment complex in Silver Spring—Spring Gardens, at 8001–8031 Eastern Avenue, on the District line—was built in 1941. The architect was Santmyers, and the developer was Morris Miller.[28]

One stand-alone garden-apartment building deserves special mention: Mount Dome, at 3304 Pennsylvania Avenue SE, designed by Bryan J. Connor and built in 1939. This three-story, red brick building has retail space at the corner; its entrance is clad in Carrara glass. But the apartment-building entrance is the memorable feature: a concrete plane with a recess containing no less than seven receding zigzag terraces at the top. The shape of the windows in the doors mimics this pattern.

Across the Potomac, in Arlington, Virginia, an extensive garden-apartment complex arose in 1941 and 1942: Lee Gardens, since renamed Sheffield Court. This complex represents an interesting and important example of the later work of Mihran Mesrobian, as well as a richly eclectic (and in many ways superbly improbable) intermixture of Art Deco, the International Style, and Colonial Revival. Lee Gardens was located along the newly constructed Arlington Boulevard, originally named Lee Boulevard. Built by the developers Fred Schnider and Melvin Schlosberg, the complex comprises thirty-seven buildings on a site bounded by Arlington Boulevard, Pershing Drive, North Barton Street, and North 10th Street. The original Lee Gardens project was built around an internal street, North Wayne Street, which serves as a central north-south axis. This street terminates within the project, thus eliminating through traffic. Another street, North 9th Street, enters from the west.

The layout is formal, symmetrical, and axial. The buildings are arranged in a peripheral crescent around North Wayne Street. They are clustered into groups of three around courtyards that open to the east or to the west, in alternating sequence, except at North 9th Street, where the courtyards open to the north or south.

The central building in each of the U-shaped courtyards has a hip roof; the two flanking buildings have flat roofs. The central building is symmetrical, with a pavilion (with its own hip roof, which intersects the building) placed on either side of the entrance that faces the courtyard. The flanking buildings in the courtyards are Z-shaped. At the entrance to the courtyard a single pavilion faces in. On the other side of the building, at the opposite end, a contrapuntal pavilion faces out.

All of the three-story buildings in the complex are clad in either red or buff brick. The central buildings in the courtyards mix Art Deco and Colonial Revival; the limestone door surrounds, for example, feature classical broken pediments with urns. Above these doorways are octagonal windows that illuminate the second story of the stair hall. The third story is illuminated either by oriel windows or by pairs of vertical windows.

The flanking buildings synthesize Art Deco, Colonial Revival, and the International Style. The inward-projecting pavilions feature wrap-around windows at the corners of the second floor. At the third floor, wrap-around fenestration runs as a continuous band of glass block that is punctuated by casement windows. Above this band of fenestration is a cantilevered roof canopy. Deco ornamentation is added in the form of stone circular panels that display a sun motif—emblazoned with a smiling, bas-relief face—surrounded by a circular pattern of chevrons. Additional Deco ornamentation consists of nonstructural two-story piers surmounted by a bas-relief sculpture of birds.

At the south end of the project is a large rectangular building that serves as the focal point of Lee Gardens. And its references to Colonial Williamsburg—a restoration project that was capturing the imagination of many Americans in the 1930s—are unmistakable. But the Colonial Revival vocabulary has a Deco quality. The center of the building is flanked by pavilions. Each pavilion has a hip roof that intersects the main roof. At the outer edge of each pavilion is a further projection, a towerlike window bay with a conical roof that intersects the pavilion roof.

The central section of the building has a ground-floor arcade. Above the arches is a limestone panel engraved with the name and date of the project. Atop the gabled roof is a cupola. But this distinctively eighteenth-century feature crowns a column of glass block, which is surely 1930s whimsy at its finest.[29]

Such playfulness was generally absent in the low-rise public housing projects that served as

Building in the **Lee Gardens complex**, Arlington, Virginia, showing
a synthesis of Art Deco, Colonial Revival, and the International Style.

Photograph by Melissa Blair.

Washington's public-sector counterpart to the privately built garden apartments. Although Anglo-American Garden City ideals—and aesthetics—were influential among the architects and planners who designed these public projects, another influence, radical modernism, was prominent as well.

Such were the aesthetics of the Langston Terrace Dwellings, built by the federal Public Works Administration. Built upon a sloping site north of Benning Road NE—the slightly irregular fourteen-acre site is bounded roughly by Benning Road, 21st Street, H Street, and 24th Street NE, though the project extends to the north and to the west. The work of an African American architect, Hilyard Robinson, and its first residents were low-income blacks.

The origins of the project date to 1934, when the new federal Alley Dwelling Authority was created by Congress to rid the nation's capital of slums that formed "hidden communities" in the alleys of the city. Concurrently, local activists formed a Washington Committee on Housing, which successfully petitioned for PWA funding to construct a model public housing project for low-income African Americans in northeast Washington.

Interior Secretary Harold Ickes laid the 1937 cornerstone for the Langston Terrace Dwellings, named for John M. Langston, a black reformer and political leader who served as a congressman from Virginia during Reconstruction and became the first dean of the Howard University School of Law.[30] The project, which opened in April 1938, comprises more than twenty groups of attached buildings that vary from two-story row houses to three- and four-story apartment buildings, containing in all 274 units.

The architecture is restrained, with rectilinear massing, straightforward fenestration, subdued cladding materials (buff and dark brown brick), and an overall plan that favors symmetry (albeit with some traces of asymmetry), especially the symmetry of the central courtyard contained within the segment of the project built between

G and H Streets. This courtyard functioned as the center of community life for the early residents.

One can certainly behold in this project some elements of the International Style, to which Robinson was exposed in his European studies.[31] But important traces of Art Deco can be glimpsed, in both massing and ornamentation. High on a hill overlooking the Anacostia River, the Langston complex is easily visible from the westbound lanes of the East Capitol Street Bridge. From there, the varying heights of these numerous attached buildings create an interplay of mass with a decidedly zigzag, almost cubistic effect. When the complex is viewed at close range, from Benning Road, this effect is even more pronounced.

As to ornamentation, the entrance to the main building from H Street NE is noteworthy. This entrance consists of an underpass that leads from the street to the inner courtyard. One passes through a rectilinear passage—in truth, a tunnel—leading through the building.

Looking back from the courtyard, one beholds a sculpted frieze of terra-cotta figures. This frieze, entitled "The Progress of the Negro Race," was produced by the sculptor Daniel G. Olney. It begins on the left-hand wall, which curves into the underpass entrance on the courtyard side of the project. One of the few curvilinear features of the project, this "streamlined" corner is not repeated on the other side. The rectilinear arch of the underpass entrance is thus asymmetrical: it has a curved corner wall on the left-hand side and a straight corner on the right. The frieze begins beside the entrance to the underpass at the left and then passes over the top of the arcade. All the figures to the left and the center are sculpted in low relief. Then, to the right, upon a separate pavilion of the building, is a high-relief sculpture of a mother and children. Additional, freestanding sculpture within the courtyard—large sculpted animals intended to serve as play fixtures—were created by Lenore Thomas (known later on by her married name, Lenore Thomas Strauss), who also made important contributions to the public buildings of Greenbelt, Maryland.

The town of Greenbelt constitutes a venture in garden-city planning and development that is internationally renowned. It was the brainchild of Rexford Guy Tugwell, a professor at Columbia University who became a member of FDR's "brain trust." After serving as assistant secretary of agriculture, Tugwell persuaded FDR to create a new agency, the Resettlement Administration (RA), in 1935. The RA combined several preexisting programs designed to assist impoverished Americans in rural areas, as well as refugees from the Dust Bowl. Tugwell added a new division to the RA: the Suburban Division. Preliminary funding came from the Relief Appropriation Act of 1935, which, out of a total RA appropriation of $126.5 million, provided $31 million for the Suburban Division to create new garden cities, or "greenbelt towns."[32] The term *greenbelt* came directly from the lexicon of Ebenezer Howard, the garden-city visionary, whose plan for the British garden city of Letchworth included "green belts" of open space surrounding the community.[33]

Once the RA was created, Tugwell held an organizational meeting from June 30 to July 3, 1935, in the resort town of Buck Hill Falls, Pennsylvania. Among those attending were First Lady Eleanor Roosevelt, the financier Bernard Baruch, the philosopher John Dewey, and the urban planners Clarence Stein and Catherine Bauer. The construction of Greenbelt, Maryland, began on October 12, 1935.[34] Since the preliminary planning session had adjourned on July 3, this construction date reveals that the preliminary designs for Greenbelt were produced in only three months.

The Suburban Division hired Hale Walker as the town planner for Greenbelt and Wallace Richards as the overall coordinator of the project. Douglas Ellington and Reginald J. Wadsworth were commissioned to design the buildings. (The plans were drawn up in the fifty-four-room Evalyn Walsh McLean mansion on Massachusetts Avenue NW in Washington, DC.) The workers who constructed the town were recruited from the WPA work-relief program.[35]

The design concept for Greenbelt derived from Clarence Stein's work at Radburn, New Jersey, in association with the sociologist Clarence Perry. Stein, who served as a consultant to the RA and advised the designers of Greenbelt, wrote that Greenbelt and the other new towns built by the RA were "among the best applications of the principles laid down by Clarence Perry, which we would have carried out at Radburn had its growth not been stunted."[36]

Stein observed that the "focus" of Greenbelt was a "planned center" made up of "school, community buildings, shopping center, government and management offices, and principal recreation activities."[37] Radiating from this civic center in a sweeping semicircle were neighborhood units laid out along the lines first developed at Radburn: residential blocks of row-house units (or garden-apartment buildings) facing inward, away from the street, toward a central green court. The residential blocks were connected to each other, as well as to the civic center of the town, through a system of pedestrian trails that crossed the roads via underpasses.

When completed, Greenbelt comprised 574 row houses, 306 apartments, 375 garages, and five single-family houses.[38] Residents were selected according to criteria developed in 1937. Applicants were screened in regard to income level, demonstrated need for decent housing, pride in the upkeep of their existing homes, and a "cooperative spirit." Quotas were established in an effort to maintain an even balance between governmental and nongovernmental workers, as well as an even distribution of religious denominations.[39]

Much of the local reaction to Greenbelt was hostile. Nearby residents in Prince Georges County feared an influx of low-income "outsiders." Plans for an adjunct community for black residents were dropped because of local opposition; consequently, the town became a whites-only project. Washington's newspapers took a unified position of editorial opposition to Greenbelt. Eugene Meyer, the publisher of the *Washington Post*, blasted "Tugwell's folly."[40] Many conservatives regarded the project as socialistic. Although Greenbelt received much favorable press coverage outside the Washington area, Tugwell became a lightning rod of controversy, and he resigned on December 31, 1936. The Resettlement Administration was dismantled, and its programs were transferred to the new Farm Security Administration in 1937.

The Maryland General Assembly passed legislation on June 1, 1937, creating a council-manager form of government for the town, as the FSA had proposed. The first housing blocks were completed on September 30, 1937, along with the civic-center buildings. The first residents began to move in. In the meantime, however, there was serious concern that the town might never be completed as designed.

The FSA had put army engineers in charge of completing the construction. Wallace Richards, the former coordinator of the project, worried that the landscaping and the recreational features, such as a swimming pool, might not be completed owing to last-minute "economizing." In October 1937 he wrote to Eleanor Roosevelt: "If I were not utterly convinced of the necessity for the full completion of Greenbelt, I would not think of begging you, as I am, to assume an even greater interest in the town." Mrs. Roosevelt, persuaded, wrote to her husband: "This seems to me most important. There is a new experiment being involved which curtailment may seriously hurt. Won't you look into it?" The president replied, "I suggest that you and Will Alexander go out to Greenbelt and see it some morning or afternoon after you get back."[41]

Will Alexander had been Tugwell's deputy at the RA, and he was familiar with Greenbelt. It bears noting that the president had visited Greenbelt shortly after his reelection in November 1936. During that visit he proclaimed, "I have seen the blueprints of this project and have been greatly interested, but the actual sight itself exceeds anything I have dreamed of."[42] The president's intervention guaranteed Greenbelt's completion. The swimming pool opened on Memorial Day 1939.

The residential buildings were similar in aesthetic terms to the buildings of Langston Terrace; the powerful influence of the International Style was obvious. The Art Deco flourishes in Greenbelt were concentrated in the civic-center buildings. The residential buildings were simple and rectangular, some constructed with cinder-block and others with wood frames clad in brick and painted white or in pastel colors. Some of the buildings had flat roofs, per the International Style convention, while others had gabled roofs. Casement windows predominated, with a vertical expanse of glass block above the apartment-building entrances to illuminate the stair halls. The entrances to most of the residential buildings had overhead canopies.

Visual interest was created in some of the buildings through the use of streamlined horizontal brick courses that created a band between the windows. Moreover, the floor plans of the units varied significantly. Among the 574 row houses, there were seventy-one different floor plans, including one-, two-, and three-bedroom layouts. Most of the row houses had two stories, but twenty-two of them were three stories high, and sixteen ("honeymoon cottages" for married couples without children) were one-story dwellings. The entrances all faced inward toward the courtyard side of the buildings, which residents often called the "garden side," while the back side of the buildings, also called the "kitchen side" or "service side," faced the street.

Each unit had an attached outside storage closet, along with a drop-lid underground garbage container, on the porch of the "kitchen side."[43] Simple but elegant maple "Greenbelt furniture," designed by artists in the Special Skills Division of the RA, was available for purchase on easy terms. All housing in Greenbelt was rental in the early years of the town. After World War II, a long series of efforts by Greenbelt residents established a housing cooperative, Greenbelt Homes, Inc.

### SINGLE-FAMILY AND DUPLEX HOUSES

Most of the "modern" homes built in greater Washington during the Depression—amid a larger trend of traditionalism—displayed the influence of radical modernism far more than the influence of Art Deco. Still, the eclectic spirit imbued some nontraditional houses in Washington with traces of Art Deco in combination with the International Style. There were even some combinations of Art Deco, the International Style, and clear-cut traditionalism—very much along the lines of the synthesis achieved by Mesrobian in the Lee Gardens project. Finally, in and around the city there were "modern" houses whose qualities can only be expressed by the term *Art Deco*.

The grandest example of Art Deco in a single-family Washington residence is without question the 1936–37 Cafritz house, popularly known as the "Cafritz Mansion," at 2301 Foxhall Road NW. Designed by the Cafritz architects Alvin Aubinoe and Harry L. Edwards, the house sits atop a hill with a breathtaking view of the city. From the back porch of the mansion, one gazes over a long wooded valley at the other end of which the Washington Monument, the Potomac River, and the Virginia shoreline are visible.

The developer Morris Cafritz and his wife, Gwendolyn, traveled around the country collecting ideas for the "dream house" they planned to build. One of the houses that caught their fancy was the Richard Mandel house in Mount Kisco, New York (1933–35), designed by Edward Durrell Stone.[44] They admired the site and the avant-garde interior, designed by Donald Deskey. While the Cafritz house exterior would be more subdued than the International Style design of the Mandel house, the interiors, designed to the specifications of the Cafritzes by Eugene Schoen (pronounced "Shane"), were dazzling displays of

Art Deco. Schoen (1880–1957) had designed the remodeled interior of the Russian embassy in Washington in 1934.

In plan, the house as designed by Aubinoe and Edwards is a V-shaped building, with the wings spread very wide apart. In front, at the center of the V, is a rounded entrance pavilion. On the back of the V, on its south wing, a long, rounded pavilion extends from the middle of the building, slightly off-center.

In front elevation the house is a two-story building with a low hip roof. The cladding is brick, painted white. The entrance pavilion has a conical roof that intersects the main roof. A large window subdivided by muntin bars—four vertical and one horizontal—is located above the entrance. Another large bay window, at the ground-floor level in the middle of the right-hand (south) wing, was the living room's picture window.

The front door of the house, designed by Schoen, contains geometric patterns. Crisscrossed lines of stainless steel delineate diamond shapes in the middle of the door. Three small, horizontal rectangular windows, each broken into rectangles with internal stainless steel trim, are vertically stacked within the door. Above the door is a stainless steel marquee. There is a horizontal band of rectangular ornament and spotlights along the bottom of the front and sides of the marquee. The fluted trim around the door is grained marble.

The house had a three-car garage at the end of the north wing, with the entrance on the side. (A photograph of the house in the 1930s shows an Auburn boat-tail speedster parked out front.) At the end of the south wing (on a downhill slope) is a half-octagonal two-story porch pavilion with long sweeping staircases, front and rear, that extend to the ground.

The upper floor of the pavilion is connected to the ground floor of the house. It served as an open-air entertainment deck off the living room. Wrought-iron railings in geometric patterns, painted white to match the house, wrapped

The living room of the **Cafritz** house soon after its
construction and furnishing.

Courtesy of the Morris & Gwendolyn Cafritz Foundation.

around the edge of the porch. Similar metalwork was used for the columns supporting the overhead canopy as well as for the staircases. Below the deck of this porch, enclosed within the pavilion's brick lower level, is a patio connecting to a downstairs game room.

The upper, entertainment deck of the porch pavilion extends around the rear of the house, but without the canopy. The pavilion's foundation and its balconies continue to the rear and form a large open porch that runs the length of the south wing of the house. The porch ends at the rounded pavilion that extends from the rear of the mansion. This pavilion encloses the dining room (on the ground-floor level) and Mrs. Cafritz's bedroom (on the second-floor level). It contains curved wrap-around windows arranged in three vertical bays on the ground- and second-floor levels. On the lower level, a staircase leading from the porch to the lawn wraps around the pavilion wall.

One entered the grounds of the Cafritz house via a circular driveway connecting to Foxhall Road. On entering the house, one stepped into a circular foyer designed by Schoen. The gray-and-white marble floor has a sunray pattern with a zodiaclike display of bronze symbolic figures. These figures represent the "arts and sciences." The rear wall of the foyer was constructed of translucent white marble that could be illuminated from the rear. The other walls had sage-colored wallpaper.

A spiral stairway wraps around the foyer. The railing has curvilinear patterns executed in aluminum, burnished bronze, and lucite. The domed ceiling, finished in gold leaf, contained spotlights that could furnish illumination in blue, red, gold, or white, depending on the color of the gown that Mrs. Cafritz selected for the evening. To the right of the foyer was a small art gallery with olive-green silk-and-satin wallpaper woven by Dorothy Lieves. This gallery contained artwork by Chagall, Dali, and Monet.

Schoen's design for the living room, which occupied most of the building's south wing on the ground floor, featured large windows at the front and the rear, doors that opened to the side and rear porches, floors of East Indian rosewood and walnut, an asymmetrical fireplace with a stainless steel mantel and an inner half-wall constructed of glass block with a silver-leaf backing, a "leather wall" composed of "silvered patent leather"—leather rubbed with silver—and two murals by André Durenceau, one of them an overmantel painting. These murals, painted on canvas, depict classical female figures, some nude and some draped. The walls of the living room were painted pastel blue to match the color of the sky in the murals.

This living room was large enough to feature multiple seating arrangements. The furniture, designed by Schoen, included sofas, lounge chairs, armchairs, end tables, game tables, and a bar cart. The furnishings, executed in rosewood, satinwood, and mahogany, came from the New York cabinetmakers Schmieg and Kotzian.

The dining room, built within the rounded pavilion on the rear of the building, has a black drop ceiling. The long dining table, designed by Schoen, was built of bleached hornbeam with macassar ebony inlays. The chairs were done in bleached hornbeam and white leather. Schoen designed this particular dining-room chair in 1934 for the exhibition *Contemporary American Industrial Art* at the Metropolitan Museum of Art. Another principal room on the ground floor was Mr. Cafritz's library. The simple modernistic desk, an elegant interplay of rectilinear and curvilinear forms, was built of sucupira wood.

Upstairs were the master bedrooms, the children's bedrooms, the servants' quarters, a private gymnasium for Mrs. Cafritz (with a cork floor), and bathrooms paneled in Vitrolite and cream-colored marble supplied by the Tompkins-Kiel Marble Company. The color of the Vitrolite was "Sun Tan." Both of the master bedrooms had asymmetrical fireplaces containing gold-tinted glass block. The windows in the circular wall at the back of Mrs. Cafritz's bedroom commanded a sweeping view of the city. Mr. Cafritz's bedroom had a walkout balcony and a cedar closet.

On the downstairs level of the house were entertainment rooms. The circular room located below the foyer was used for card games. It has a multicolored terra-cotta floor (done in brown, orange, and cream) and red ornamented wallpaper with silhouettes of trees. This room contained torchères, a white couch, a white upright piano, and white card tables.

Toward the rear of the lower level, underneath the dining room, was a "night club," or bar. To the right of the entrance is a long asymmetrical fireplace with copper mantel. An overmantel mural of gypsy figures, by Domenico Mortellito, was constructed of multicolored panels of carved linoleum. This off-center mural extends outward to the left of the fireplace. To the right of the mural is a copper decorative panel with vertical folds in a wavelike pattern, illuminated from behind by hidden yellow neon lights.

The walls of the nightclub were finished in blue-grey wallpaper with gypsy figures and leatherette banquettes. The bar itself was finished in Bakelite and panels of red leather arranged in horizontal stripes with a zigzag pattern. The nightclub also featured a dance floor constructed of large glass blocks that could be illuminated from below. Among the guests who danced upon the modernistic floor were the Duke and Duchess of Windsor.

Beneath the living room, in the south wing of the house, was a larger ballroom or game room. This room had a black linoleum floor with images of game boards (such as shuffleboard). The wallpaper bore a whimsical design that suggested the seats of an amphitheater. Simple faceless figures in the bleachers appeared to be cheering on the guests as they engaged in whatever pastime struck them as amusing.[45]

Morris Cafritz died in 1964, and Gwen Cafritz died in 1988. In the 1990s their heirs decided to sell the mansion and its furnishings. Most of the Schoen furniture went to the Dallas Museum of Art. The mansion and its superb grounds became the premises of the Field School, a private secondary school.

The officials of the school have done a conscientious job of preserving the mansion and its principal public rooms. Though stripped of their original furnishings, the foyer, living room, dining room, and nightclub survive almost totally intact. The other rooms have been remodeled. Even the aforementioned preserved rooms serve as classrooms.

As adaptive use, this is better-than-average treatment, but the best of all possible outcomes in terms of preservation values would have been the purchase of the house by a wealthy family. Then the furnishings could have been retained and the house to this day would remain the *Gesamtkunstwerk* that the Cafritzes and Schoen intended. Instead, the finishes in the Cafritz house are now subjected to the hard wear and tear that comes with institutional use, which is truly a shame.

If the Cafritz Mansion represented Art Deco for the elite—which it surely did—a different use of Art Deco in single-family houses emerged from the studio of John Joseph Earley, the son of an Irish ecclesiastical stone carver. By the 1920s Earley was a recognized master in the art of exposed concrete aggregate. He produced polychrome panels emblazoned with patterns formed of colored stone.[46] During the Depression he began to build inexpensive prefabricated houses. Washington was his proving ground.

In the 1930s Earley's products gained nationwide attention. He was honored in his field by being elected president of its trade association, the American Concrete Institute, and through commissions in a number of cities. In Washington, numerous buildings were graced by one or more of his precast, multicolored concrete mosaic panels, created by the staff of the Earley Studio in Rosslyn, Virginia. At least

The fireplace in the bar of the **Cafritz** house, with
the overmantel painting in carved linoleum.

Courtesy of the Morris & Gwendolyn Cafritz Foundation.

one architectural firm, Porter & Lockie, used the panels supplied by Earley on many of its Deco buildings.

Earley's "polychrome houses"—his term—in the Washington area were prompted by a social vision, the redoubtable Jeffersonian vision of independent freeholders, reworked during the Depression in back-to-the-land movements. Some of these visions, like the one in the 1934 King Vidor film *Our Daily Bread*, were communalistic. Others, like that of the social theorist Ralph Borsodi, entailed retreat from profane cities to self-sufficient homesteads. Earley described his vision as follows:

> Everyone is seeking security. Labor has always sought security but has not achieved it. Capital has assumed security and is now in danger of losing it. The present social movement is a leveling one and it is entirely possible that we all will come to understand that the security which we desire for ourselves and our dependents lies in the nation's ability to provide food and shelter for everyone. It seems to me that the simplest way in which security can be achieved is to enable everyone to procure a small house and a plot of ground, which can be cultivated and which will produce sustenance.[47]

The medium he chose to employ, prefabricated concrete mosaic, "will make strong and beautiful walls," wrote Earley. It offered a possibility "the like of which has never been known before, and the limits of which are the limits of human ingenuity," he proclaimed.[48]

In 1934 Earley and his partner, Basil Taylor, started work on their first prefabricated house. Polychrome House Number One was constructed at 9900 Colesville Road in Silver Spring, Maryland. It was followed the next year by a second one-story house next door and by three two-story houses around the corner on Sutherland Road.

Polychrome House Number One was designed by the architect J. R. Kennedy to Earley's specifications. A simple L-shaped plan, the house featured hip roofs on each wing. Thirty-two slabs were employed to construct the house. Metal casement windows were cast into the slabs. The framework of the house, behind the outer concrete walls, was built of wood. The prefabricated concrete panels were anchored on small structural concrete columns cast in place at each joint. The main background color for the mosaic panels was obtained using aggregates of red jasperite, a form of quartz. Other colors were derived from crushed natural stones and various ceramic and vitreous enamels. The brilliant colors have lasted down the years with no apparent signs of fading.

All of the Polychrome houses in Silver Spring are protected on Montgomery County, Maryland's Master Plan for Historic Preservation. The houses are just beyond the Capital Beltway, whose construction providentially spared them years before official protection arrived.

A polychrome mosaic frieze surrounds Polychrome House Number One below the roofline. Buff-colored quartz was used in the fluted columns flanking the door, which contain three square inset panels, vertically stacked, with swirling crosses in the middle of ornamented discs. In the second polychrome house, Earley made less extensive use of color. Instead, relief patterns were applied, along with large porthole windows, whose frames were embedded in the panels before casting.

Another polychrome house was built in a secluded neighborhood in southeast Washington. This house, at 2911 W Street SE, is perhaps the most beautiful known residence created by Earley. The adaptability of concrete prefabrication is illustrated in the lower-level garage constructed on the sloping front yard.

Earley's vision of low-cost prefabricated houses had a counterpart in the Usonian houses of Frank Lloyd Wright, elongated single-story houses with flat roofs—and without attics or basements—that were designed to make the residential ideals of the famous architect affordable. Greater Washington has an example: the

**Polychrome House Number One**, at 9900 Colesville
Road in Silver Spring, Maryland, 2011.

Photograph by Melissa Blair.

Pope-Leighey house. Commissioned by the journalist Loren Pope, of the *Evening Star*, in 1938, the twelve-hundred-square-foot house at 1005 Locust Street, in Falls Church, Virginia, was completed in 1941. The second owners, Robert and Marjorie Leighey, who purchased the home in 1946, were informed by the state of Virginia in 1961 that the house would have to be torn down to make way for highway construction. The Leigheys decided to donate the house to the National Trust, and it was relocated to Woodlawn Plantation in Alexandria, Virginia.[49]

A number of houses in and around Washington from the 1930s and 1940s possess unmistakable Art Deco qualities. One spectacular example is the house at 2915 University Terrace NW, designed in a collaborative effort by Howard D. Woodson, an African American civic leader and structural engineer, and William Nixon, a black art teacher at Dunbar High School. Nixon and Woodson designed the house for Nixon's daughter, Dr. Ethel Nixon-Mounsey, in 1949.[50] The house is sited on a slope; the front elevation is two stories high above grade on the north side and three stories high on the south. A lower basement story curves around behind the house on the south side and becomes fully visible in back. A curvilinear and flat-roofed composition, the house blends symmetry and asymmetry. A rounded entrance pavilion is flanked by wings. The south wing is recessed; the north is not.

The entrance pavilion is subdivided, with the right third recessed behind a rectilinear corner. The central third contains the entrance, which sits atop a staircase whose curving stairs ascend in gradually narrowing steps to form a ziggurat. Above the entrance is a curved marquee. Most of the windows are casement windows, but glass-block windows are used at the rounded corners of the first and lower levels. Two glass-block windows curve around the left side of the entrance pavilion on the first and second stories. On the right-hand side—the recessed side—a long, vertical glass-block window spans the first

and second stories, shaped at the bottom into an ascending zigzag pattern. This remarkable house has a shiplike compactness on its sloping site. The cladding is blonde brick.

Two other unmistakably Deco houses are duplicates. Built by their owners in the late 1940s from mail-order plans supplied by the Garlinghouse Plan Service of Topeka, Kansas, founded by Lewis Fayette Garlinghouse, the houses are located at 5516 Auth Road in Camp Springs, Maryland, and at 6911 21st Avenue in the Lewisdale section of Hyattsville, Maryland. The design was number 6692 in the Garlinghouse catalog.

The two-story house with a flat roof is asymmetrical. The main block is rectilinear. At the second floor on the front elevation the left-hand side of the block is recessed in a zigzag pattern to form a sun deck. On the ground floor, a single-story entrance wing projects forward by means of a rounded corner and extends away to the right. The left-hand side of this pavilion has a recessed portion at the bottom to accommodate the entrance. To the right of the door is a glass-block window. The fenestration of the house consists of casement windows, except for two portholes, one to the left of the entrance and one at the back of the recessed portion of the second floor. This cubistic house, with its streamlined and zigzag massing, exudes the spirit of Art Deco. The Camp Springs house is built of brick clad in stucco. The Hyattsville house is clad in blonde brick.

In addition to these striking Deco houses, scores of "modern" or "contemporary" houses were built in and around Washington in the 1930s and 1940s. Some of them exist within the same "middle range" of design as Art Deco, though without being clear-cut examples of Deco design in the manner of the houses just described.

The legacy of Frank Lloyd Wright is extended in the greater Washington area through the work of a disciple. Charles Callander, an architect trained by Wright at his Taliesin Fellowship, designed a modern two-story residence in the

The streamlined house at **2915 University Terrace NW**,
southwest of American University in Washington, DC, 2011.

Photograph by Melissa Blair.

Seminary Hill section of Alexandria, Virginia. Designed for Haven Page, the house at 1213 Key Drive was built in 1940. Clad in red brick, the house features decorative brick courses, bands of casement windows, a second-story sun deck, and a flat roof.[51]

A comparable modern house was built in Bethesda, Maryland. Featured in the November 1941 issue of *Architectural Forum*, the residence of Charles and Helen Baldwin was designed to their taste by Francis Palms Jr. and Lewis E. Stevens. An irregular, L-shaped brick-clad house, it featured sweeping horizontal lines, casement windows that extended at the second-floor level right up to the eaves, and hip roofs on the principal wings. In many ways the aesthetics of the house are reminiscent of Frank Lloyd Wright's earlier Prairie Style houses.[52]

Then there was the house Mihran Mesrobian designed for himself in Chevy Chase, Maryland. Built at 7410 Connecticut Avenue in 1941, this two-story painted brick house is rectangular with a single-story pavilion on either side. The pavilion on the south side has a ground-floor window bay. The top of the pavilion forms a walkout porch from a second-floor bedroom. The pavilion on the north side of the house has a two-car garage. Mesrobian designed his house with a hip roof and casement windows. In front elevation, the central block contains a recessed entrance bay flanked by chimneys. These chimneys are flush with the facade and contain horizontal belt courses. The entrance is asymmetrical, with the door on the left-hand side and a curving wall of glass blocks to the right.

The list of "modernistic" houses in and around Washington, houses that combine the International Style with elements of streamlining, could go on indefinitely.[53]

An account of Deco residential architecture in Washington, DC, must also include the duplex houses built in the northwest section of the city. A block of these attached houses was constructed in the middle of the large Deco garden-apartment district, at 6101–6121 14th Street

NW. These houses, built in 1935 and designed by Harry Sternfeld, a professor of architecture at the University of Pennsylvania, are eclectic compositions that synthesize Art Deco with traditionalism of a vaguely Jacobean character.

Each two-story building consists of a central block with short projecting wings and a single-story entrance pavilion. Clad in red brick, the houses feature fenestration that combines traditional sash windows and portholes. Both the central blocks and the side wings have hip roofs. The entrance pavilion is arcaded and rectangular. The four rectilinear arches, two at the front and one on each side, are surrounded by limestone trim, and there is a curvilinear keystone at the center of each arch. Two chimneys, one for each residence within the duplex, run back to back at the center of the front elevation. The interiors contained maple paneling divided by aluminum trim. Frank Koplin was the developer.

Another row of modernistic duplexes designed by Joseph Abel, was constructed in 1940 at 4116–4136 Arkansas Avenue NW. These very interesting buildings are unambiguous examples of the International Style. The developer was J. B. Tiffey.

## BALTIMORE

Only a small portion of the residential architecture built in Baltimore between the wars displayed the influence of Art Deco. For the most part, builders of large apartment buildings stuck to traditional design vocabularies. Garden apartments were primarily built in the Colonial Revival idiom. Only a handful of single-family houses in Baltimore displays the Art Deco spirit, and they are examples of cautious designs by architects who worked mostly in a traditional vein. While Baltimore will not be known for high-style Deco residential architecture, subtle hints of the movement exist throughout the city in many residential forms.

Baltimore has no clear-cut examples of large Art Deco apartments. In fact, Baltimore has a limited number of large apartment buildings of any type from the interwar years. Apartment living in general did not take hold in the city during this period to the extent that it did in Washington. At the beginning of the twentieth century, Baltimoreans observed this new style of residential living as a handful of large-scale luxury apartment buildings went up in the neighborhoods of Mount Vernon and Bolton Hill and along a boulevard on the south side of Druid Hill Park, across from Druid Lake.

Construction of large apartment buildings moved uptown after World War I. The Homewood Campus of the Johns Hopkins University drew large and mid-rise apartment buildings north of downtown. Baltimore's Tuscany-Canterbury neighborhood, located directly north of the Homewood Campus, features a triangle of large apartment buildings, known to realtors as the "golden triangle," that date from 1928 to 1988. Within this neighborhood are the majority of the high-rise apartment buildings that appeared in the years between the world wars. They include the Warrington, 100 West University Parkway, the Ambassador, and the Northway. While none of these towers are explicitly Art Deco, they nonetheless display massing and design elements that were common to the Deco apartments of Washington, DC. Their eclectic style is similar to that of contemporaneous Washington buildings such as the Shoreham Hotel and Sedgwick Gardens.

A very good example is 100 West University Parkway (1927), designed by Wyatt & Nolting. The apartment occupied the last parcel of the original 210-acre colonial land grant, Merryman's Lott, purchased from a member of the original landholding family, Mrs. Henry Lucas, née Merryman. Promoters touted it as a million-dollar apartment building with seventy-four suites. This ten-story, T-shaped building over-

looks the Hopkins athletic fields. Its brick facade is broken by several limestone belt courses. The first three stories feature limestone quoining at the corners and limestone trim around doors and windows. These details are executed in a bold geometric fashion, resulting in a look that is more modern than traditional. The main entrance to the apartment building is located off University Avenue within an inverted V created by two of the building's three wings. A limestone balustrade with simple turned balusters partially encloses the V, creating a small courtyard in front of the entrance, which consists of French double doors recessed in a thick limestone surround with a segmental pediment. The use of glass block on first-story fenestration further emphasizes the building's modern character.

Another example, the Northway Apartments (1932), illustrates the tensions between traditional and modern design in the Art Deco era and demonstrates one architectural firm's attempt to mediate between the two. Here, Palmer & Lamdin applied Georgian Revival decoration to a thoroughly modern building form. A Deco effect results from the apartment's large-scale, setback massing, reminiscent of the skyscraper style so prevalent in the new buildings of larger cities. This form was the result of a zoning battle: the congregation of the Cathedral of the Incarnation opposed the construction of a high-rise building on the opposite side of Charles Street.[54]

Numerous design elements in the Northway, such as brick cladding in a traditional bond pattern, robust classical door surrounds, large first-story windows topped with fanlights, segmental arched windows with keystones, ocular windows on the twelfth story, and two massive corbeled brick chimney stacks jutting up from a hip roof, which is pierced by round arched dormers, were no doubt intended to harmonize with the Colonial Revival–themed campus of Johns Hopkins University, located directly south of the Northway. While Hopkins's contempora-

The **Northway Apartments** on North Charles Street, October 1932.

Photograph by Consolidated Gas, Electric Light, and Power Company of Baltimore.
From the BGE Collection at the Baltimore Museum of Industry.

neous buildings are fairly standard yet no doubt superb expressions of Colonial Revival—red brick structures with balanced composition, hip roofs surmounted by spires and cupolas, and accentuated by small-pane windows and centered ornamented entrances—the Northway is more unusual. The building's step-back facade represented a compromise brought on by a zoning battle; presumably it was not the architects' first choice. Yet Palmer & Lamdin fashioned a design that interpolates the elegance and proportional grace of Georgian architecture with the energy and scale of a Deco form, allowing traditional elements to transform into something fresh. The apartment building is an important example of "the Moderne traditionalized" in a city that has far more examples of "the Traditional Modernized."[55]

While downtown Baltimore does not feature any large Deco apartment buildings, the 1928 Lord Baltimore Hotel, on the northeast corner of the intersection of Baltimore and Hanover Streets, is one of city's larger buildings with Art Deco tendencies. William Lee Stoddart, a hotel architect who maintained offices in Atlanta and New York City, produced a design that reflected a synthesis of Deco and classicism. Twenty-two stories high, the hotel featured seven hundred rooms (with baths). It was the largest hotel built in Maryland at the time of its opening.[56]

Like many of the grand Beaux-Arts apartments along Druid Park Lake Drive, the building is U-shaped, having the appearance of two identical eighteen-story towers joined at the base. Floors 19 through 22 are housed in the building's distinctive octagonal crown, which is set back toward the rear (or north) elevation of the building. The French Renaissance Revival–style crown features a copper mansard roof with elaborate dormers. A 1920s rendering of the hotel indicates that the architect intended to use projecting gargoyles on the upper stories (similar to the famous stainless steel gargoyles on New York City's Chrysler Building), but these were not included in the built design.

The hotel's design is transitional. In some respects it reads as a Beaux-Arts composition, for example, in the tripartite base-shaft-capital arrangement of the main block. Yet in other respects it shares characteristics with Baltimore's Art Deco masterpiece, the Baltimore Trust Company building, located just one block to the east, for example, in the upward thrust of the lavish crown. Many of the decorative details throughout the brick and stone building are stripped classical elements, but some ornamental motifs are clearly Art Deco in spirit, motifs such as low reliefs depicting Indian chiefs, griffins, and other evocative symbolic figures. Decorative detailing continues on the hotel's interior, most notably in the lobby and ballroom, the latter featuring murals by John and Mable Giorgi.

## GARDEN APARTMENTS AND PUBLIC HOUSING

While construction of garden apartments in Baltimore's outer neighborhoods (and in adjacent suburban counties) proceeded at a rapid pace after World War II, this building type was less popular than the Baltimore row house during the interwar years. Daylight rows fulfilled the desire of many city residents for small front yards, deep porches, and airy four-square plans.[57] Generally similar in size to garden apartments, daylight row houses had the advantage of keeping homeownership in reach of families of modest means—families that would likely be renters in more expensive cities such as Washington. The developers and architects who designed Baltimore garden apartments in the 1920s and 1930s tended to stick to traditionalistic schemes. In contrast to the designers of garden apartments

(*opposite*) View of the **Lord Baltimore Hotel** and other buildings from the twentieth floor of the Lexington Building, October 1929.

Photograph by Consolidated Gas, Electric Light, and Power Company of Baltimore. From the BGE Collection at the Baltimore Museum of Industry.

The **Samester Parkway Apartments** on Park Heights Avenue, September 1940.

Photograph by Park & Hull, Baltimore City Life Museum Collection, courtesy of the Maryland Historical Society.

that wished to use Housing Authority funds, to overcome the mayor's opposition. Although Jackson and his backers initially opposed the creation of a housing authority in Baltimore, those in the city who supported public housing, known as "public housers," rallied to make sure that Baltimore would not miss the boat a second time.

The Baltimore Citizens Housing Committee, a conglomerate of thirty-two black and white fraternal groups, religious and civic societies, and organizations that represented the unemployed, pressed for a housing authority for Baltimore. This committee eventually prevailed. Daniel Ellison, a member of the city council, proposed legislation creating a local housing authority that could apply for USHA funds. In response, the mayor reluctantly introduced a bill of his own to create the authority. In 1937 the Baltimore Housing Authority (BHA) was created, and in early 1938 it gained federal approval to build five projects.[62]

Baltimore's first public housing project, Edgar Allen Poe Homes, broke ground in 1939. Bounded by Fremont, Saratoga, Amity, and Lexington Streets in the west Baltimore neighborhood of Poppleton, this complex contained 298 units designated for low-income African Americans. The project opened on December 31, 1940. The buildings are unambiguous examples of radical modernism. The architect, James R. Edmunds, was also the chairman of the BHA. Unfortunately, the overall design of the complex has been marred by the replacement of the original flat roofs with gable roofs.[63]

The BHA's third "slum clearance" project was Latrobe Homes, built on a twenty-three-acre site in east Baltimore. More than twice the size of the Poe Homes project with 701 homes, Latrobe was for low-income whites. It is a clear case of a federally funded program not just supporting segregation in the city but actively creating it. Both blacks and whites lived in the residential blocks that were slated for demolition. In August 1939, when a *Sun* reporter asked

Edmunds why the area had been chosen for an all-white project, he replied that the BHA was hoping to enhance the value of a white residential area slightly to the north.[64]

The BHA acquired the properties through condemnation. School No. 129, a black school, was left standing until the city could provide a new facility in the vicinity of the project. Reed Memorial Church was spared the wrecking ball and stands to this day. William D. Lamdin & Associates, including William D. Lamdin, L. McLane Fisher, Lucien E. D. Gaudreau, and Carroll R. Williams, were the project's architects. Both the demolition and the construction were to be completed in 456 days. The first units were supposed to be opened by June 1941, but shortages of material and laborers as a result of America's defense mobilization, which began well before Pearl Harbor, delayed work on the project. At the end of the summer, residents finally moved into the first section of Latrobe Homes.[65]

The site for the project, on land sloping slightly to the south, is bounded by Eager, Aisquith, and Madison Streets as well as McKim and Homewood Avenues. One-, two-, and three-bedroom units were available. Each unit had a private entrance sheltered by a cantilevered cement canopy and included a galley kitchen with a gas range and a porcelain sink, a living room, and one bathroom. The floors were cement. The project's manager, Clarence W. Burrier, touted the "rat-proof" construction.

Latrobe Homes is one of Baltimore's strongest examples of the modernism employed in New Deal–era public housing. The overall site design exemplifies the concept of *Zeilenbau*, developed in early twentieth-century German worker housing. As Spiro Kostof explains, the concept eliminates street-facing houses in favor of rows of apartment buildings spaced for maximum exposure to the sun.[66] Individual buildings within the Latrobe project reflect both the influence of the International Style and the streamlining fad. Notable design elements include corner windows, cantilevered canopies, and horizontal dark brick courses that project slightly from the overall red brick facades.

World War II cut short Baltimore's experiments in public housing. Many of the early projects remain, but they are marred by new gable roofs with cheap vinyl siding at the ends. Latrobe Homes has been spared this fate, but Poe Homes has not. This attempt to make older public housing projects appear more traditional is perhaps a sign that Baltimoreans now view these once-bold modernistic projects as a stigma. Perhaps people regard the buildings as nothing more than houses the government built for poor people.

### SINGLE-FAMILY AND DUPLEX HOUSES

The majority of Baltimore's houses from the interwar period can be characterized as examples of academic eclecticism, a wide-ranging architectural movement that drew from a variety of historical sources.[67] Baltimore houses of this era exhibit traditionalism more than they do modernism. Yet tucked within certain neighborhoods are examples of Art Deco single-family residences and duplex houses.

The neighborhood of West Arlington is a sea of bungalows and other modest 1920s-era houses. But the house at 3606 Marmon Avenue is quite different. Built in 1936 by an unknown builder for Dr. and Mrs. William Schuermann, this two-story, rectangular red brick building has a flat roof. The main block of the house has an entrance with a decorative streamlined brick surround. On the right-hand side of this facade is a long, vertical glass-block window between the first and second stories. The original steel casement windows have been replaced, with the exception of one on the second story of the south elevation. To the right of the main building block is a single-story section containing two garage bays, one a carport and the other a one-car garage. This section of the house supports a second-story terrace and sun deck with a brick parapet. Were the red brick walls of this house to be painted white, the residence would stand out prominently for what it is: a stunning example of Art Deco residential architecture.

The house at 3707 St. Paul Street in Guilford manages to blend in with the surrounding neighborhood of traditional-style homes while expressing the forwarding-looking aesthetics of the era.

In October 1936 George Streeter, director of the Department of Embryology at the Carnegie Institute of Washington, and his wife, Julia Streeter, purchased one of the last remaining vacant lots in the Roland Park Company's successful Guilford residential development. The couple hired John Ahlers, of the Roland Park Company, to design their new home. The F. E. Wurzbacher Corporation completed its construction in the spring of 1937. Before the Streeters occupied their house, the Roland Park Company used it as an exhibition house, which they dubbed "The House of Tomorrow." For an admission fee of ten cents, members of the public could tour the house, which had been furnished and decorated by the Stewart & Company department store for the exhibition. Promoters touted the "restrained modern influence" on both the interior and the exterior. The house received the Good Housekeeping Shield for excellence in the Good Housekeeping Program of Better Standards in Building.[68]

"The House of Tomorrow" is a two-story, white-painted brick house that uses elements of modernized classicism, though without the disciplined rigor of classical symmetry. An L-shaped building, the house has a low hip roof clad in copper that looks almost flat from certain vantage points. Copper downspouts drop from the roof at each corner. The facade, facing south, is symmetrical; a central door is flanked by large, fifteen-pane casement windows on the first story, and a long vertical expanse of glass block directly above the door is flanked by eight-pane windows on the second story. The door is recessed and surrounded by glass block. This entrance no longer serves as the primary entrance;

The **Schuermann House**, on Marmon Avenue, 1936.

**The House of Tomorrow**, on St. Paul Street, 1937.

it leads to a patio, sheltered by a large awning. The house is now accessed by what was once a secondary entrance on the north facade. Off-center, to the left, within the two inner elevations of the L shape, it has a solid wood door with a multipane transom and sidelights. To the right of the door is a large, imposing chimney stack.

The ornamental program of the house includes a cornice with brick dentil, scored pilasters at the corners, and vertical glass-block sidelights at both of the entrances. A two-car, flat-roofed garage is banked into a slope and connected to the house by a covered walkway.

Edward Palmer, the architect of so much residential architecture in north Baltimore, designed three modern duplexes at 333–335 Belvedere Avenue and 5905–5907 and 5917–5919 Bellona Avenue, on the edge of the Homeland neighborhood. Kelly & Sadtler built the duplexes in 1939.[69] A notable departure from the trademark styles of Palmer's firm, these two-story, white-painted brick houses have simple rectangular plans and hip roofs originally covered with standing-seam sheet metal. The chimneys are placed on the sides of the duplex units. The symmetry of these buildings, along with the placement of particular design elements (the end brick chimneys) and the use of certain ornamental details (brick belt courses), helps them to blend in nicely with nearby Colonial Revival houses, which were also designed by Palmer & Lamdin and built by Kelly & Sadtler.

At the center of the front facade of each building is an entrance section with a long metal canopy supported by thin, round metal posts. Centered below the canopy are two side-by-side, vertical sidelights of glass block separated by a thin brick partition wall, giving privacy to each unit To the left and the right of the sidelights are the doors.

The second story of the buildings has a central, horizontal glass-block window flanked by four-pane casement windows. More casement windows are located near the corners of the building. Brick belt courses wrap around the corners of the buildings, thus connecting the windows on the different facades in a manner suggestive of quoining. A few original casement windows remain in these houses.

One of Baltimore's most interesting Deco houses is the Eisenberg residence on Erdman Avenue, in the neighborhood of Mayfield, just a block southeast of Lake Montebello. In 1945 Benjamin Eisenberg, a Baltimore attorney known for his attempt to turn Fort Carroll Island into a casino, designed and built his own home. This one-story stucco house has an asymmetrical plan and a flat roof. A wide metal canopy below the roofline encircles the building. The facade features glass block and two large, curved steel-frame windows. Three horizontal stucco bands run the length of the front facade. At the foundation, a stone planter follows the curve of the overhead canopy on three sides of this futuristic house.

Built in 1947, the house at 5502 Charles Street is a two-story brick building painted white. It has a low hip roof with asphalt shingles. The entrance, which is centered on the facade, features a wood door scored with a diamond pattern and flanked by wide sidelights. A small, flared copper canopy shelters the door, and Deco metal lanterns are attached to either side of the sidelights. There are corner windows with red brick sills on each corner of the first story. An octagonal window is centered over the door. Overall, the appearance of the house represents a blend of Art Deco and the International Style.

As in Washington, a number of single-family houses from this period combine the International Style with elements of streamlining. At least a half-dozen of them survive around the city.[70]

The **Edward L. Palmer Duplex**, on Belvedere Avenue, 2011.

Photograph by Melissa Blair.

The **Eisenberg Residence**, on Erdman Avenue, 2012.

Photograph by Melissa Blair.

**WASHINGTON**

Art Deco began to influence commercial architecture in Washington with the construction of the Chesapeake and Potomac Telephone Company building at 730 12th Street NW in 1928. Through the years, an enormous number of Deco commercial buildings arose in the city and its suburbs. Shockingly, most of them are gone. Although Washington can boast of significant commercial Deco buildings that survive—the Hecht Company Warehouse, the Greyhound Bus Terminal, the Uptown theater, the Silver Theater and Silver Spring Shopping Center complex, the Sears Roebuck store—most were the focus of intense, at times ferocious, preservation battles in the 1980s and 1990s. Without this preservation action, most of the above-referenced buildings would have long since been destroyed.

Why is the retention of historic commercial buildings in Washington (and elsewhere) difficult, while the survival rate for residential buildings is impressive? Some of the reasons are obvious and economic: the great profit to be made by replacing low-density commercial buildings with higher-density buildings if the zoning and market conditions allow it—what the real estate attorneys call the "highest and best use" of the site, though it is usually nothing of the kind—creates a powerful destructive momentum. But there are other reasons as well—cultural reasons—for the wholesale destruction of historic commercial buildings in Washington, Baltimore, and elsewhere. Americans venerate history—with a capital *H*, so to speak—and they make it something of a cult, but they also long for the inspiration of contemporaneity. They love to anticipate the future, especially when they conceive it in the iconography of science fiction.

Because of some cultural quirk, these opposite-tending impulses are often dichotomized in the built environment: our love of history is enshrined in our residential neighborhoods, while our disdain for history is reflected in our business districts. That is to say, Americans are more at home, figuratively as well as literally, with the cozy continuities of life in their neighborhoods and resentful of everything that seems out of date (shabby, passé) in commercial settings.

In the 1930s the American building industry used the image of an up-to-date cityscape to push the theme of inspirational remodeling—modernization as uplift. One of the most influential of these campaigns was the Modernize Main Street Competition, held by the

Libbey-Owens-Ford Glass Company in 1935. This competition was followed by the traveling exhibition of modern store fronts sponsored by the Pittsburgh Plate Glass Company in 1936. In 1937 the Pittsburgh Glass Institute sponsored another competition.

All of these campaigns were obviously *sales* campaigns: the executives of the glass companies were building up an image—a vision of a sleek new America—that they could use to sell products. Exemplary products such as Vitrolite and glass block were fraught with *message* in the 1930s. And this message was probably sincere as well as opportunistic. In all likelihood, the businessmen found their own vision attractive as well as profitable. They were missionaries of progress. There was fervor in the drive to spruce up the old storefronts. But the forces of irony could not be held off forever. With the passage of time, even newer images—visions that made the older ones passé—were put forward. So the cycle continued, and the vast majority of storefronts created in the thirties, with their porcelain enamel neon signs and their Carrara glass trim, were destroyed.

In addition to these cultural and pecuniary factors, the destruction of commercial buildings can be attributed to straightforward factors of functionality and logic: enterprises go out of business, and their premises, frequently custom designed, do not suit the future tenants and owners. Premises can fall into disrepair, and most people are averse to setting foot in what appears to be a dirty establishment. Renovation provides a quick solution.

But to muse upon the lost world that Washingtonians and Baltimoreans possessed in their Art Deco commercial establishments is mournful: a wealth of great design was thrown carelessly away, and the destruction continues. To gaze upon surviving photographs of these demolished buildings is to glimpse a lost netherworld of "up-to-date American style" that revivalists are often eager to salute through vari-

ous "retro" efforts that are obviously not the real thing.

New preservation efforts in the 1970s attempted to address this problem. The National Main Street Center at the National Trust, for example, and preservation tax credits created by Congress were helpful. But the destructive forces continued to rage in the commercial sections of Washington. And the preservation movement, for a great many reasons, generally grew weaker in the 1980s and 1990s. Thus, much of this chapter constitutes an elegy and an epitaph.

## COMMERCIAL OFFICE BUILDINGS

Washington never possessed an abundance of Deco commercial office buildings, for a simple reason: the construction of office buildings tapered off by the 1930s. The Depression accounted for part of this trend, but a more significant factor was the completion of the Federal Triangle: when the government started to move its agencies into the newly completed buildings, it relinquished office space previously leased in commercial buildings, which created a glut on the market. But the relative paucity in Washington of Deco commercial office buildings is counterbalanced by the positive survival rate for these particular buildings.

The first commercial Deco office building in Washington, though a corporate facility instead of a rental project, was extremely important. The 1928–29 C&P Telephone Company building, at 730 12th Street NW, was designed by Ralph T. Walker, who also designed one of the first Deco buildings in America, the celebrated Barclay-Vesey Building (also a telephone company building) in New York City. The C&P Telephone Company, incorporated in 1883, built a six-story central operations building at 722 12th Street NW in 1903. The 1928 building was an addition. To design it, the company commissioned the prestigious New York firm Voorhees, Gmelin & Walker, which held a monopoly on corporate architecture for the New York and New Jersey Bell Systems. By 1928 Ralph T. Walker was the firm's principal designer.

A seven-story building (plus attic) clad in buff brick trimmed in limestone, the C&P building appears rectangular in plan when viewed from 12th Street. But the building has a hidden south wing to the rear that together with the main building block forms an L shape. The front elevation is six bays wide and symmetrical, except for the entrance, which is to the right. The middle four bays of the facade are contained in a slightly projecting pavilion with a pediment that features a sculpted eagle in high relief. Fenestration consists of recessed sash windows, and a gable-end pitched roof crowns the main section of the building.

Limestone trim is featured at the bottom and top of the facade, with a brick middle section in between. The ornamentation in the limestone trim is complex. Faceted vertical lines run the length of the piers and erupt into foliated patterns. But the upward dynamism is counterbalanced by the vertical lines, which suggest a downward-flowing drapery as well. Ornamentation, in the form of floral patterns, was also employed in the spandrels. These sinuous forms link the repertoires of Art Nouveau and Art Deco.

The ornamented sections have ziggurat terracing as well. At the upper edge of the bottom section, a ziggurat shape is created atop each window. In the upper trim section, a ziggurat is formed on the underside of each pier. These pyramid shapes give a sense of vertical thrust. The ornamental program of the building continues in the foyer, where ziggurat forms cap the upper edges of the marble wainscoting. Zigzags also define the upper edge of the ventilator grillwork. The plaster walls feature vertical facets tilting inward at the ceiling. The building is a designated District of Columbia historic landmark.[1]

A contemporaneous corporate office building arose at the west edge of McPherson Square.

The 1928 Southern Railway Building, at 920 15th Street NW, was the work of the classical architect Waddy B. Wood. Though the massive building lacks overt Deco ornamentation, its lines contain setback elements suggestive of Deco massing.

But another contemporaneous office building—a rental project—synthesized modernized classicism with full-blown Art Deco expressiveness. The 1928–29 Tower Building, at 1401 K Street NW, was the work of the architect Robert F. Beresford. A twelve-story H-shaped building clad in limestone with a granite base, it sits atop an east-west ridge at the corner of 14th and K Streets NW, overlooking Franklin Square. In the middle of the east elevation, on 14th Street, is a deep courtyard. The projecting wings that frame it are three bays wide and two bays deep. The central section is five bays wide. The flat south elevation of the building, on K Street, contains eight bays.

The upper stories have setbacks, creating, on the east elevation, ziggurat shapes at the top of the projecting wings. On the inner wall of the courtyard is a three-bay pavilion that surges upward into a tower. Recesses articulate the mass of the tower, and additional setback terraces are added at the top. The tower culminates in a slate-clad pyramidal roof clad capped by a lantern. In the upper portions of the building are sash windows grouped in pairs. At the top of the tower, the windows run in vertical bands, surmounted by rosettes.

The one-and-a-half-story base of the building runs continuously. It has a regular pattern of recesses surrounded by ornamented bronze frames. At the top of each frame is a pediment with acroteria. Most of the recesses contain fenestration, but several contain entrances for commercial space. Much of this space was designed to accommodate a bank. There are two lobby entrances, one at the center of the K Street facade and the other in the right-hand wing on 14th Street. The L-shaped lobby is clad in cream and orange travertine with black pilasters and bronze trim.

The developers of the building were Colonel William L. Browning and Bates Warren. When the Tower Building opened in June 1929, it was the tallest office building in the city. In 1995 the building was listed in the National Register of Historic Places.[2]

A more modest example of a late-1920s commercial Deco office building survives in nearby Alexandria, Virginia. A corporate facility, the 1929 Virginia Public Service Company building (the company later evolved into the electric utility VEPCO), at 117 South Washington Street, was designed by Frank D. Chase Inc., of Chicago. A horizontal, rectangular, three-story building clad in limestone, it is a modernized classical composition with a richly ornamented Deco entrance.

Equally modest in scale is the two-story office building at 2001 Massachusetts Avenue NW, near Dupont Circle. Designed by Gertrude Sawyer, who specialized in residential work, and built in 1936, this building expresses the streamline aesthetic in subdued terms. The cladding is limestone, with a surface of textured veining produced by "shotting." The rounded corner at the intersection of Massachusetts Avenue and 20th Street NW is framed by narrow vertical piers. These piers consist of engraved fluted lines in ascending levels. Fenestration consists of metal-frame sash windows grouped in pairs. In the rounded corner are wrap-around ensembles of windows. The principal original tenant was the Junior League.[3]

A handsome five-story office building was constructed at 1627 K Street NW in 1936. The Heurich Building (demolished) was the work of the architect Frank Russell White. The developers were Anita Eckles and Karia King. A rectangular building clad in limestone, the building was three bays wide. Four pilasters with capitals were placed between the bays. Fenestration consisted of metal-frame casement windows. The spandrels were adorned with vertical lines of aluminum ornamentation on a darker background.

These patterns, aligned with the segments of the casement windows above and below, were arranged in an alternating sequence of unadorned shafts and narrow piers with floral motifs. The recessed, central walk-up entrance was flanked by aluminum torchères on stone pedestals. From the pedestals extended aluminum railings with a decorative pattern that echoed the pattern in the spandrels. These railings framed walk-down entrances to commercial space in the basement of the building.

In 1937 an interesting Deco office building was constructed in the 15th Street commercial corridor, around the corner from the White House. The Walker Building, at 734 15th Street NW, was named for the developer, W. M. Walker. The firm of Irwin Stevens Porter and Joseph Lockie, who designed the building, specialized by the 1930s in commercial and institutional buildings. They made John Joseph Earley an associate for this project. This dignified office building was constructed between larger buildings. It is twelve stories tall and three bays wide; the top two floors are set back. Except for the entrance, which is placed at the right, the building is symmetrical.

At the ground-floor level, each bay is recessed between piers. Windows extend to the base within the recesses, except for the right-hand recess, which contains the entrance. Identical panels of Earley concrete mosaic were placed at the tops of the recesses. These panels tilt outward and upward to make a diagonal connection between the recesses and the rest of the facade. Every panel has, along with other ornamentation, a wing motif with a circular medallion in the center containing the letter *W*. In the transom window above the entrance is a grille with ornamentation. It employs a vocabulary reminiscent of the Arts and Crafts Movement, though rendered in an Art Deco manner. Motifs from the grillwork are reproduced in the concrete mosaic panels.

At the second-floor level, tall windows containing three vertical muntins span the space

The **Heurich Building**, which stood at 1627 K Street NW, [1930s?].

between the piers. Fenestration above this level consists of metal 1/1 sash windows in pairs. The ornate lobby features marble-clad and mirrored walls, geometric crown molding, and elevator doors emblazoned with intricate Deco patterns.[4]

A more subdued large Deco office building arose on K Street in 1941. The Commonwealth Building, at 1625 K Street NW, resulted from a collaboration between Alvin Aubinoe, the prominent designer and developer of apartment buildings, who was starting to diversify, and the architect Harvey Warwick Sr. A twelve-story building clad in limestone, it is symmetrical and rectangular; the top story is set back. The facade is composed of a wide, central six-bay section flanked by smaller sections.

At the bottom of the central section is a two-story base containing the simple but expressive entrance. It runs the length of the six-bay central section and is subdivided by a pier into two bays of doors. It is framed by a border of polished gray stone with curvilinear edges, rounded inward. These curves are convex at the sides and concave at the top. Above the doors—the original doors have been replaced—is a band of tall windows intersected by a horizontal bar of gray stone. Above the windows is a row of large letters spelling "Commonwealth." The fenestration of the central section is vertically aligned, but in the outer two sections the windows are horizontal, meeting at the corners as wrap-around windows with rectilinear edges.

Developers eventually defaced the original lobby of the building. The terrazzo floor, containing black and red bands that formed rectangles, may survive underneath the new floor veneer, but the polished marble walls, which had an undulating band at the top, were probably destroyed.

Alvin Aubinoe resumed his role as architect to design an office building for the developers Preston and Raymond Wire in 1948. The Wire Building, at 1000 Vermont Avenue NW, above McPherson Square, is devoid of Deco orna-

mentation, but its rounded corner and ribbon windows were surely a late manifestation of the streamlining vogue.

### STORES, SHOPPING CENTERS, AND RETAIL SERVICE FACILITIES

Many Deco retail establishments in Washington and its suburbs have vanished. The comparatively few that survive, aside from a handful that escaped demolition through happenstance, were the objects of preservation campaigns.

The most transient stores were the one-of-a-kind proprietorships that were once so plentiful in Washington. The list of these demolished local Deco stores is a gloomy litany. Older Washingtonians may still remember some of them. Examples include the streamlined M. S. Ginn & Company stationery store, at 919 E Street NW in downtown Washington; the nearby coffee emporium of M. E. Swing & Company, at 1013 E Street NW, whose Deco cabinetwork and equipment survived almost totally intact until the 1980s; the Wilbur-Rogers clothing store, at 1211 F Street NW, designed by the architect Solomon Kaplan and built in 1931; the Ross jewelry and optometry store, at 1331 F Street NW, built in 1936; Herzog Men's Wear, at 10th and F Streets NW, designed by E. Paul Behles and built in 1948; W. H. Brewton & Sons Stationers, at 3256 M Street NW, in Georgetown, designed by the architect Dana B. Johannes and built in 1938; the Quality Shop, at 3028 Wilson Boulevard in Arlington, Virginia, built in 1935, and Yeatman's Hardware, just across the street; the Lustine Oldsmobile showroom, at 5600 Baltimore Avenue (Route 1) in Hyattsville, Maryland; and the Aero Chevrolet showroom, at 1101 King Street in Alexandria, Virginia.[5]

To this list should be added the premises designed for the local firm Hahn Shoe Stores, premises that have been altered beyond recognition or else demolished, at the following addresses: 7th and K Streets NW, designed by Porter & Lockie and built in 1938; 1207 F Street NW, architect and year unknown; 4483 Connecticut Avenue NW, designed by the architect William M. Denton Jr. and built in 1938; 3101 Wilson Boulevard in Arlington, Virginia, designed by the architect Raymond G. Moore and built in 1941; and the northeast corner of the intersection of Georgia Avenue and Colesville Road in Silver Spring, Maryland, designed by the Philadelphia firm Thalheimer & Weitz and built in 1949. Almost all of these one- or two-story buildings used the signature emblem of the chain, a wide clock tower at the entrance with freestanding metal letters at the top spelling "Hahn." This feature was probably derived from department-store design; for decades, clocks had been a common feature at the corner entrances of department stores.[6]

Among the earliest Deco stores in Washington were two commercial buildings commissioned by the local Brownley's confectionery company and built across the street from each other in 1932. One of them survives. The confectioner Walter Brownley opened a candy store at 12th and G Streets NW in 1905. In 1920 he purchased buildings at 1300 and 1309 F Street. He moved his candy business to 1309 F Street and sold fruit and nuts across the street at 1300. After Brownley's death in 1932, his family commissioned Porter & Lockie to design new buildings at the sites.

The building that the Brownleys constructed at 1300 F Street NW, at the southwest corner of the intersection of F and 13th Streets, was a two-story, horizontal and rectangular creation clad in limestone. Thanks to the downward slope of 13th Street, the architects included a basement with a prominent entrance. This building was a highly sophisticated example of modernized classicism. The ground-floor level on F Street had entrances and display windows for leased shops. The exterior of the second floor exterior was a colonnaded composition of alternating vertical windows and pilasters. Above each window and between the pilasters, which rose much higher than the windows, was a rosette. The top of the building had a cornice.

The retail space in this building was preliminarily leased by the Gordon Millinery Company, the Shapiro Company (a women's clothing chain), and De Young Shoes. Ewart's Cafeteria, of Richmond, Virginia, leased the basement. In the 1980s this building was destroyed by the federally chartered Pennsylvania Avenue Development Corporation (PADC) to clear the site for the enormous National Place complex.[7]

Across the street, at 1309 F Street, is the four-story vertical building designed to house the confectionery, including the candy store, the kitchen, and the bake shop. The original entrance was removed years ago, but the ornamental trim around the entrance has been largely replicated and restored in recent years. The building survives as a brilliant example of early Art Deco design. The Brownley's building is perfectly symmetrical and clad in limestone. The one-and-a-half-story base contained a recessed entrance. The inner glazed wall of the recess was divided into sections by aluminum trim. Within the lower portion of this wall were two doors with a small glazed display pavilion in between. Flanking the entrance on the front facade were two vertical display windows. And surrounding the entire ensemble—the entrance recess and the windows—was aluminum trim containing intricate Deco ornamentation.

The most striking ornamental section rose above the entrance. This rectangular section was bordered by a narrow band of ornamentation. Within the upper corners of the rectangle were quarter-round curves shaped like descending fans. Within these curves were concentric lines with a wider band at the border. And in the very center of the rectangle, between the upper curves, "Brownley's" was written in aluminum script against a background of vertical lines. Another flamboyant touch was a lower section draped downward at the sides to frame the top two corners of the entrance recess in descending zigzags.

At the top of the one-and-a-half-story base was an aluminum cornice. Above, a central

**Brownley's**, at 1309 F Street NW, soon after its construction in 1932.

Photograph by Theodor Horydczak, Theodor Horydczak Collection, Prints and
Photographs Division, Library of Congress.

glazed section of the building had five bays of casement windows surmounted by transoms, with aluminum piers in between. Aluminum spandrels with intricate ornamentation are placed between the windows. The spandrels become progressively smaller as the building ascends. At the top of the third-story windows are aluminum panels with pediment forms at the crown. The aluminum cornice at the top of the building has a slightly higher, denticulated central section. The Brownley's confectionery building was listed in the National Register in 1994.

Another surviving Deco store built by a local retail firm is the former Dobkin's (later Morton's) clothing store at 2324 Pennsylvania Avenue SE, across the Anacostia River. Designed by Evan J. Connor and built in 1938, this painted brick, rectangular building features ornamentation that combines geometric Deco panels and streamlining. The ground-floor level has two entrances, one on the south facade, which fronts Pennsylvania Avenue and the other at the southeast corner, and a series of display windows. The original fenestration on the second story of the building has been largely bricked over. This section features long, parallel stringcourses of brick. Between them at the rounded southeast corner are wrap-around windows. At the roofline above this corner is a parapet with vertical chevrons.[8]

One of the most interesting Deco-era retail buildings in downtown Washington was built by a manufacturing firm to serve as a sales outlet. At the southeast corner of the intersection of 13th and F Streets, just across the street from the two-story Brownley retail building at 1300 F Street, a remarkable building, the Remington Rand Building at 1230 F Street NW (demolished), was completed in 1935. Designed by the Chicago firm Holabird & Root, this three-story, rectangular building took cues from Porter & Lockie's two-story Brownley building. The ground-story level of the newer building used the same organizational formula: display win-

dows and doors for retail tenants on F Street and a basement level around the corner on 13th Street containing a restaurant, the Mayfair Restaurant, "Café of All Nations."

The two upper floors of the Remington Rand Building were devoted to sales. The builder was the Remington Rand Corporation, a manufacturer of office machines, which made use of the upper floors to display and sell its products. *Architectural Forum* explained that since "the upper floors of the Remington Rand building are sales, not office space . . . the client considered it essential somehow to express this fact on the exterior."[9] The result was an interesting fenestration program.

The second- and third-story windows were contained within rectangular horizontal sections, one on each elevation. The fenestration had alternating outer and inner surfaces. The outer ones consisted of vertical piers arranged like crystalline pilasters. They flowed uninterrupted except for internal metal trim between the panes. The inner surfaces consisted of 1/1 sash windows hung at the second- and third-floor levels in groups within the vertical recesses between the outer piers. Each recess was divided in half vertically by a projecting pier of trim. This extremely sophisticated composition was destroyed when the Remington Rand Building was demolished by the PADC.

The PADC also demolished the 1940 Lansburgh department store at 418 7th Street NW. The firm Lansburgh & Brother hired Porter & Lockie to design this rectangular, limestone-clad building on the site of their existing premises. The newer building was a modernized classical composition with streamlined features. The facade was developed above the ground-floor level as a colonnade of recessed window bays. Press coverage at the time announced that "entrances will be streamlined in the new front and doors will open with the slightest touch."[10]

Other regional department-store chains made important contributions to the heritage of Art Deco commercial architecture in Washington. In particular, the accomplishments of the Baltimore-based Hecht Company were outstanding. The firm made its first appearance in Washington in 1896. In the 1920s, Hecht's opened a large department store in the 7th Street commercial corridor. Notwithstanding the Depression, the firm continued to grow. In 1936, for its fortieth anniversary, Hecht's announced a three-part program to expand and improve its operations in Washington: the installation of air conditioning in the main store, the creation of a six-month installment purchase plan, and the construction of a large new warehouse.

The warehouse site chosen by Hecht's, at 1401 New York Avenue NE, provided easy access to a motor route between Baltimore and Washington as well as to adjacent railroad lines. It exemplified an important new trend in department-store operations, the remote-delivery station or purpose-built warehouse. The concept was bold: with loading and storage consolidated at a warehouse constructed on cheap land, precious retail space at the department stores would no longer be required for this purpose. For twenty years after its construction, the Hecht Company Warehouse would be hailed within the industry as a model of the building type.[11]

The warehouse is also a masterpiece of Art Deco. Not only did this majestic building fire the imaginations of Washingtonians, it also garnered national attention. The cornerstone was laid on November 23, 1936, and the building was completed the following June. At the cornerstone laying, Alexander Hecht, the firm's president, was joined by several other dignitaries, including the DC commissioner Melvin Hazen and US Senator Millard Tydings of Maryland. Tydings, according to press accounts, "praised the company officials for the 'do and dare' philosophy that led them to build the huge new warehouse, which . . . will stand as a monument to the 'business genius which has made America the country it is.'"[12] Upon the building's completion, the *Washington Herald* declared that it epitomized an "architecture that is destined

to precipitate a revolutionary transformation in the appearance and utility of buildings in this country."[13]

The Hecht Company Warehouse was the work of the designer Gilbert V. Steele, of the New York engineering and architectural firm Abbott, Merkt & Company, founded by Hunsley Abbott and Otto Merkt in 1921. Its specialties included industrial buildings, power plants, and warehouses.[14] Steele's earliest design for the warehouse was utilitarian, but it developed into a stunning composition suggestive of an actual department store. Indeed, the building was designed for conversion into a store if the market conditions made such a conversion advantageous.[15]

The Hecht Company Warehouse made spectacular use of a revolutionary new building product, glass block. Walls constructed of glass block were translucent, not transparent. They provided abundant illumination without sacrificing privacy.[16] The Hecht's Warehouse was regarded in the thirties as a nationally significant demonstration of this material. The brand of glass block employed was Insulux Glass Block, produced by Owens-Illinois. It has a slightly greenish hue.

The base of the warehouse has visual weight: its cladding of black glazed brick contains internal trim of blonde brick. Cream-colored lines form continuous stripes; they are also developed as patterns of concentric rectangles with a tracery below and in between. The rectangles punctuate structural bays, including loading bays that take the place of the rectangular decoration without disrupting its pattern.

Above the base, the warehouse facade consists of horizontal bands composed of alternating ribbons of glass block and blonde brick. At the edges of the brick bands, narrow courses of black glazed brick provide additional emphasis and definition. These alternating bands sweep around the building with tremendous horizontal thrust. On the topmost band of blonde brick are black "pinstripes." These bands are an obvious expression of the 1930s streamlining. Their hori-

of Historic Sites. But it ceased to be a department store—it was merged into the City Place retail mall—and the county's Historic Preservation Commission approved cosmetic additions that rob this building of its character.[20]

The template for the Silver Spring Hecht's was replicated in Washington. The four-story, windowless Neisner Brothers store, at 1112 G Street NW (architect unknown, 1948) had slightly more decoration: some recessed blank bays in the limestone facade and vertical letters spelling "Neisner's" at the rounded corner. This building—store number 125 in the Neisner Brothers chain, based in Rochester, New York—was demolished in the 1980s.[21]

Other national chains built stores in the greater Washington area in the Deco era, not least the five-and-ten stores that used the well-established strategy of price-point retailing. These one- and two-story premises used Deco design in the storefronts and interiors. Some exterior features have survived in the following stores: the F. W. Woolworth store at 3111 M Street NW, in Georgetown, built in 1940; the S. S. Kresge store at 434 7th Street NW, built in 1934, whose facade was dismantled and reinstalled in a PADC project; and two Woolworth stores built across the Anacostia River—at 3932 Minnesota Avenue NE and 4001–4005 South Capitol Street SW—in 1947 and designed by the same corporate architect, Frank Beatty. While both of these stores have been heavily altered, their parapets with floral and geometric Deco ornamentation survive. But the 1936 Kresge store at 666 Pennsylvania Avenue SE, on Capitol Hill, became a "facade project"—saving a thin, cosmetic slice of a historic building—that denatured most of the store.

The greatest contribution of a national retail chain to the Deco heritage in Washington was made by Sears Roebuck. The mail-order firm began to open department stores in the 1920s. These early Sears buildings were explicit expressions of Art Deco. The firm Nimmons, Carr & Wright designed buildings for Sears that featured setback massing, decorative piers, and soaring signature towers that epitomized Deco aesthetics. One of these buildings was constructed at 911 Bladensburg Road NE in 1929.[22] It was demolished in the 1980s.

In the 1930s, Sears began a vigorous program of design experimentation. The mastermind of this program was Leslie S. Janes, who ran the new Store Planning and Display Department. Under Janes's leadership, Sears began to use in-house design talent. Among the bold innovations of the thirties were built-in service centers for automobiles and rooftop parking. The interior planner John Gerard Raben and the architect John Stokes Redden turned these programmatic ideas into blueprints. Redden was appointed chief architect in 1938.

Perhaps the most spectacular example of Raben and Redden's work was the Sears store built in 1939 at 4550 W. Pico Boulevard in Los Angeles. In 1940 the team developed plans for three other new stores, one in Washington.[23] The Washington store, constructed at 4500 Wisconsin Avenue NW, in the neighborhood of Tenleytown, was completed on October 2, 1941.[24] This five-sided building is surrounded by four roads. The intersection of Wisconsin Avenue and Albemarle Street NW formed the major corner of the building.

Constructed on a ridge upon a highly irregular site, this store was designed in three sections that were linked by expansion joints. Reinforced concrete was the principal material. Redden's design for this building was brilliant: large and irregular, the store is a sweeping composition with a light line that almost "floats." It was a store with a motor-age design par excellence. Rooftop parking was accessed by four ramps built into the walls. The experience of shopping at Sears was almost futuristic; one drove straight up to the roof and took an escalator down to the sales floor. Essentially a one-story building with a mezzanine and a basement level, this building has a very low profile. Below a uniform parapet, the wall heights vary with the grades sloping downward toward the intersection of Wisconsin and Albemarle. This corner of the building is the "tallest."

The long elevations on Wisconsin and Albemarle contain display windows and entrances; the principal entrance—there were five—is on Wisconsin Avenue. Above the show windows are canopies that run continuously and surge outward into graceful curves. The Wisconsin elevation is dramatically intersected by a ramp between parallel walls. The outer wall, which climbs upward with the ramp, from right to left, is complex. At ground level the wall lines up within the horizontal sequence that contains the entrance and the windows. Then it starts to ascend in a progression of zigzag edges to the roof. At the corner of Wisconsin and Albemarle, the display windows give way to a display pavilion that rises sixteen feet. The window panes of this pavilion meet at a rectilinear corner. Above them is a rounded canopy that surges out to form an overhang. Tall, freestanding letters spelling "Sears" were placed atop the canopy.

One of the finest aspects of Redden's design was the use of textured concrete panels. These formboard panels were imprinted with woodgrain patterns. The rusticated rhythm of alternating vertical and horizontal panels gave an interesting finish to the building.

The 1941 Sears building is a designated landmark in the District of Columbia. However, the building has been altered with permission from the local government. A large condominium apartment house now rises from the middle of the building. This is one of many preservation-development compromises in Washington that reflect the great power of real-estate developers and the power-broker law firms that represent them. Even the best of these compromises are in absolute terms rather tragic, but they offer an alternative to total loss through demolition. At their worst, however, in the form of facade projects, they are arguably worse than demolition.

Washington's Deco-era retail architecture encompassed another important building type:

the neighborhood shopping center. Washington became a major proving ground for this building type. Shopping centers with a planned mix of tenants had appeared near suburban residential developments before the 1930s. But in 1930 a Washington developer combined this concept with automobile accessibility. The new Park-and-Shop center built in 1930 by Shannon & Luchs in Cleveland Park (Arthur B. Heaton, architect) set a bold new retailing precedent. Two potent ideas were combined: a recessed parking lot permitting shoppers to drive right in and a planned and coordinated mixture of tenants. This shopping center broke with the prevailing conventions by giving up valuable frontage for construction of a parking lot. But the experiment succeeded: shoppers loved the convenience of gliding right in rather than having to park parallel on the street.[25]

The experiment was such a success that it was copied. Though the Park-and-Shop center was designed in the Colonial Revival style, many subsequent centers in the Washington area were influenced by Art Deco. One of them was truly unique. In the planned community of Greenbelt, Maryland, the architects—Douglas Ellington and Reginald Wadsworth, who also designed the residential buildings of Greenbelt—included a "market square" in which two streamlined commercial buildings were placed right across from each other at the sides of a pedestrian mall. These two-story buildings, constructed of brick painted white, featured wrap-around windows at the corners. Short canopies were placed above the ground-floor entrances and display windows. Car accessibility and pedestrian-friendly dynamics were harmonized, with large parking lots placed behind the buildings. Additional parking was offered in a lane curving inward from Crescent Road. A movie theater was included in the Greenbelt commercial center.[26]

In 1937 the Consumer Distribution Corporation (CDC), founded by the Boston department store magnate Edward Filene to encourage cooperative enterprise, leased the Greenbelt

The **Greenbelt** theater and an adjoining portion of
the **Greenbelt Shopping Center**, December 1941.

Photograph by Arthur Rothstein, Prints and Photographs Division,
Library of Congress.

commercial center from the federal government. The CDC helped the Greenbelt residents start a cooperative owned through shares. The coop established a credit union, a grocery store, a gas station, a drugstore, a barbershop, and a movie theater.[27]

Most of the other new neighborhood shopping centers in Washington replicated the Park-and-Shop precedent more directly. In 1935 the developer Garfield Kass took advantage of the Sheridan theater project on Georgia Avenue by persuading Warner Brothers to join forces with him; the result was a shopping-center complex (now altered beyond recognition) comprising six stores and a parking forecourt. Another center in the Deco idiom was the 1936–37 Bethesda–Chevy Chase Shopping Center (demolished), designed by Porter & Lockie at the intersection of Wisconsin Avenue and Leland Street.

In 1938 Kass Realty constructed the Chevy Chase Park and Shop at 4433–4465 Connecticut Avenue NW (altered). The architect was James F. Hogan. In addition to a market, a drugstore, and clothing stores, this U-shaped two-story building clad in blonde brick with stripes of black brick included bowling-alley lanes and an auditorium, the Chevy Chase Ice Palace, that rose high above the street-level retail. In addition to ice skating, the "palace" was designed to host special events.[28]

Among the other Deco shopping centers in Washington and its vicinity were the 1939–41 Westmont Shopping Center, at 3233–3263 Columbia Boulevard in Arlington, Virginia, designed by Evan J. Conner; the 1940 Westover Hills Shopping Center, at 5841–5853 N. Washington Boulevard in Arlington, designed by Kenton D. Hamaker; the 1937 shopping center at 7415–7423 Baltimore Avenue (Route 1) in College Park, Maryland (architect unknown); and the Arlandria Shopping Center, in the 3800 block of Mount Vernon Avenue in Alexandria, Virginia (architect and year unknown).

The most spectacular and most significant Deco shopping center in greater Washington was the 1938 Silver Spring Shopping Center, which included the Warner Brothers Silver Theater. This complex triggered a building boom that made Silver Spring a regional nexus of commerce. The center was built on the southeast corner of the intersection of Georgia Avenue and Colesville Road. Both roads were commuting corridors.

In 1936 the realtor C. H. Hillegeist, joined by associates Albert Small and S. E. Godden, did a market study of Silver Spring as the possible site for a park-and-shop center. Then the Hillegeist company commissioned architectural feasibility studies by Raymond G. Moore. One of Moore's preliminary schemes depicted an ornate Deco commercial building with a clock tower at the corner of Georgia and Colesville. But it was not a true park-and-shop center, for it occupied the full commercial frontage. Then Hillegeist attracted a developer, William Alexander Julian, an erstwhile shoe manufacturer and friend of Franklin D. Roosevelt's who was serving at the time as treasurer of the United States. Julian hired an old friend, the famous theater architect John Eberson, to design the shopping center.

The design of John Eberson's firm was a virtuoso performance, a composition blending symmetry and asymmetry. The center was designed as a one-story, U-shaped building with the wings spread very wide apart. A parking lot is framed between the wings, which flow downward to the corner of Georgia and Colesville. Small terraces make the limestone parapet ascend by imperceptible degrees to adjust to the slope. Within the parapet are recesses to accommodate signs. On the canopy are roll-down awnings and bell-shaped pendant lights. In the middle of the parapet's central section is a clock framed by three black "speed stripes."

To the rear of the shopping center was another parking lot. The front and rear lots connected through a shallow underpass. The shopping center had nineteen units, including two grocery stores, which were placed in the middle. Other tenants, selected for strategic sales value—a drugstore and a variety store—were placed at the end of each wing. In the front parking lot was a gas station. And adjacent to the shopping center, connected to it on the left-hand side, was the principal anchor of the whole ensemble: the Silver Theater, with its entrance on Colesville Road.

The theater is turned sideways in relation to the center, so the bulk of its long auditorium has decorative use in the overall pattern of the complex. The entrance pavilion of the theater, facing Colesville Road, has a limestone facade, but the long auditorium is clad in blonde brick. The theater has a vaguely nautical feel. The back of its auditorium is sculpted round, like the stern of an ocean liner. Ornamental black stripes run the length of the auditorium's continuous wall. The same materials—blonde brick with stripes—appear on the very tall chimney that rises at the back of the building in terraces. It suggests a skyscraper, but the nautical references suggest an alternative reading, namely, a mast. Another nautical touch is the curved enamel sign tower at the theater's entrance, which in some ways suggests a sail. A "porthole" of glazed black brick is inserted on a pier between the entrance pavilion of the theater and the auditorium wall. This theater–shopping-center complex possesses both horizontal dynamism and equipoise. The near-symmetry of the shopping center and the asymmetrical "weight" of the theater are blended effortlessly.

When the center opened on October 27, 1938, the *Washington Post* ran a twelve-page special section to cover the event. Six thousand people attended the opening-night ceremonies, which featured an appearance by the baseball legend Walter Johnson, who declared that the scene "reminds me of Broadway." The *Washington Post* took cognizance of the shopping center's role in the suburbanization of Washington. "Designed to Serve Needs of 50,000," ran a column title near the front page of the *Post*'s special section; "Planned for Future in Line of D.C. Growth, Extends Urbanization," ran another headline.[29]

The coverage was prophetic. The construction of the complex triggered a boom that led business observers to declare by the early 1950s that Silver Spring was the "second great city of Maryland." Among the architectural contributions to the boom were the Hecht Company branch store of 1947, the Hahn shoe store of 1949, and a J. C. Penney store of 1950, designed by Clifton B. White, now converted (as a facade project) for use as the Fillmore, an entertainment venue.

When it opened, the Silver Spring Shopping Center had the following tenants: S. S. Kresge, the Sanitary Grocery Company (the future Safeway), the Atlantic & Pacific Tea Company (the future A&P), Barker's Bakery, Modern Radio, Robinson's ("Robby's") Men's Wear, Lilyan's Lingerie Shop, George's Furniture Store, the Venerable Grocery Company, Lee's Tea Garden, Peggy's Hall of Beauty, Irene's Women's Wear Shop, Ethel's Millinery Shop, Gross's Novelty Shop, Alexander Jewelry and Gift Store, the Silver Barber Shop, and People's Drug Store. The Silver Theater and Silver Spring Shopping Center complex was almost lost to demolition in the eighties. It survived because of a preservation struggle by the Art Deco Society of Washington and its allies, a struggle that lasted twenty years.

Other retail buildings from the Deco era in Washington survive in the form of small premises stripped of their original interiors, signage, and fixtures, but with some Deco ornamentation intact. These buildings may be found either in commercial sections of neighborhoods or along the arterial commuting corridors in pockets zoned "commercial." The Mount Vernon Avenue corridor in the Del-Ray section of Alexandria, Virginia, for example, has a rich collection of these minor but interesting buildings. And the commercial blocks of Connecticut Avenue that intersect the uptown neighborhood of Cleveland Park retain a substantial number of the premises constructed there during the thirties.

The **Silver Spring Shopping Center** from the intersection of Georgia Avenue and Colesville
Road, November 4, 1938. The developer commissioned a series of photographs, including
this panoramic picture, to document the project from ground-breaking to completion.

SILVER SPRING SHOPPING CENTER
SILVER SPRING, MARYLAND
ALEXANDRIA REALTY CO., OWNER
JOHN EBERSON, ARCHITECT
MOHLER CONSTRUCTION CO., BUILDERS
NOV. 4, 1938          No. 12

The attrition rate for Deco movie theaters in greater Washington has been staggering. Only two other types of commercial buildings from the Art Deco era in the region—gas stations and hamburger stands—have fared worse. Of the thirty Deco movie theaters built in Washington and the vicinity, only three—the Greenbelt, the Uptown, and the Silver—still function as movie theaters. And the Silver's survival resulted from a grueling preservation battle in the course of which civic groups and a powerful developer induced the local government of Montgomery County, Maryland, to buy the theater and recruit (and subsidize) the American Film Institute as operator. Three other Deco movie theaters—the Cheverly, the Atlas, and the Bethesda—function as performing-arts centers. But thirteen others were demolished or converted into facade projects (the auditoriums have been destroyed). The others have been either gutted and put to adaptive use or abandoned.

In the Washington area, the Warner Brothers studio had acquired scores of existing movie theaters by the middle of the 1930s. Naturally, their own films received top billing. Nonetheless, through cooperative agreements most films produced by the other Hollywood studios were shown as well. Warner Brothers had local competitors: the Sidney Lust chain, the Wineland chain, the Alexandria Amusement chain, and the K-B chain, created by Fred S. Kogod and Max Burka. Warners showed the first-run films—the new releases—and the other chains showed the same movies later on.[30]

The Great Depression had devastating effects on the entertainment market in most parts of the United States. Among the various immediate results were the drastic downscaling of theaters from the "picture palaces" of the twenties to much smaller premises; the creation of new revenue-generating spin-off activities and products, especially popcorn and candy concession stands; and the introduction of raffles and gimmicks such as "bank night."

But thanks to the New Deal workforce, the Washington market continued to support new movie-theater construction throughout the 1930s. Once again, the nation's capital served as an important proving ground for the latest new methods, conveniences, and luxuries, including air conditioning. Many memoirs of life in Depression-era Washington include the reminiscence that the only real refuge from summertime heat was the ice-cold auditorium of a new movie theater.

Most of the new Deco movie theaters in Washington were designed by one of two theater architects: John Eberson, whose firm was based in New York, and John Jacob Zink of Baltimore. It was Eberson who had the big reputation at the time; he was known in some circles as the dean of American theater architects. And he had a special working relationship with Warner Brothers.

Eberson was famous in the 1920s for his "atmospheric" movie palaces, which were immense (they seated up to 3,800 people), ornate, and eclectic. In 1930 Eberson approached Warner Brothers with some standard new designs for more compact and economical theaters. He called these new designs the "Warner Brothers Standard Theatres," and he offered four schemes, designated, in order of size, A, B, C, and D, with D the largest.[31]

In 1930 Warners commissioned Eberson to design a new movie house to be constructed on Capitol Hill in Washington. But the plans were delayed. When it opened in December 1935, the Penn Theatre, at 644 Pennsylvania Avenue SE, became—with one exception, to be noted—the first Deco theater in Washington. It seated fifteen hundred.

The Penn's large, rectangular buff brick auditorium, with two parallel courses of blonde brick at the top, contained a section that projected forward toward the entrance and its limestone facade. Some two and a half stories high at the center, this facade spread outward at the sides to accommodate one-story shops. The entrance, with its eight glazed doors and its ticket booth placed at the center, was recessed underneath the marquee. Both the booth and the walls within the recess, which contained four display windows for posters, were clad in tan travertine.

The marquee was an exuberant expression of streamlining. Cantilevered, with a tan-colored surface of cement plaster, it was a graceful rounded shelf above the street. Parallel strips to which electric lights were attached flowed around the underside. Five more were included in a central band that surged outward from the top of the ticket booth along the underside of the marquee, which flipped jauntily upward at the front.

Above the marquee, on the limestone facade, three recesses were adorned with reeded lines capped by horizontal elements with concentric curves. This part of the building had a modernized classical feel. At the top of the facade's central section were freestanding letters—painted blue and with neon tubes—spelling "Penn." At each side of the facade's central section were recesses with vertically stacked smaller letters—again painted blue—spelling "Penn Theatre." This theater's overall effect on the streetscape was extraordinary. Notwithstanding the auditorium's bulk, the composition sat gently on the street; it had a lightness of line that was surprising.

The lobby of the theater featured tubular railings, molded ceiling bands, blue walls, and inner doors with curvilinear designs created in Formica. The auditorium, which contained a balcony, was bold and simple. Along the center of the ceiling, from the back to the front, ran a long, descending "shield" that was designed to cover circulation ducts. It was decorated with zigzag terraces. The ceiling curved directly downward to merge with the wall where the fifty-three-foot screen was mounted. Accord-

ing to descriptions in the press at the time, this ceiling was "dark maroon near the screen" but "gradually lightens as it approaches the back of the auditorium."[32]

At the edge of the screen was just a simple black border; there was no proscenium arch. Along the edges of the ceiling were three continuous bands of sculpted plaster that flowed from the ceiling down the edges of the wall where the screen was mounted. These bands, painted blue, purple, and red, were staggered in zigzag terraces. The side walls were sheathed in a special acoustical plaster. They featured sweeping horizontal lines that were "sliced away" as they approached the screen to form niches.

When the theater was dedicated on December 27, 1935, Warner Brothers officials—the general zone manager, John J. Payette, and the theater manager, Dan Reynolds—welcomed local dignitaries, including the DC commissioner Isaac Gans. The film shown was *Captain Blood*, starring Errol Flynn. A private dinner was held at the Willard Hotel, with John Eberson himself in attendance. The *Washington Times* praised the "practicality" of Eberson's "new gem," with "its lovely and unusual decoration."[33] In the 1980s, the auditorium was destroyed and the theater was reduced to a facade project.

Only one movie theater could vie with the Penn for the distinction of the first Deco theater in the city: the Circle theater, at Pennsylvania Avenue and 21st Street NW. The Circle was an older and smaller establishment. It was remodeled in 1935. The new architect, Luther R. Ray, gave the building a limestone facade with a zigzag pattern at the top. Above a stainless steel marquee was some vertical ornamentation, together with a finial with ziggurat qualities. An attempt to preserve this building by the Foggy Bottom/West End Advisory Neighborhood Commission was defeated in 1986, and the Circle was demolished that year.[34]

Almost a year after the dedication of the Penn, the next Deco theater in Washington opened: the Uptown, at 3426 Connecticut Avenue NW, in Cleveland Park. This time Warner Brothers commissioned the Baltimore architect, John Jacob Zink.[35] Like the Penn, the Uptown seated fifteen hundred. But unlike the Penn, which was a delicate presence, Zink's Uptown was bulky and majestic. One reason for this was that the Uptown's lot was smaller; there was less room to set back the auditorium. Consequently, the bulk of that structure comes close to the street, and the entrance facade has to hold its own against the mass. So Zink gave the facade of the Uptown powerful, massive wall planes.

The rectangular auditorium was clad in red brick, with the important exception of the tall front wall, for which blonde brick was employed. The upper edge of this wall contains zigzag terraces, and its surface is adorned with brick courses. In front of this wall is the entrance pavilion, whose facade is composed of three limestone sections. The middle section, set back between the others, is the tallest. Its verticality is heightened further by ornamentation above the marquee and the theater entrance: bands of vertical lines, two piers protruding forward at the ends, and tall windows. At the top of this section are freestanding letters, painted red and with neon tubular lighting, spelling "Uptown." At the ground level of the section is the entrance. To the left and right of this middle section, shorter wall planes project slightly forward. At the ground level these outer sections are designed to house leased shops. Above the theater entrance is a long, rectangular marquee. Its outer edges are sheathed in stainless steel, with horizontal striations. Three narrow vertical bands, painted red, intersect the front edge.

Although the Uptown's interior has been altered, contemporaneous accounts provide vivid descriptions of Zink's original interior scheme, which was subcontracted to the New York interior-design firm Rambusch. According to a description in the *Washington Herald*,

The walls of the auditorium are laid off in invisible panels, each with an allegorical figure in low bas-relief, which treatment is carried to the proscenium opening, which is blended imperceptibly into the ceiling, the main feature of the decoration. There in parallel rows are hundreds of concealed lights of various hues and colors, which, when lighted and blended, will produce a veritable sunrise of color. . . . The lighting fixtures, designed exclusively for the Uptown, are most unusual and combine the double purpose of lighting and ventilating, thus doing away with all ventilating grilles and plaques.

This account provided further details about the mezzanine corridors, which were embellished with "a decorative scheme which can only be described as Pompeiian . . . with several massive urns and columns."[36] The Uptown's auditorium has a balcony. A photograph of the original auditorium reveals that what the journalist called an "imperceptible" blending of proscenium and ceiling resulted from peripheral banding like Eberson's scheme for the auditorium of the Penn. Large abstract shapes formed repeat patterns on the ceiling.[37]

At the inaugural opening on October 29, 1936, the honored guests included Major Albert Warner, vice president of Warner Brothers; John Payette, the general zone manager; the DC commissioner Melvin C. Hazen; Harry C. Grove, president of the Cleveland Park Citizens Association; and the architect, John J. Zink. *Cain and Mabel*, starring Clark Gable and Marion Davies, was the film shown.

The Uptown was part of a $4 million expansion program for Warners, a program to build six "neighborhood" theaters in outlying sections of Washington. In the course of a visit in December 1935, the corporation's president, Harry M. Warner, announced the program. These theaters would be "second-run" houses, showing films that already had been screened in the huge picture palaces that Warners had acquired downtown. Although the Uptown was opened as a second-run house, in recent years its status has improved.

By default, the Uptown has come to play a valuable role in the nation's capital as the "presentation house" for the Hollywood block-buster films. With the single exception of the late-blooming Silver Theater, which in 2003 became the new East Coast home of the American Film Institute, all the other major "screens" in the area are multiplexes, and most of the great old theaters have been demolished, gutted, or abandoned. (The busily destructive PADC can take credit for destroying the magnificent 3,500-seat Fox theater, renamed the Loew's Capitol, at 1328 F Street.)[38] One fortunate factor helped the Uptown survive: its inclusion during the 1980s in the newly created Cleveland Park historic district. Not only were the leaders of that neighborhood successful in gaining historic-district status but they also achieved a significant "downzoning" of its commercial blocks.

In 1937, arguably the most beautiful example of Deco theater design in Washington arose just a few blocks from the White House: the Trans-Lux theater, at 734 14th Street NW. Designed by the New York theater architect Thomas Lamb, the Trans-Lux was the latest addition to an East Coast chain of newsreel theaters. For a quarter, patrons could sit in air-conditioned comfort watching *March of Time* newsreels of current events, along with short features and travel-ogues. The $50,000 translucent ("trans-lux") screen featured backlit projection, so the lights in the auditorium did not need to be dimmed completely. On the buff-and-brown walls were drawings and murals depicting generic news events, with an emphasis on sports. These murals were the work of Andres Hudiakoff.[39] In the lobby, on an azure background, was a map of the world.

The theater was part of the overall Trans-Lux Building, which swept in a continuous horizontal line down the western slope of 14th Street to New York Avenue. At the top of the hill it was two stories tall, with a third story added below. The expansion from two to three stories began below the entrance to the theater. The Trans-Lux Building was clad in limestone. While the Penn and the Uptown theaters had tenants, the Trans-Lux Building was a multipurpose creation, with space for retail and offices as well as a theater. Display windows and entrances ran the full length of the ground floor; the early tenants included a drugstore. Ribbon windows flowed uninterrupted at the second and third stories. The National Broadcasting Company leased the second floor for the use of radio stations WRC and WMAL. A transmitting tower with RCA thunderbolt script rose from the roof at the south end of the building.

But the dominant vertical feature was the tower above the entrance. Above a short marquee with two shelves containing upswept "teeth," a tall, illuminated tower soared seventy-five feet upward. It had panes of frosted glass within a network of narrow metal bars. The panes in the front tilted slightly backward from the center; smaller panes were set in place along the sides. At the top of this tower was a narrow metal reeded "capital." And tilted outward and forward at the sides of the tower were two mirrored wings to reflect the tower's light. Vertical letters on the outside edges of the wings spelled "Trans Lux."

This elegant, futuristic building had a beauty and economy of line that were breathtaking. It would surely stand today as one of the most accomplished Art Deco designs in the United States. At the time of its dedication, its visual qualities were obvious to all. Jay Carmody, of the *Evening Star*, called the building "a delight to the eye . . . a sort of H. G. Wells architectural dream come true."[40] The theater opened on March 13, 1937. The first newsreel was about the Spanish Civil War, a speech by FDR on his fight to reform the Supreme Court, and the Academy Award ceremonies.[41] Honored guests included

The **Trans-Lux** theater, October 1959.

Emil A. Press Slide Collection, The Historical Society of Washington, DC.

the DC Commissioner Melvin Hazen and Major Lester E. Thompson, president of Trans-Lux.

The extraordinary Trans-Lux Building was demolished in 1975 and replaced by a dull office building. There was no historic-preservation ordinance at the time in Washington. The demolition was widely decried, and the loss of the theater was something of a protest or rallying point for the DC preservation movement, much as the loss in the 1960s of Pennsylvania Station helped to spur the passage of a tough preservation law in New York City.[42] But however consoling it is to consider the good that arose from the evil of these demolitions, there is no way to palliate the brutal blow to Washington's architectural heritage that occurred when the Trans-Lux vanished.

From 1937 right up to America's entry into World War II, the construction of new Deco movie theaters in Washington continued. Warner Brothers delivered another new creation by Eberson in January 1937: the Sheridan theater, at 6225 Georgia Avenue NW, in the Brightwood neighborhood. Built in partnership with Kass Realty, the new Sheridan seated one thousand. It was a sedate composition, with the low-slung lobby and entrance pavilion stepping up to a gable-roofed auditorium. At the top of the terrace of the buff brick entrance pavilion, freestanding white letters spelled "Sheridan."[43] This theater was gutted in the 1980s.

When the Sheridan opened, work had already started on another new Warners "neighborhood" theater by Eberson, the Calvert (demolished), at 2324 Wisconsin Avenue NW, in upper Georgetown. The Calvert opened on May 7, 1937. The exterior design was even more low-slung than that of the Sheridan; the entrance pavilion barely rose above the retail shops that surrounded it. But it was bright: old photographs reveal a dazzling color scheme of cream, light blue, and red. The entrance featured panels of light blue Carrara glass with cream trim above a red-and-cream marquee. Above the parapet were freestanding letters spelling "Calvert." The theater was hailed in the press as "ultra modernistic."[44]

The lobby looked almost like a spaceship. Aluminum horizontal banding was connected to curvilinear aluminum display cases for posters. A large, tubular light fixture was suspended across the ceiling. And the Formica doors contained tremendous round central portions that were linked ornamentally by swirling trim that flowed across them, loop-de-loop.[45]

Another new Eberson theater for Warners, the Beverly (demolished), was built at 517 15th Street NE in 1938. The marquee was identical to that of the Penn, but the entrance pavilion took cues from the Uptown scheme. The brick facade was enlivened by rectilinear courses that turned at right angles, surging up to form a zigzag parapet. Rising above the marquee was a large, vertical sign adorned with vertical letters spelling "Beverly."[46] Flowing banded lines ran across the auditorium ceiling and converged at the proscenium arch, sweeping down. This particular feature was becoming almost standard in Eberson's Deco theaters. And there were murals with gazelles above the prominent emergency exits.[47]

Two Eberson movie theaters were opened in Montgomery County, Maryland, in 1938: the Boro (renamed the Bethesda theater within a year) and the Silver. Both of these theaters survive. But the Boro/Bethesda survives in a form that raises philosophical questions for historic preservation.

The Bethesda theater, at 7719 Wisconsin Avenue, was built on a downward-sloping site. The auditorium, slightly irregular in mass and with a very tall chimney at the back, was clad in red brick. The facade of the entrance pavilion is clad in blonde brick with short ornamental courses of black glazed brick in the middle and at the corners. The entrance, which is flanked by retail space for shops, contains a centrally situated ticket booth, eight pairs of doors, and aluminum-trimmed display cases. The base of this entrance, including the base of the ticket booth, is trimmed in green serpentine, a stone that is similar to marble. A thick, grooved band of aluminum trim rises up from the poster cases that front the sidewalk and turns into the entrance recess, swooping down to the bottom of the doors. There is a matching panel of this aluminum trim over the front window of the ticket booths. More curvilinear ornamentation extends to the bottom of the doors themselves.

The large curved marquee contains complex rectilinear trim, including tracks for electric lights, on the bottom. The front and sides of the marquee serve as sign boards to advertise attractions. Above the marquee is a tall sign mast, or marquee tower, in the form of a miniature skyscraper with "Bethesda" spelled in vertical letters. Above the entrance pavilion is a parapet wall of blonde brick with intermittent black stripes. Farther back, where the entrance pavilion was attached to the auditorium, a larger parapet wall of blonde brick marked the division. On the south elevation of the building, this wall turned the corner and extended back approximately twenty feet.

The floor of the lobby descends with the slope of the land. The green serpentine used on the theater's facade extends into the lobby, all the way to the foyer doors. On the walls of the lobby are rounded projections upon which were mounted additional display cases. These cases feature Deco details, such as terraced finials. The plaster ceiling of the lobby has prominent undulating waves that were dramatically illuminated with indirect lighting. At the bottom of the lobby were eight pairs of Formica-inlaid doors leading to the foyer. The foyer was a general-purpose transitional space containing entrances to the other key destinations: lounges, restrooms, and of course the auditorium, which had a balcony.

Eberson's design for the auditorium was flamboyant: the parts of the room were linked visually by surging lines. Wooden moldings almost race down the walls, plunging "over the brink," like waterfalls. Rounded mirrors with lights punctuate the design. On the ceiling, more horizontality flowed from the ventilation shield running straight down the middle. And

lines of painted plasterwork swept around the edge of the ceiling to the point where the walls curved in to the proscenium. These inward-curving walls contained arched recesses, or niches, that led to emergency exit doors. Above the doors were aluminum canopies with dark striations. And above the canopies were vertical murals featuring "astral" swirls—forms of comets, stars, and constellations—on a background of deep blue. At the proscenium edges were bundles of simplified columns gathered into clusters of futuristic beauty; they were representations of machine-age art, of the shimmering forms that mass production was creating in America. This fantasy palace in Bethesda was the work of the Sidney Lust entertainment chain, which included five theaters in suburban Maryland, three in Virginia, and two in the District of Columbia. The new Boro theater had its gala premier on May 19, 1938.[48]

In the 1980s, this building received protection through Montgomery County's definitive Master Plan for Historic Preservation. But the owners applied for permission to build a large house building directly over the theater. Despite the opposition of preservationists, a deeply divided Preservation Commission gave permission for the project. While the theater interior was partially restored and converted for use as a performing-arts center, the original building is largely swallowed up by the apartment tower. Only a narrow slice of the original building— the front of the entrance pavilion—is visible. The project was denied preservation tax credits by the National Park Service, which administers this federal incentive. Today, the Bethesda theater as such does not exist as an identifiable building. Though it is not an actual facade project, it looks like one. In protest, the Art Deco Society of Washington urged the state preservation review board to recommend the theater's removal from the National Register. The state board was deadlocked—evenly divided—so the protest failed.[49]

The opening of the Silver Theater in 1938 was

eagerly anticipated. The planning of the theater was publicized with the planning of the Silver Spring Shopping Center, of which the theater was the principal anchor. But the Silver got separate publicity.[50] When it opened, the Silver was featured in motion-picture-industry trade journals. One of them, *Better Theatres*, compared it to a new movie theater in London.[51]

The Silver was another creation of the Warner Brothers studio, which had worked with the developer Garfield Kass to combine the new Sheridan theater with a park-and-shop center in 1937. Thus, the Silver Spring project was built upon a recent local precedent. Perhaps John Eberson suggested to Warners that they locate one of their new neighborhood theaters in the Silver Spring Shopping Center after William Alexander Julian hired him as architect. In any case, the theater opened a month before the shopping center, on September 16, 1938, with the film *Four Daughters*, starring Claude Rains.

The Silver is unique among the Deco cinemas of Washington in that the mass of the theater's auditorium was used for ornamental purposes. The Sheridan, for instance, was attached to its shopping center at a right angle, and the auditorium was just a utilitarian box. The Silver auditorium, with its curved rear wall, its stripes, and its large terraced chimney, was original, at least in the greater Washington area. It was the grade elevation to the rear of the shopping center that made this composition possible. Sitting higher on the hill, the large mass of the theater was a visual layer added to the shopping-center profile.

The front of the theater is similar to that of the Bethesda. Once again, the outer edge of the curved marquee serves as a signboard. There is a marquee tower, but while the Bethesda's tower is rectilinear, the Silver's tower has gently rounded edges, a prominent curve in the back, and curved step-down pieces at the sides. It suggests a sail—in keeping with the nautical whimsy that characterizes the project. This porcelain enamel sign was painted tan. Upon

its surface, red vertical, neon-illuminated letters spelled "Silver."

The facade of the entrance on Colesville Road is clad in limestone, but the auditorium is clad in blonde brick with black stripes. These materials extend straight back along the auditorium wall. On the opposite side of the auditorium (which faces an alley) the cladding is red brick, though a faint vestigial stripe pattern was retained. The theater doors were finished with a Formica veneer. The design of the doors possessed a nautical touch because of undulating lines at the bottom suggestive of waves.

The lobby of the theater is ascending. The ceiling has sculpted and cantilevered ledges, as did the Bethesda. On the underside of these ornamental ceilings were patterns painted on with stencils. The lobby had a very warm feeling, thanks to Eberson's choice of materials. Rich wood veneer with narrow horizontal trim was employed for the wainscoting. Around the poster cases were borders of precision-cut stone. Both the color of the stone—a delicate shade of rose red—and the variations of its mineral patterns added visual appeal. On the floor were rubber mats with geometric patterns. The foyer doors echoed the doors in the entrance. The color scheme was turquoise, silver, and cream.[52]

The foyer was arranged like that of the Bethesda, with portals to the restrooms and lounges. The wallpaper bore a swirling motif that again suggested ocean waves. The colors were dark and light blue. The pattern in the carpeting was more complex, though it harmonized with the walls. Much of the interior décor of the Silver Theater was subcontracted to Rambusch.

The Silver auditorium (which did not have a balcony) seated one thousand. Toward both the back and the front, the side walls bore the same wallpaper as the foyer. But in the middle of each side wall was a horizontal section divided into three subsections. In each of these subdivisions was a turquoise-and-orange mural that depicted exotic foliage and peacocks. These murals continued into small arched sections that

The lobby of the **Silver Theater**, September 16, 1938.

John and Drew Eberson Archive, The Wolfsonian, Florida International University.

"bled" into the edges of the ceiling. Surrounding these murals at the bottom and the sides were concentric plaster bands that were terraced and painted pale yellow, pale blue, and two contrasting shades of grey. These bands were connected at the top to horizontal bands that ran the full length of the walls and draped down beside the proscenium arch (and around the projection alcove as well). Within the bands below the central murals were disc-shaped lights, and between the murals were plasterwork piers that were reeded into convex curves between horizontal bands.

The ceiling had the typical ventilator shield with painted stripes. At the edges of the ceiling were painted narrow lines that swirled inward, forming halos around individual spotlights that ran in two parallel lines beside the shield. At the front of the auditorium, bands of terraced plasterwork traversed the outer edges of the ceiling in convex arcs and then plunged straight down at each side of the proscenium arch. On the ceiling, they defined the sections of the room that contained the emergency exits.

Below these arcs at each side of the room were five shelves of cove lighting executed in plaster. The way that they extended from the sides of the proscenium suggested the internationally ubiquitous emblem of outspread wings. They extended in convex curves to match the curvature of the rounded exterior wall at the back of the auditorium. The wings and the plasterwork arcs on the ceiling formed a pattern that can best be described as "convexo-convex," convex curves joined at the outermost points.

This beautiful theater was preserved and partially restored after twenty years of bitter fighting. The ultimate treatment that the building received at the hands of the tenant recruited by Montgomery County, Maryland—the American Film Institute—has been in most respects admirable. But some of the AFI's decisions were (and are) questionable, in a few cases regrettable. The AFI constructed new "screens" to supplement the Silver. Additional theaters were placed next door to the Silver in a building designed by

the Gensler firm, which Montgomery County retained as the overall architect. The original 1938 theater is connected to the newer building through a sublobby that occupies what used to be the Silver's foyer.

Despite preservationists' request that the Silver be restored and used only to present classic films (after all, there was plenty of additional theater space next door), the AFI made a nonnegotiable decision to adapt the Silver for presenting films from all periods. Thus a full restoration was impossible. The negative results were twofold. Since a larger screen was required for wide-screen films, the original proscenium arch is now hidden by a larger screen. And to certify the theater for films that use "THX" technology, a coating was applied to the ceiling that prevented Eberson's color scheme from being reproduced in full. Although chemical analysis revealed that the original scheme had used dozens of colors, only two-thirds were reproduced, because for technical reasons the chemical coating on the ceiling would not permit more. Perhaps in two or three generations this room can be returned to its full and authentic grandeur.

Other changes were equally regrettable. The requirement of handicapped access prevented the original foyer doors recovered by the Art Deco Society from being reused. The AFI leaders displayed no interest in pursuing alternative methods to address this legal requirement. Lastly, the re-created marquee tower—the original had been destroyed—was higher than that in Eberson's design. This alteration was proposed so that "AFI" could be written just above "Silver." The resulting alteration in Eberson's proportions, though small, seems myopic.

Still, the Silver Theater is free of any new exterior construction of the sort that has entombed the Bethesda theater in a condominium apartment building. The Silver and the Uptown are thus the last remaining crown jewels of a once-lavish heritage of Art Deco movie-theater design in this locale.

Two more Eberson theaters were built in

The auditorium of the **Silver Theater**, 1938.

John and Drew Eberson Archive, The Wolfsonian, Florida International University.

greater Washington before the United States entered World War II: the 1940 Highland, at 2533 Pennsylvania Avenue SE (altered for adaptive use), and the 1939 Hyattsville, in Prince George's County (demolished). The Hyattsville, at 5612 Baltimore Boulevard (Route 1), was a low composition, like the Calvert. This theater, built by Sidney Lust, seated eight hundred patrons.[53]

While Eberson was working on his Washington commissions, John Zink was also kept busy. In the very same year that the Uptown theater opened—1936—two other Zink theaters were constructed adjacent to Washington: the Sidney Lust Milo theater, at 120 Commerce Lane in Rockville, Maryland (demolished), and the Reed theater, at 1723 King Street in Alexandria, Virginia (also demolished).[54] In Washington, Zink designed the 1937 Newton, at 3601 12th Street NE (demolished), and the 1938 Atlas, at 1313–1331 H Street NE.[55]

The Atlas survives, though it has been converted for performing-arts use. The original theater, which seated one thousand, opened on August 31, 1938. This was the first new movie theater built by the K-B partnership of brothers-in-law Fred S. Kogod and Max Burka.

Zink's design was creative. The entrance was placed at the left of a long elevation that contained enough retail space to accommodate eight stores. The limestone facade contained bands of Carrara glass on the parapet. This portion of the project is divided into three smaller sections of storefront bays, which in turn are subdivided by pilasters. The theater is L-shaped, with the auditorium extending in a parallel line behind the stores, but unlike the Silver's auditorium, it does not play an ornamental role.

The entrance to the Atlas is complex. The marquee has extruded aluminum banding, and its front outer edge contains a panel of Carrara glass. The facade of the entrance is L-shaped. At the left-hand side is a projecting pylon that holds a vertical sign—an aluminum plane. Red letters spelling "Atlas" are stacked upon its sides. The other side of the L-shaped facade contains three receding limestone panels with curved upper corners. These panels create a large zigzag pattern stepping back from the edge. Backlit with neon, they attach at the left-hand side to the pylon. The Atlas is a District of Columbia landmark.[56]

Zink designed two more Deco theaters for the K-B chain in the years that preceded Pearl Harbor: the 1940 Apex theater, at 4813 Massachusetts Avenue NW, in Spring Valley (demolished), and the 1941–42 Senator theater, at 3950 Minnesota Avenue NE (partially demolished). The Apex was Zink's greatest masterwork in Washington. Its demolition in 1977, just two years after the terrible loss of the Trans-Lux, was a source of additional outrage among preservationists.

The Apex theater was a grand and imposing composition, in a class with the Uptown. But the grace of this building put it truly in a class by itself. There was no separate pavilion for the entrance and lobby; the auditorium was equaled in size by the limestone-clad facade. The marquee's four, terraced levels were scalloped at the outer corners. These levels were painted in shades of blue that got lighter as the terraces rose. Above the marquee was a tall, colonnaded recess. Four rectilinear columns, flush with the facade, delineated bays containing vertical windows. Above the colonnade was another horizontal recess that contained large letters spelling "Apex." Like the columns below, these limestone letters were flush with the facade; it was the chiseled recess that set them off. To each side of this upper composition was a large recessed circle. Three metallic speed stripes extended straight across these circles.

To the left and right of the facade's central section were subsidiary sections with retail space. In the middle of the facade of each of these sections was a round enameled medallion. These ornamental discs, painted brown and cream, depicted classical female figures, recumbent, each holding a crystal ball in the palm of her upturned hand.

The **Reed** theater, at 1723 King Street in Alexandria, Virginia, soon after its construction in 1936.

Courtesy of Theatre Historical Society.

The **Apex** theater, at 4813 Massachusetts Avenue NW, August 1964.

The Apex lobby had a circular terrazzo floor. A large cross spanned the vertical and horizontal axes of the floor, which had concentric rings, along with smaller rings at the periphery. The auditorium, which seated one thousand, was dignified and subdued.[57] Over great local protest, the owners of K-B Theatres destroyed this magnificent building in order to construct an almost featureless office building.[58]

Zink's Senator theater—not to be confused with the Baltimore theater of the same name, also designed by Zink—was another K-B creation. Designed to be attached to a park-and-shop center that was never built, the theater opened early in 1942. Its auditorium facade had the same pattern of blonde brick and stripes that both Eberson and Zink had employed in so many other theaters. The Senator's entrance pavilion, also clad in blonde brick, extended forward. Its facade contained a formidable tall central mass, a freestanding monolithic wall with thick piers at the sides. Multicolored brick courses rose along these piers. A horizontal band near the top of the wall terminated the courses and created an upper section where neon-illuminated letters spelled "Senator." In the middle of the wall, a large plane of glass block was intersected by a white sign board.

The long lobby had a fine terrazzo floor, along with wainscoting of highly polished wood veneer containing decorative mirrors and poster cases. Within the auditorium, above the emergency exits, were murals with classical figures. To the sides of the murals, long, fluted wood panels with brilliant gold leaf extended from floor to ceiling.

In 1989, when the Art Deco Society of Washington sought to protect the Senator through landmark designation, the theater possessed a remarkable degree of integrity. Most of Zink's interior—lobby, foyer, auditorium—was intact. But in a cowardly decision made for political reasons, the DC Historic Preservation Review Board ruled that the pavilion containing the entrance and lobby was a separate building. So the entrance pavilion was protected as a "landmark," and the auditorium was razed, which meant that the owners could do what they liked with the largely cleared site. This farcical episode shows what happens when appointed officials are afraid to confront bad politics.[59]

In the early forties, Warner Brothers commissioned Mihran Mesrobian to remodel some older neighborhood theaters in Washington. The Savoy, at 3030 14th Street NW (demolished), was remodeled in 1942. Mesrobian gave it a new facade with an off-center tower. This tower was crowned with a glass-block lantern that was similar in spirit to the cupola Mesrobian designed for the principal building in his Lee Gardens complex.[60]

In 1941 Mesrobian remodeled the Home theater, at 1230 C Street NE. The Home's new facade was a three-story composition with concrete mosaic ornamentation. There can be little doubt that the panels Mesrobian designed were products of the John Joseph Earley studio.

The facade was divided vertically into three sections, with the tallest section in the middle. Over the entrance was a large stainless steel marquee supported by cables. To the left and right of the entrance were display cases. Above the entrance rose the tall middle section, which contained a high vertical recess with fenestration. Three fluted pilasters subdivided this recess into bays. At the second-story level the bays contained windows above concrete spandrels, and above each window was a band of concrete mosaic. Above the second story were vertical planes of glass block. Within these planes, in the outer two bays of the recess, single metal-frame windows were embedded. The overall recess was topped by a horizontal band of concrete mosaic. Above the recess were metal neon-clad letters spelling "Home."

The two outer sections of the theater's facade each contained a metal-frame, 6/6 sash window at the second story. Intersecting these

The **Home** theater, 2011.

Photograph by Melissa Blair.

windows were five horizontal bands. Above the second story, centered over these two windows and aligned with the upper two windows of the middle section, were rectangular medallions of concrete mosaic.[61]

This Deco-renovated theater survives, though it has been converted for use as a church. It is completely intact, with the following exceptions: the marquee is gone, the entrance has been altered, and the openings for the display cases have been bricked over.

The construction of Deco movie theaters resumed at the end of the war years. Among the new examples were Eberson's 1944 Atlantic theater, at 21 Atlantic Avenue SW (closed); the 1945 Kaywood, at 2211 Varnum Street in Mt. Ranier, Maryland, designed by the architect Frank G. Ackerman for Sidney Lust (altered for use as a church); Zink's 1945 Naylor theater, at 2834 Alabama Avenue SE (altered beyond recognition); Zink's 1945 Langston theater, at 2501 Benning Road NE (demolished), a superb design that featured curvilinear walls and auditorium murals depicting horses and deer in woodland settings; Zink's 1946 MacArthur theater, at 4859 MacArthur Boulevard NW (gutted); Eberson's 1947 Anacostia theater, at 1415 Good Hope Road SE (demolished); his 1947 Virginia theater, at 601 1st Street in Alexandria, Virginia (demolished); two theaters named Carver, both designed by Zink: the 1947 Carver, at Fayette and Queen Streets in Alexandria, Virginia (altered), and the 1948 Carver, at 2405 Nichols Avenue SE in DC (altered); Eberson's 1948 Cheverly theater, at 5445 Landover Road in Cheverly, Maryland (converted for performing-arts use as the Prince George's Publick Playhouse); his 1948 Coral theater, at 4907 Marlboro Pike in Capitol Heights, Maryland (altered for use as a church); and Zink's 1950 Flower theater, at 8725 Flower Avenue in Silver Spring, Maryland (altered).[62]

In addition to theaters, other types of recreational buildings in Washington bear the unmistakable influence of Art Deco. Besides the previously mentioned Chevy Chase Ice Palace, a Deco bowling alley by an unknown architect opened in Bethesda, Maryland. The Bethesda Bowling Center (altered beyond recognition) opened in January 1942 at the northwest corner of the intersection of Woodmont Avenue and Old Georgetown Road. This two-story composition had a streamlined corner at the intersection, and its cladding was blonde brick. Pairs of metal-frame windows were aligned within a banded pattern on the second story, and a vertical porcelain enamel sign bore a simple invitation: "Bowling." This 40,000-square-foot building contained forty lanes.[63]

In 1946 a large roller-skating rink opened at 1649 Kalorama Road NW, in the Adams-Morgan section of Washington. Designed by the firm Frank Grad & Sons, the "America on Wheels" rink was a stunning irregular composition placed upon a hill. Built of concrete, this enormous building shows the unmistakable influence of John Stokes Redden's design for the 1941 Sears Roebuck store in Tenleytown.

The building's central section has a half-cylindrical roof supported by buttresses. On the second floor was the skating rink, lit by a long, horizontal expanse of fenestration. Below were two entrances, for a garage and a bowling alley. At the top of the hill was the principal entrance, recessed below a canopy. Within the recess, which was subdivided by piers, is a long staircase. Above the entrance is a parapet wall with four ascending terraced wall planes. This feature was perhaps inspired by the entrance of the Atlas theater. The tallest of the planes extend high above the roof to form an upward extension of the parapet. At the left-hand edge is a porcelain enamel sign bearing neon-clad letters that form the words "Roller Skating." At the top of the canopy were letters in script that spelled "America on Wheels." At the bottom of the hill is a lower section of the building with a rounded corner. In the 1980s this building was converted for use as a sound stage and movie studio.[64] An-

The **Langston** theater, at 2501 Benning Road NE, late 1970s.

Photograph by Hans Wirz.

other roller-skating rink developed by the same chain and also designed by Frank Grad & Sons was built in Alexandria at 807 North St. Asaph Street. The year of construction is unknown, and it has been demolished.

And now a word or two about the Glen Echo Amusement Park in Montgomery County, Maryland. This establishment was founded in the 1890s, and some Art Deco structures were added in the 1930s. The entrance to the 1931 Crystal Pool featured terraced slabs and a pair of tall piers beside the doors. This aboveground pool was the largest public pool in the metropolitan area. The 1933 Spanish Ballroom, a popular venue for Big Band concerts and jitterbug dances, featured Deco trim around the stage and the bandstand.

But the most significant Deco features were added in 1939: a streamlined entranceway, positioned next to the trolley line that ran along MacArthur Boulevard; an administration building, linked by a long curvilinear canopy to the amusement arcade placed to the left of the entrance; the "Cuddle Up" ride, near the arcade; and the popcorn sales pavilion. All these facilities were custom designed by Alexander, Becker, & Schoeppe, an architectural firm in Philadelphia.

The arcade contained towers with upper sections of glass and medallions of concentric circles. The "Cuddle Up" was an oval-shaped pavilion with a streamlined canopy. The popcorn pavilion, also oval-shaped, had distinctive letters in its sign—letters spelling "Pop Corn"—that corresponded with elevated lights above the roof. The *C* in "Pop Corn" was a circle with a horizontal wedge carved out at the right. The elevated fixtures made use of the same shape.[65]

Glen Echo Amusement Park was closed permanently in 1968. The federal government acquired it in 1971. For a while, budget cuts made this ownership a tragic situation, and a number of the buildings fell into disrepair. Then, through a partnership between the National Park Service, Montgomery County, and a non-profit group, restoration work began. The arcade was repaired and reconditioned in 2003.

### RESTAURANTS

As with retail premises and movie theaters, so with restaurants dating to the Art Deco era in Washington: most of them are gone. Aside from some diners, only two or three Deco restaurants survive, and with substantial alterations. Among the earliest examples of Deco design in establishments providing food and drink for Washingtonians were hotel lounges. Period photographs reveal that the 1930 Shoreham Hotel contained a handsome bar and lounge with a linoleum floor, aluminum urns, a circular bar that appears to have been sheathed in porcelain enamel, and tables that might have been constructed of black-and-white Bakelite.

A more expressive Deco bar and lounge, the Carlton Club and Garden, was added to the older Carlton Hotel, at 923 16th Street NW, in 1934. The designer Nat Eastman created a spectacular room that contained among its Deco embellishments circular mirrors with tubular and vertical light fixtures and with speed stripes at the sides; murals of classical figures mounted in medallions with speed stripes extending top and bottom; a fireplace with mock flames executed in neon; modern banquettes and chairs upholstered in multicolored leather; and a modernistic bar in which the bartender sat concealed. This bar, called a "servidor" in press accounts, was a three-tiered apparatus projecting from the wall; its outer edges were rounded. It was clad in burnished metals, and the top and bottom tiers had a series of etched-glass panels with depictions of classical figures and grapes. In the middle tier were revolving canisters in which the drinks appeared as if by magic, a feature perhaps inspired by the automats of New York City.[66] At the top of the bar was a fountain, above which there was a metal sculpture depicting Diana and the Hunt.

The *Washington Herald* described the room as follows: "The new rendezvous features murals of striking color, red and white chairs of modernis-

The bar in the **Carlton Club** soon after its creation in 1932.

Photograph by Theodor Horydczak, Theodor Horydczak Collection, Prints and Photographs Division, Library of Congress.

tic shape, and a hidden bar which adds genuine novelty to the room. . . . The cocktail room opens out onto a garden which completes the setting. In the afternoons it is a colorful spot, gay with awnings and tables while in the evenings carefully lighted fountains give an added effect to the whole."[67] *Fortune* magazine proclaimed that "the small and exquisite Carlton Club has the smartest bar, as well as a series of rooms famous as birthplaces of New Deal legislation."[68] The most substantial coverage appeared in the *Washington Post*:

> Continentalism is found at the Carlton's cocktail room. Red and white leather furniture, gold mirrors, murals amazing and at the same time subtly subdued, and best of all, the "hidden bar." There are odd bits about the room. The murals are painted on wood by special process. The leather furniture can be washed only in the soap that is 99 44–100 per cent pure. How does the bartender, Louis Meyer, get into his gilded cage? If you arrive just at the right time, you'll see one of the green glass panels open, and Mr. Meyer's heels disappearing within. . . . For ladies: try the Carlton cocktail, a mixture of gin, maraschino, and grenadine.[69]

The Carlton Club no longer exists; it was apparently destroyed as part of a hotel renovation that was performed in 1958.[70]

In 1935 a smart new restaurant opened in the new Remington Rand Building: the Mayfair Restaurant, "Café of All Nations." According to a write-up in *Architectural Record*, the Mayfair used a "novel method" of operation: before being seated, patrons walked along a counter in the dining room where all the dishes on the menu were displayed.

Joseph Urban Associates designed the restaurant in collaboration with the architects Irving L. Scott and Otto Teegen. One entered the place on the 13th Street side of the Remington Rand Building. Above the entrance was a stainless steel marquee that was curved at the left. To the right-hand side of the marquee was a vertical

sign bearing neon-illuminated letters spelling "Mayfair." A short horizontal sign flowing along the upper edge of the marquee bore neon-illuminated letters spelling "Café of All Nations."

The dining room featured a terrazzo floor, large circular columns attached to a black, rectangular drop ceiling, and murals. The murals featured simplified maps of different parts of the world, and within the different maps were illustrations of scenic attractions. *Architectural Record* provided additional description and commentary:

> The benches along three walls are upholstered in a deep blue-green facricoid, as are the chairs. The woodwork of the chairs is white, while the tables have black formica tops and chromium plated pedestals. All wainscoting and bench woodwork are painted in black lacquer. Along one of the long walls an arrangement of circular alcoves provides an intimate grouping for parties of six to eight persons. These alcoves are separated from each other by vertical sheets of black glass, reaching from the top of the benches to the ceiling. . . . The entire source of light comes from the ceiling fixtures. Not only does each free-standing column in the main room terminate in a glass fixture comprising three sheets of projecting frosted glass, but a continuous fringe of two layers of frosted glass follows the perimeter of the suspended ceiling.[71]

The Remington Rand Building, which contained the restaurant, was demolished by the PADC.

In 1936 an Italian restaurant with Deco features, the Roma, was opened at 3419 Connecticut Avenue NW, in Cleveland Park, directly across the street from the 1936 Uptown theater. These premises have been successively occu-

(*opposite*) An ornamental fireplace with mock flames of neon tubing in the **Carlton Club.**

Photograph by Theodor Horydczak, Theodor Horydczak Collection, Prints and Photographs Division, Library of Congress.

The **Mayfair Restaurant**, "Café of All Nations," 1930s.

Photograph by Theodor Horydczak, Theodor Horydczak Collection,
Prints and Photographs Division, Library of Congress.

call the "fast food" industry—originated in luncheonettes and lunch wagons. In the early 1920s the hamburger stand appeared. An early prototype was the White Castle chain, which originated in Wichita, Kansas, in 1921. By 1926 the White Tower chain had been founded in Milwaukee, and it gradually built stands across the eastern United States. At first the White Tower designers simply mimicked the White Castle formula: rectangular, brick-clad buildings with a tower suggesting a castle. By the 1930s, however, the iconic White Tower had become "moderne."[78] Many of the newer White Towers were similar in spirit, though not of course in scale, to the contemporaneous Sears Roebuck stores, designed by Nimmons, Carr & Wright: Deco buildings with a signature ziggurat tower. The towers of the White Tower hamburger stands featured clocks.

With the switch to Deco aesthetics came a change in materials, from white brick to white porcelain enamel, with additional features such as stainless steel marquees, extending "gooseneck" lamps, and increasingly—by the mid-1930s—ribbon windows. The interiors included black-and-white tile floors, white counters with black countertops, black-upholstered stools with tall metal bases, and rows of black-upholstered booths.

About a half-dozen White Tower stands were constructed in Washington during the mid-1930s, most of them downtown. Then in 1938 the second in a series of new "deluxe" White Tower prototypes—the first of them constructed in the same year in Camden, New Jersey—was built in Silver Spring, at the northeast corner of the Georgia Avenue and Colesville Road intersection, across from the Silver Theater.[79] The deluxe White Towers were full-service fast-food restaurants. The Silver Spring model had a wrap-around stainless steel marquee, a side pavilion for carhop service, and a streamlined, neon-clad horizontal sign—the neon letters spelled "restaurant" in capital letters—that jutted forth atop the vertical tower. The deluxe White

Tower in Silver Spring was torn down in 1949 to make way for the Hahn shoe store that was built upon the site. By the 1990s every White Tower stand in and around Washington and vicinity had been destroyed.

White Tower's major local competitor was the Little Tavern. Its founder, Harry F. Duncan, began with a carry-out business in St. Louis in 1924. In 1927 he moved to Louisville, Kentucky, where he built the first Little Tavern stand. In 1928 he started building Little Taverns in Washington. At the height of his success there were more than thirty in Washington and Baltimore.[80]

Duncan's first Louisville stand was yet another imitation of the White Castles. But with the move to Washington, the Little Tavern formula emerged: a white-painted cottage with a green tile roof illuminated by gooseneck lamps and neon signs. By the early thirties, Little Tavern—like White Tower—had changed its cladding from brick to porcelain enamel. Duncan's designers, the engineer Charles E. Brooks and the architect George E. Stone, were in Baltimore.[81]

The first Little Tavern in Washington was built at 3701 New Hampshire Avenue NW in 1928. By 1981, when Duncan sold the business, Little Taverns were ubiquitous in Washington. The new Little Tavern owner tried to restore the stands with new porcelain enamel panels in the 1980s, but the transition failed, and the new owner sold the premises. Today just a few of these hamburger cottages survive, altered beyond recognition.

The Little Tavern formula—traditional in its massing and ornamental references but produced with futuristic materials—related to the major new national example set in the thirties by the Howard Johnson roadside restaurant chain. Even the color schemes were comparable: a white building with a roof of colored tile (the Howard Johnson roofs were orange). The Howard Johnsons related in an obvious manner to Colonial Revival, with their cupolas, broken-pediment signs, and hip roofs. By the forties, however, the signs were done in porcelain enamel, with rounded corners and a neon-clad motif depicting Simple Simon and the Pieman added at the top.[82] Washington had several Howard Johnson restaurants by the time the firm reached its heyday. Almost all have been demolished or altered beyond recognition.[83]

The Washington entrepreneur J. Willard Marriott copied Howard Johnson with his regional Hot Shoppes chain. Marriott entered the food business in 1927, when he opened a food stand—the Hot Shoppe—at 14th Street and Park Road NW selling A&W root beer, chili, and tamales. In the 1940s and 1950s Marriott built a chain of family restaurants that replicated the Howard Johnson design, even down to the orange tile roof. Almost all of the original restaurants have been closed, demolished, or altered beyond recognition.

All the aforementioned restaurant chains employed design devices to attract the attention of motorists; green or orange roofs turned the buildings into three-dimensional billboards. Perhaps the quintessential pioneer roadside-restaurant architecture was the diner. Diners evolved from the lunch wagons that emerged in the late 19th century. By the 1920s, "lunch cars" or "dining cars" appeared all over America. The internal design took its cues from the dining cars of trains. Diners—the term steadily crept into use—were shipped from the factory by rail and then towed or delivered by truck to their destinations, where they sat upon foundations of poured concrete or brick. By the 1930s, diner design had become streamlined, with aluminum, Formica, glass block, and porcelain enamel neon signs standard.[84]

A number of diners from the Deco era survive in the Washington area. One local chain in particular survives as a suburban presence in Maryland and Virginia: Tastee Diners, founded by "dinerman" Eddie Warner in 1938.[85] Three Tastee Diners remain in suburban Maryland— in Bethesda, Silver Spring, and Laurel—as

does a fourth in Fairfax, Virginia. The Bethesda diner, at 7731 Woodmont Avenue, was heavily remodeled years ago. The Silver Spring diner, assembled at 8516 Georgia Avenue in 1946, was relocated in the 1990s and increased in size by means of extremely large, disproportionate extensions. But the Laurel diner, at 118 Washington Boulevard, and the Fairfax diner, at 10536 Lee Highway, are relatively intact.

## OTHER COMMERCIAL DECO SERVICE BUILDINGS

Commercial buildings in Washington that delivered a service were also influenced by Art Deco. Some were created in abundance, while others were unique in the city. Of the latter, the most significant is the 1940 Greyhound Bus Terminal, at 1110 New York Avenue NW. Designed by William S. Arrasmith, of the Louisville firm Wischmeyer, Arrasmith, & Elswick, it was hailed when it opened as the "super terminal," the "Grand Central of the Motor Bus World." As late as 1952 it was called a "brilliant solution of the city bus terminal" in *Forms and Functions of Twentieth-Century Architecture*, a study prepared under the auspices of the School of Architecture at Columbia University.[86]

After two slightly older terminals in Washington became inadequate for the burgeoning operations of Greyhound, the company chose Wischmeyer, Arrasmith and Elswick to design a new state-of-the-art "super terminal" in 1938. This firm had come to specialize in bus station design. By the late 1930s, William S. Arrasmith was the principal designer.

The Washington terminal would be an island unit, a freestanding station of the type that Arrasmith pioneered. The station was designed for boarding in the rear: buses pulled in to the rear yard of the station from 11th Street NW, pulled up to the loading docks, received passengers, backed out of the docks, and then pulled forward to the west and entered 12th Street NW. Unlike earlier stations, where boarding and departure were combined on the street, the newer stations

Loewy) in shots of scenic America. The ceiling of the waiting room had a domed recess with an oculus window at the top. The acoustical plaster was painted in coral hues.

Construction of Washington's "super terminal" began in March 1939, and the building was completed a year later. The *Washington Post* published a nineteen-page special section, and twenty-five thousand people toured the building. Greyhound's founder and president, Carl Eric Wickman, led a delegation of company officials, and he urged the public to regard this new transportation portal as the "doorway to all America." This was close to the truth, for the terminal was linked to thousands of cities and towns that did not have railroad connections to Washington. Greyhound's regional manager, L. C. Major, was quoted by the journal *Bus Transportation* as saying that he "was anxious to have his company get into the new terminal . . . to ease the Easter rush. It was his belief that better care could be taken of the thousands of school children who come to Washington each spring aboard chartered Greyhound coaches."[87]

When it opened, the terminal had some commercial tenants: the Gray Line travel service, Seaton's Barber Shop, the Jean Karr & Company bookstore, the Greyhound Grill and Restaurant (with an adjacent drugstore and soda fountain). Other regional bus lines used the terminal with Greyhound's permission; Blue Ridge Lines and Peninsula Lines, which served the Mid-Atlantic seaboard and the Midwest, had such arrangements.[88]

During World War II the terminal had special importance not only as a transportation hub that was put to substantial use by the military services but also as a "little Ellis Island," through which thousands of blacks came north on their way to better jobs in northern cities. In 1943 Wilson L. Scott, of the *Washington Times Herald*, wrote that the bus terminal was a "wartime mecca. . . . If you wish to find out what kind of people come in and out of Washington . . . there is never a dull moment there day or night." The

terminal boasted "the only bookstore in Washington to stay open until 2 a.m. . . . . A good part of this time, book-manager Samuel Pevsner, historian, polyglot and former Russian journalist, is on hand."[89]

By the 1980s, bus transportation had declined, and Greyhound's site was the single most valuable piece of commercial real estate in the city. The terminal closed its doors on August 4, 1987. Greyhound had already sold the property to a developer, and the property was subsequently sold and resold as the preservation fight unfolded. The terminal was saved in a six-year battle led principally by the Art Deco Society of Washington. Some salient facts are worth mentioning.[90] First, the front and sides of the terminal had been covered in a 1976 renovation. Never before had protection been secured for a historic building whose original surfaces could not be seen. To meet this challenge, the Art Deco Society found copies of the cover-up plans, which proved that the original exterior of the terminal remained intact underneath the covering. The landmark designation of the "covered bus terminal" (in 1987) set a national precedent in preservation law.

Second, development pressure on the site was so intense, and the preservation politics at the time were so bad under the administration of then mayor Marion S. Barry, that developers kept trying to reduce the Greyhound Terminal to a facade project—to save just a ten-foot sliver and paste it onto the front of a full-scale office building. This is not the place for a detailed account of how this outcome was averted, but the situation was resolved when Manufacturers Real Estate agreed to save the building while constructing their office building over the rear portion—the portion that contained the rear drum and the loading docks. As it was, the developer gave up roughly $10 million worth of air rights and spent another $5 million to remove the 1976 covering and restore the terminal inside and out. Only future generations will be able to decide whether this Washington preservation compromise was justified. But the terminal remains an identifiable building.

Another Deco commercial service building that was also related to motor-age transportation opened in the same month as the Greyhound Terminal: the 1940 Star Parking Plaza, at 10th and E Streets NW. The builder was none other than the publisher of the *Evening Star* newspaper, whose offices were around the corner on Pennsylvania Avenue. Company vehicles were parked in the basement; the rest of this commercial parking deck was open to the public.

A long, rectangular building designed by Porter & Lockie, the Plaza was three stories tall; it included five levels of parking at the north end and four at the south. A wide entrance-and-exit bay was placed on each side. On 10th Street was a vertical section with a ziggurat parapet projecting above the roof. This probably covered a stairwell. At the ground-floor level of the building, at the intersection of 10th and E Streets was rental space for a store.

The distinguishing feature of this parking garage was the cladding produced by the John Joseph Earley studio. Earley created the panels with perforated latticework in a pierced-screen design, which provided both ventilation and light, in lieu of windows. These panels were hung upon the frame of the building like a "lace curtain." Other concrete panels framed the entrance-and-exit portals, in the upper two corners of which were ascending zigzag terraces. On the lintels were Deco letters spelling "Star Parking Plaza." This creative design was destroyed by the PADC.[91]

Another Deco-era building type served motor-age needs in greater Washington: the gasoline station. All the Deco gas stations in and around Washington have been destroyed or completely altered. Here and there one can still glimpse one-story buildings that might long ago have housed a streamlined Texaco or Esso station—one example can be found at 1729 Bladensburg Road NE—but that is all.

Only a long search of corporate records, if they still exist, could provide the basis for a comprehensive survey of Deco gas stations in Washington. But within the trade literature are glimpses of what used to exist: in the May–June 1937 edition of a corporate Gulf Oil publication, *The Orange Disc*, are photographs of then-new Gulf stations in Washington. While most were in the Colonial Revival style, two exemplify Deco commercial design. The Gulf station at Georgia and Eastern Avenues, for example, featured a row of three service bays and an office pavilion crowned with a Deco parapet emblazoned with a course of geometric ornamentation with setback terraces above. There were similar ornamental courses above the service bays, and between the bays were fluted pilasters. Another station, at 12th and Franklin Streets NW, was a smaller version of the same scheme, with one service bay and a restroom section adjacent to the office pavilion. Another version was constructed at 14th and L Streets NW; a picture of this particular Gulf station was included in a 1937 ad for terra-cotta siding.[92]

Although the 1937 Hecht Company Warehouse received national publicity for its use of glass block, another Washington building, the 1936 Manhattan Company laundry building at 1326 Florida Avenue NW, made extensive use of the same material a year earlier. Designed by Bedford Brown IV, son of the architect and past AIA president Glenn Brown, this rectangular building made substantial use of porcelain enamel as well.

The facade of this three-story building was classical, but its use of modern materials made it seem futuristic. The ground-floor base featured six long bands of white porcelain enamel; on the upper band were black letters that spelled "Manhattan Company." On the middle two bands were smaller letters advertising services: "Launderers, Dry Cleaners, Rug Cleaners, Storage." A large entrance bay at the center was flanked by windows. Around the border of the entrance

One of the entrances to the **Star Parking Plaza**,
at 422 10th Street NW, late 1970s.

Photograph by Hans Wirz.

ran a narrow black band with a Greek-key pattern, and above the doors was a large horizontal transom.

The upper two stories had a glass-block "wall of light," a long horizontal section dominated by glass-block fenestration. Perhaps Brown was inspired by the fenestration program of the 1935 Remington Rand Building, though his choice of materials was different. The building's top stories had a long expanse of glass block with embedded metal-frame windows. On the second-story level, the windows were narrow, tall, and vertical. Above each window was a green-and-yellow porcelain enamel spandrel (with a water lily motif) within a band of glass blocks tinted black. This remarkable building was restored for adaptive use by the developers Fran and Jeffrey Cohen in the 1980s.[93]

In what was then a distant suburb on the outskirts of Washington, another futuristic commercial building arose in 1939 and 1940: the WJSV (later WTOP) radio transmitting station, designed by E. Burton Corning. This sleek white building was constructed on a large open site along University Boulevard in Wheaton, Maryland. It is in some respects a radical modern design with streamlined curves. The central mass of the building is a three-story windowless block with a curved front corner.

Along the second-story wall is a long horizontal pavilion. This pavilion, with its rounded front corner, mimics the larger block that contains it. But this corner is pushed behind the building's front corner, and its rear portion trails behind the building. Within the pavilion is a narrow horizontal window composed of glass block. The pavilion is supported by narrow, simplified columns in a manner that suggests the work of Le Corbusier.

Inside the building, a curving staircase leads to a large round room lit by recessed illumination. Within this room is a large, circular "well" containing radio equipment; the well is surrounded by an elevated circular walkway. This

important building received protection from Montgomery County, Maryland, in 1991.

No account of Deco commercial buildings in Washington would be complete without a mention of the soft-drink bottling plants in Silver Spring. Two were constructed across the street from each other near the Maryland-DC boundary: the 1941 Coca Cola plant at 1110 East-West Highway and the 1946 Canada Dry plant at 1201 East-West Highway. The Canada Dry plant, designed by the New York architect Walter Monroe Cory, was a blonde brick building with metal-frame ribbon windows and a rounded entrance corner with a light wall of glass block. This important building was turned into a facade project in a redevelopment scheme approved by Montgomery County.[94]

One other Deco commercial building in Montgomery County should be noted: the 1930 Farmers Banking and Trust Company building at 4 Courthouse Square in Rockville, Maryland. Designed by the Tilghman-Moyer Company of Allentown, Pennsylvania, this two-story building was clad in granite on its north and west facades. Carved reliefs at the upper corners feature eagles with radiating lines. A colonnaded pattern is established by tall window bays—three on the west facade and five on the north—with black spandrels bearing ornate octagonal medallions. The pilasters between the bays contain capitals with Deco ornamentation. Around the bank's entrance is a black stone frame with ornate Deco ornamentation and a pediment containing three smaller, ascending pyramidal forms.[95]

## BALTIMORE

### COMMERCIAL OFFICE BUILDINGS

Central Baltimore maintains a number of Deco office buildings in fair to excellent states of preservation. The crown jewel of Baltimore's Deco buildings, indeed one of the city's most impressive buildings from any era, is the Baltimore

The **Radio WSJV (later WTOP)** transmitting station on University Boulevard in Wheaton, Maryland, late 1970s.

Photograph by Hans Wirz.

Trust Company building. The building has had many subsequent names, including O'Sullivan Building, Mathieson Building, Nations Bank building, Maryland National Bank building, and Bank of America building. This 1929 structure is by far the most distinctive building on Baltimore's skyline. Two Baltimore firms, Taylor & Fisher and Smith & May, partnered to create the design. The internationally renowned Art Deco artist Hildreth Meière designed mosaic floors, and the local artist R. McGill Mackall painted murals for the grandiose lobby. The ironwork, including the tellers' cages and day gates, were designed by the Philadelphia ironworker Samuel Yellin.

During the planning stage, the building's promoters promised prospective tenants "A Distinctive Address for Men of Vision." Promotional brochures invoked the theme "Faith in a Greater Baltimore." This building would symbolize stability, denote leadership, "inspire respect and confidence," and carry prestige. Tenants were to be selected with careful discrimination, protecting against "undesirable neighbors" and further ensuring that the building would be "Baltimore's finest and largest office building." The architects designed the building to be readily adapted so that a tenant could rent a single office, a suite of rooms, or an entire floor.[96]

The building included many modern features that are taken for granted in office buildings today, as well as some services that have long passed from office environments. Underfloor electric wiring systems with outlets every two feet provided for the easy installation of plentiful electric floor plugs, telephones, and call bells. Large plate-glass windows provided natural light, and every floor had a double mail chute and "ample toilet facilities, with central rest rooms for ladies." Workers would reach their offices by ten high-speed elevators, which were fully enclosed to reduce the sensation of speed and had a self-leveling feature. The Chesapeake Club, a lavish members-only dining room and lounge, occupied the entire twentieth floor and

part of the nineteenth. Workers who could not afford the club fees could eat at a sandwich shop in the basement. The Tower Service Club, occupying the coveted top floor, provided businessmen who had evening engagements with a convenient place to get a shave and manicure, exercise, and a shower, even "a few minutes in bed" before donning a freshly pressed suit. The building also had a three-bed infirmary staffed by a graduate nurse.[97]

The first four floors were devoted to the banking operations of the Baltimore Trust Company, which was a consolidation of five financial institutions—the National Exchange Bank, the Atlantic Trust Company, the National Union Bank of Maryland, the Century Trust Company, and the original Baltimore Trust Company. This consolidation made the Baltimore Trust Company the largest financial institution in Maryland at the time of the building's construction. No doubt the building's most lavish interior treatments were for the Baltimore Trust Company's own premises, including the Board Room, inspired by a Florentine palace, and the stunning main banking lobby on the ground floor.[98]

The lobby is one of Baltimore's finest interiors. The room extends two hundred feet from Baltimore Street to Redwood Street and reaches up to a fifty-foot ceiling. It is adorned with massive columns of Pyrenees, Levanto, Rouge Roja, Verde Antique, and Marion marbles. A neck of Tennessee marble topped with a gilded and colored beam bracket takes the place of the conventional capital in these columns. Hildreth Meière's lobby floor features multicolored marble borders that weave around marble mosaic scenes depicting zones of commerce and the Baltimore Trust Company's corporate values. In three bays female figures symbolize Land,

(*opposite*) The **Baltimore Trust Company building** under construction, September 1929.

Courtesy of Enoch Pratt Free Library, Maryland's State Library Resource Center, Baltimore, Maryland.

The **Baltimore Life Insurance Company** building,
at Charles and Saratoga Streets, ca. 1930.

Photograph from Special Collections, courtesy of the Maryland
Historical Society.

**Baltimore Life Insurance Company** building, ornamental detail, 2011.

Photograph by Melissa Blair.

it, forming a towerlike central element. The overall massing effect suggests a setback. Next door, at 309 North Charles Street, the stripped classicism of the four-story Eastman Kodak Stores building (1930), now the Royal Oak building, is a nice contemporaneous counterpart to this building.

Decorative elements of the Baltimore Life Insurance Company building include incised stylized scrolls, fluted piers, cast-metal panels, and wrought-iron balconies on the second floor. The fluted piers between bays on the upper three floors of each facade extend above the cast-metal cornice to intersect terraced finials with plaques. Between the second- and third-floor fenestration are limestone spandrels with intricate floral and geometric motifs.

Edward Palmer and William Lamdin selected Charles Nes from their staff to design the firm's new offices at 1020 St. Paul Street. Nes was in his eighth year of practice when the building was constructed in 1938. Essentially a hybrid synthesizing radical modernism and streamlining, the firm's two-story office building was one of the first buildings in Baltimore to reflect the influence of the International Style, surely a forward-looking statement for a firm known primarily for residential architecture built in various revival styles.[102]

The deeply recessed front entrance has a bull-nose door surround composed of twin quarter-round and reeded columnar elements. The street address, 1020, was painted in a Deco-style font; moreover, an octagonal metal medallion with a sunflower design on the entrance ceiling shows a lingering Deco influence. The entrance is reached by shallow concrete steps with curved metal "ship's railing" handrails flipping forward from the building like concentric waterfall lines. A shallow projecting marquee runs the length of the building above the first floor. There are large, eight-pane steel or wood casement windows throughout the building, and there is a concrete planter along the base of the facade. On the second story, the windows are arranged

in horizontal recesses and divided by pilasterlike piers containing horizontal grooved lines that intersect the muntins.

During several twentieth-century building campaigns, Baltimore's Monumental Life Insurance Company expanded over a large block north of Chase Street and east of Charles. The company has roots in Maryland dating back to the mid-nineteenth century. In 1858 the Maryland General Assembly issued a charter to the Maryland Mutual Life and Fire Insurance Company. In 1879 the company changed its name to Mutual Life Insurance Company of Baltimore. Because the names of so many insurance companies included the word *Mutual*, the company became the Monumental Life Insurance Company in 1935. Earlier, in 1926, the fast-growing company erected the first stage of its office complex. Taylor & Fisher designed the original six-story limestone building in a Beaux-Arts classical style.[103]

The company continued to grow during the Depression, leading to cramped office conditions. In 1938 Taylor & Fisher designed a large, six-story addition to be attached to the Monumental Life building's north side. The addition was completed in late 1939, providing forty thousand square feet of additional space.[104]

The addition to the Monumental Life building is set back from Charles Street, with a courtyard in front of the entrance. The structure is brick faced with limestone. Taylor & Fisher continued several of the design elements of their 1926 building, but made them more streamlined. The 1926 building has half-round fluted columns that are four stories high on both of its street-facing facades; the addition features pilasters approximately the same width and height. The original building has metal bas-reliefs and carved-limestone classical ornamentation; the addition is largely devoid of such detail, with the exception of the main entrance's two-story surround, which picks up on the classical motifs of the original building, but in a streamlined fashion. The original building has an entablature at the fifth story; the addition has a simpler version at the same location. The sixth story of the addition features "Monumental Life" in gold letters. Side by side, the 1926 building and the 1939 addition provide a good example of 1920s classical commercial architecture and the more austere, modernized classicism of the 1930s, thus showing how an important Baltimore architectural firm updated its aesthetic.

In 1940 the number of telephones in Baltimore was approximately 160,000, twice the number in 1920. To keep pace with growing demand, the Chesapeake & Potomac Telephone Company planned a new Baltimore headquarters. Completed in 1941 at a cost of approximately $1 million, it was the first large midtown building constructed after the Depression. Taylor & Fisher designed the building, its austere look a sharp contrast to their exuberant work on the Baltimore Trust Company building; the C&P Telephone building is similar to buildings in New York City designed by Raymond Hood in the early 1930s. Moody & Hutchinson, of Philadelphia, served as consulting engineers; Frank Kress, also of Philadelphia, served as structural engineer; and Cummins Construction Corporation was the general contractor. The building was originally six stories high, with eight floors added in 1949. In 1943 the Association of Commerce gave the building an award for architectural excellence.[105]

Rising at the corner of St. Paul Place and Pleasant Street, the fourteen-story brick-and-steel structure of the C&P Telephone building is clad in Indiana limestone. The projecting rectilinear main entrance pavilion, on St. Paul, has a recessed entrance containing a revolving door below a stainless steel marquee. There is a massive vertical, multipane transom above the door, with a vertically tripartite composition of geometric metal grilles. "Telephone Building" is incised in the limestone above the transom.

Black granite panels incised with shallow reliefs divide the first and second stories. Limestone piers separate window bays and give a vertical emphasis to the central portion of the facade, which is fourteen bays wide and rises twelve stories. This central section is flanked by one-bay extensions that rise only ten stories, thus achieving the first of two terraced setback effects. Black granite spandrels separate the sash windows between stories. The building steps back above the twelfth story. The upper story has carved panels with geometric designs in place of windows.

## STORES, SHOPPING CENTERS, AND RETAIL SERVICE FACILITIES

National and regional retailers built Deco stores in Baltimore's shopping districts, and local merchants updated storefronts across the city. Although built at an earlier date and stylistically different from the Hecht Company Warehouse, the Montgomery Ward Warehouse is Baltimore own architectural marvel of a warehouse. Designed by the Montgomery Ward Company's construction engineer, W. H. McCaully, and built by Wells Brothers Construction Company, the warehouse was the seventh of nine large warehouses built by Montgomery Ward across the United States in the early twentieth century. As with the Hecht Warehouse, loading and storage were consolidated at a warehouse built on relatively cheap land. The land was inexpensive because of efforts by the Baltimore city government and the Industrial Bureau of the Association of Commerce to persuade Montgomery Ward to locate its East Coast headquarters in Baltimore. The company required land near a railroad and a park. The city offered up a ten-acre parcel belonging to Carroll Park, the site of the Carroll Mansion, valued at $11,500 per acre. The building included a retail outlet, but its major purpose was servicing the company's well-known mail-order business. The site incorporated a train shed in the building to ease shipping and handling of goods.[106]

The Montgomery Ward Warehouse is a massive, eight-story concrete building in the northwest quadrant of the intersection of Washington

column topped with a flame flanked with wings. The relief includes the date 1931. Cast-bronze panels of an interlocking sunrise pattern frame the area over the entrance. The black granite above each recessed entrance features a carved cartouche depicting a seated figure of Justice. She sits on a base carved with the letters "AEQ" to the left of her legs and "TAS" to the right; her legs obscure the missing letters "UI." *Aequitas* is a Latin word meaning "just or equitable conduct toward others." This cartouche also contains the Roman numeral MDCCCLVIII, for 1858, with "MDC" visible to the left and "LVIII" to the right. Directly above each cartouche a flat cornice splays out to accept a black granite carved urn. Above the twin entrances large windows light the second and third stories; each window is flanked by quarter-round reeded marble columns.

Fifty thousand people attended the opening of the new addition. Baltimore mayor Howard Jackson spoke, as did Maryland governor Albert D. Ritchie, both men praising the company as a great Baltimore institution. A reporter covering the event observed that the expansion of the store—accompanied by the creation of new jobs—lifted the city's mood: "In these days when so many are finding it hard to keep their chins up, and when men forget the stamina that the American people have shown in all their periods of stress and the victories the stamina has won, it is refreshing and encouraging to turn one's eyes to what Hutzler Brothers' Company has done. In the midst of the Depression that Baltimore firm has flung a challenge into the faces of the Jeremiahs, has affirmed its faith in the future."[111]

Years later, Edmunds designed a department store with a streamlined aesthetic for Hutzler Brothers competitor Hochschild, Kohn & Company.[112] Built in 1948, the two-story brick building located on the southeast corner of York Road and Belvedere Avenue has some elements of post–World War II modernist architecture,

yet other elements speak to Edmunds's affinity to 1930s modern design. Most notable is the building's main entrance, a rounded corner with a two-story, glazed curtain wall that reveals the interior's dramatic curved staircase with streamlined metal handrails. The exterior is sheathed in light-colored brick with dark marble trim. Horizontal bands of display windows flank the entrance. A secondary entrance on the west elevation consists of plate glass double doors with streamlined vertical metal handles.

Other local retailers with downtown roots were able to expand both locally and regionally during the Depression. In 1883 William H. Read established a drugstore at Baltimore and German Streets, moving a few years later to Howard and Lexington Streets.[113] There were eventually ninety-nine Read stores in the Mid-Atlantic states when Rite-Aid purchased the company in 1977.[114] In 1934 the company built a grand new building at its original Howard Street location. The firm Smith & May served as architects, and the Engineering Contracting Company oversaw the construction. The new store featured a cigar counter, a luncheon counter, a grill, a liquor store, a surgical department staffed by a registered nurse, a photographic studio, a beauty salon, a watch-repair department, and twenty-five phone booths.[115]

The now heavily altered four-story brick building has a square plan and a flat roof. The two main facades (on the north and west elevations) were nearly identical. Each originally featured large, two-story steel-frame windows and had two large entrances sheltered with a canopy that ran the width of the facade. Centered above each canopy was the company's slogan, "Run Right to Reads," in large steel letters. The fourth story features four nautical-themed bas-reliefs, and there is a chevron-shaped flagpole holder at the corner of the building. But such subtle details are the only Deco features still visible today. Stripped of its original street-level treatment, it is no longer apparent that Read's was once a

**Hochschild, Kohn's Belvedere Avenue** store, 1949.

Photograph by the Hughes Company, Special Collections, courtesy
of the Maryland Historical Society.

**McCrory's** five-and-ten-cent store on Lexington Street, 1929.

Photograph by Consolidated Gas, Electric Light, and Power Company of Baltimore. Courtesy of Enoch Pratt Free Library, Maryland's State Library Resource Center, Baltimore, Maryland.

The windows on the second story are at this writing boarded shut, but the third-story windows appear to be original. "Schulte-United" is inscribed across the top of the building, and the inscription is flanked by bas-relief panels showing eagles standing on shields. A parapet with four domed finials tops the facade. In style, the Schulte-United building utilizes design motifs more typically seen on civic buildings. The McCrory Building and the Schulte-United building belong to the handful of remaining Baltimore storefronts with terra-cotta tile. Like Read's Drugstore, they are within the bounds of the much-debated "Westside Superblock" project, and their fate currently hangs in the balance.

Retailers located outside the downtown district modernized as well. In East Baltimore, in the Fells Point neighborhood, an unknown retailer employed Art Deco for a small store at 1900 Fleet Street. The building's scale is in keeping with the row-house neighborhood in which it is located, but the design elements are distinctly Deco. The two-story building has a rectangular plan and a flat roof and is clad in buff-colored brick. A large display window that projects from the facade wraps around the south and west elevations and features dark granite cladding at the base. The display areas are backed with elaborate burled-maple panels and mirrors. The front entrance is reached by a slight terrazzo ramp patterned with a chevron shape that points to the center of the door. The wood-and-glazed door has a large peaked transom. The second story of the facade has two double-hung sash windows. Centered above each window are chevrons of projecting brick topped by short piers of cast stone that pierce the roofline. The roofline is stepped and capped with cast stone. At the time of this writing, the building's first story had been boarded over; we can only hope that a sensitive renovation is under way.

East of Fells Point, in Highlandtown, are several stores that exhibit Deco elements. A two-

story, tan-colored brick building located at 3320 Eastern Avenue, on the northwest corner of the intersection of Eastern and Highland Avenues, is one. Another, down the block, is Bolewicki's Appliance Center, at 3222 Eastern Avenue.

North Baltimore is dominated by row houses and single-family homes built primarily in various traditional styles. There are a few Art Deco stores in the area's small commercial hubs, such as the small collection of shops and restaurants clustered around the intersection of Cold Spring Lane and Kittery Lane in the Roland Park vicinity. The Heidelbach Company building (1933), designed by Lucius R. White Jr., occupies 411 and 413 West Cold Spring Lane. The one-story brick building with a rectangular plan is banked into a slope, allowing the rear portion to rise two stories. The facade is clad in polychrome concrete-aggregate panels, which may have been produced by the Earley Studio. The building accommodates two storefronts. The east side still features the original indented entrance and plate-glass display windows, but the west side has been altered. A horizontal band of alternating Greek keys and sunbursts tops the store fronts. The upper level of the facade is divided by three vertical bands of black, red, and beige chevrons. There is a second horizontal band with red striping across the top of the facade. A sign with "The Heidelbach Co." in red lettering projects from the roofline.

The store at 415–417 33rd Street, formerly Michael's Rug Gallery, in the Waverly neighborhood's commercial center is a two-story brick building with a rectangular plan and a flat roof. The facade, clad in light-colored brick with black Vitrolite trim, is divided into three sections by pilasters topped with stepped limestone capitals. The front entrance is central and flanked by large display windows. Between the first and second stories is a horizontal band of Vitrolite with a subtly shaded geometric pattern of alternating triangles and cones. Second-story fenestration consists of five double-hung windows. The parapet features a herringbone brick design. Benjamin Frank designed this building, which was constructed in 1936.

Across the city can be seen numerous examples of stores that modernized nineteenth-century buildings by updating the ground level with an Art Deco–style facade, though they are probably only a fraction of what once existed. The storefront of 525 North Charles Street, now the Doll House clothing store, has managed to survive intact in a stretch of the city's main north-south artery that has consistently been a viable commercial area. The first and second stories of this four-story classical building were remodeled sometime in the 1930s. The storefront is clad with Carrara glass and enamel tile. A unique, B-shaped display window extends across the first and second stories. The entrance consists of a glazed double door topped with a large glass-block window. Farther north on Charles Street an altered Italianate row house at 930 North Charles features a limestone storefront with a simple scored design of six boxed lines centered over a recessed entrance. In the late 1930s the building was home to Carl, Inc., a high-end beauty salon.[119]

The store of Charles Fish & Sons, once a clothing and furniture store, sits in a largely abandoned retail area less fortunate than Charles Street. Located at 429 North Eutaw Street, this nineteenth-century three-story brick building was remodeled in the 1930s. The streetfront facades on the north and west elevations are clad with black Carrara glass. There are large steel-frame display windows, and "Charles Fish & Sons" is etched in glass on both facades. Other storefronts in the vicinity of Charles Fish & Sons that feature Vitrolite or Carrara glass cladding and other Deco-era materials and styling include those at 427 North Eutaw Street, 421 North Howard Street, and 115 West Saratoga Street.

A final example of a Deco-era storefront is the Buck Appliance Company, at 1814 Fleet Street

in Fells Point. The ground level of the facade is clad in large, cream-colored ceramic tile with maroon trim. A large plate-glass display window curves toward the entrance, and a tiled floor leads up to an original wood and glazed door with a decorative metal handle. "Buck Appliance Co." is spelled above the door in a Deco font.

There are quite a few small-scale stores with Deco qualities in the commercial hubs of Baltimore neighborhoods not covered in these pages, such as Catonsville, Pimlico, Hampden, Waverly, Belair-Edison, Hamilton, and the East Monument Street business district. Not fully known is how many Deco retail establishments we have lost. One sees remnants, such as the side elevation of Eddie's Market on Roland Avenue. Other premises remain, but they have been altered beyond recognition—buildings such as Baltimore's 1938 Sears Roebuck store, designed by Nimmons, Carr & Wright, on the corner of North Avenue and Harford Road, now the Eastside District Court.

### MOVIE THEATERS AND OTHER RECREATIONAL BUILDINGS

Quite a few of Baltimore's Deco theaters remain, although many are in a fragile or heavily altered state. Even iconic theaters central to the city's identity seem to be continually at risk. Urban church congregations, with their need for large meeting spaces, have ensured the survival, though not necessarily the pristine preservation, of many of the city's theaters.

The Senator theater, designed by John J. Zink, is one of Baltimore's best-known Art Deco buildings. In 1939 E. Eyring & Son constructed the theater for Durkee Enterprises at a cost of $250,000. Unlike most of the city's theaters from the 1920s and 1930s, the Senator is remarkably well preserved and continues to be used as a movie theater, having undergone a recent $3.5 million renovation.

The eye-catching landmark juts up from the west side of York Road in the heart of the neighborhood of Govan's commercial district, now known as Belvedere Square. An irregular mass of cylindrical and rectangular shapes composed of brick, stucco, and glass block, the Senator looks almost like a temple, yet surely not a temple that adheres to a historical prototype. A truly unique composition by Baltimore's best-known theater architect, it evokes the excitement, glamour, and exoticism of Hollywood's golden era, while maintaining a welcoming scale in harmony with the surrounding suburban neighborhood.

The quadrangle-shaped lot that the Senator occupies must have represented a challenge to Zink, since it has no parallel sides. His solution was to set the front third of the building, which houses the lobby, flush with the street, and to angle the remainder of the building, which houses the 929-seat auditorium, to the northwest. The front section contains the building's most elaborate exterior detail, while the rear section's walls are brick laid in common bond with a handful of unadorned windows and emergency-exit doors and one large, square chimney on the north slope of the auditorium's front-facing gable roof.

At the theater's front, a large semicircular marquee juts over a wide, colorful sidewalk made up of concrete squares inscribed with the names of late twentieth- and early twenty-first-century movies with Baltimore ties that premiered at the Senator. The marquee was designed to allow for backlit lettering around its full extent to advertise featured films; it is edged in horizontal bands of red neon. Distinctive, freestanding letters in a Deco font attached to the front top edge of the marquee spell "The Senator." The marquee's underside has recessed lights that draw attention to the memorable sidewalk.

Below the marquee, the theater's entrance is a symmetrical composition recessed in a wall clad in black marbleized Carrara Glass segmented by metal horizontal bands. Another band of green marble extends along the base of

the wall. A central ticket booth is flanked by a pair of double plate glass doors, followed by two display cases set to the outer edges of the facade. Fluted aluminum moldings trim the doors and display cases. The ticket booth has an aluminum base and a curved glass ticket window, which is also trimmed with aluminum.

An elegant glass-block and stucco form rises up behind the marquee. Zink's masterful design is essentially a drum squared off by four thick and prominent piers. Panels of glass block on both the drum and the piers provide vertical emphasis, while continuous horizontal stucco molding at the top unites the upper reaches with the marquee and entrance. At night, the building glows from within when the expanses of glass block are backlit with green and red neon.

The Senator's interior is as striking and well preserved as its exterior. The entrance doors open into a two-story circular lobby featuring a patterned terrazzo floor, murals by Paul Roche, and bas-reliefs of bronze and aluminum. The lobby leads to a concessions area, or foyer, with walls covered in a warm wood veneer. Men's and ladies' lounges and an office are accessed from this inner lobby. The ladies' lounge features a circular sitting room. The massive auditorium achieves a feeling of monumentality through strong vertical lines and the spare use of stylized decorative details.[120]

The Senator was not Zink's first Baltimore theater, nor it was it his grandest. Earlier in the decade he designed two Colonial Revival theaters on the west side of town, the Edgewood and the Bridge (both 1930), the latter with a grand Art Deco interior. But the Ambassador (1935), at 4604 Liberty Heights Avenue, is perhaps Zink's most ambitious Art Deco exterior. Unfortunately, today the theater is vacant and in great decay.[121]

Unlike the Senator, the Ambassador occupies a rectangular lot that allowed Zink to compose a straightforward plan. The bulk of the building consists of a large rectangular auditorium with brick exterior walls sheltered by a front-facing

The **Senator** theater on York Road, 1954.

Photograph by the Hughes Company, Special Collections,
courtesy of the Maryland Historical Society.

gable roof. Zink achieved complexity through the execution of the theater's facade, which is anchored by the front wall of the auditorium. This facade is clad in buff brick interspersed with horizontal bands of black glazed brick; it terminates in a stepped parapet. Stepped walls and pylons project from the center of the theater's facade to form pavilions for the entrance and retail space. This towering arrangement of shapes features vertical and horizontal banks of black brick, a tube-shaped metal and glass light, and a vertical sign mast to the left-hand side of the entrance pavilion with letters spelling "Ambassador." The mast is balanced on the right by a shorter pier with ziggurat terraces.

The theater has been marred by asphalt-shingled roofs that obscure original features. The original thin, streamlined black marquee with white banding has been replaced by a thick, corrugated, and unsympathetic marquee. Some octagonal white-marble medallions are still visible along the tops of the retail pavilions. The entrance has been heavily modified over the years, though six poster cases remain. In early July 2012 a fire blazed through the Ambassador, causing significant damage to the front entrance and the interior, yet most of the historic exterior survived. The current owners hope to restore the building.

Built in 1937, the Northway theater, at 6701 Harford Road, was another Zink creation, though smaller in scale than the Senator and the Ambassador. Located to the northeast of two major thoroughfares, Northern Parkway and Harford Road, the Northway forms an L shape around a single-story commercial building that occupies the corner lot (and appears to have been built in conjunction with the theater). This arrangement provides for entrances to the theater on both streets. The main entrance and the lobby front Harford Road, while the auditorium abuts Northern Parkway. The theater has brick walls painted white. In 1941 Zink was hired to design additions to the building, including the tall glass-block tower over the lobby. The original

marquee remains more or less intact. The letter N is placed atop the sides of the marquee, but the original freestanding letters spelling "Northway" across the front of the marquee have been removed.[122]

The architect John Eyring designed a number of Baltimore's Art Deco neighborhood theaters. Located not far from Zink's Northway, and built in the same year, 1937, the Earle, at 4847 Belair Road, is a low-slung and visually arresting design. Like the Northway, the Earle cradles a one-story, corner-lot commercial space that is incorporated into the theater's design. When the Earle opened, the store was home to the Atlantic Confectionery, an appropriate neighbor for a movie theater.[123] An additional contemporaneous commercial space flanks the Earle's opposite wall.

As with Zink's designs, this theater's visual interest is achieved by the marquee, the arrangement and materials of the street-level entrance, and the sculptural forms above the lobby. A large triangular marquee maintains its form, but the neon tubes that once provided emphasis have been removed. The plate-glass double doors are replacements, but the theater's grand front entrance still contains the ticket booth, some black-and-green marbleized Carrara glass panels, and a Carrara glass band with a geometric pattern of alternating triangles and wavy lines.

Rising above the marquee is a low, buff-colored brick wall with rounded corners detailed with bands of black-glazed brick and topped with a molding painted green. Freestanding letters that spelled "Earle" have been removed from the top. The wall is part of a series of stepped-back pavilions that lead to the facade of the auditorium. This facade has a terraced parapet; the terraces contain curved edges, creating a soft, streamlined crown for the building.

Eyring also designed the Pikes theater, which was built in 1938, a year after the Earle. The Pikes, at 1001 Reisterstown Road, shares the Earle's gentle massing with stepped-back

The **Ambassador** theater, on Liberty Heights Avenue, 1935.

Photograph by Consolidated Gas, Electric Light, and Power Company of Baltimore.
From the BGE Collection at the Baltimore Museum of Industry.

forms and rounded corners. The facade is clad in blonde brick trimmed with accents of black-glazed brick. A glass-block light wall occupies the central plane of the facade, just above the marquee. The building was converted into a restaurant in the late 1990s.[124]

Eyring continued to develop his rounded, streamlined aesthetic in another theater, the Uptown (1941), at 5010–5018 Park Heights Avenue. The Uptown was significantly larger than his other theaters, accommodating eleven hundred seats. The original set of three double doors has been replaced with a single entrance. The facade's main section is a powerful presence in the theater. A symmetrical design of buff brick and cast-stone piers—the striations of internal fluting that were used in between the piers was echoed in a set of receding side planes—once held the theater's name in vertical letters. Three marquees, one attached to each section of the theater's facade, have been removed. The largest of these marquees, above the entrance, was semicircular.

Radio Centre, on North Avenue near Charles Street, once housed the WFBR studios and the Radio Centre theater. The owner, Morris A. Mechanic, who was also proprietor of the New Theater, decided to unite America's two most popular forms of entertainment, radio and movies, in one location. The building cost $400,000 and opened in 1939. The theater, which seated one thousand people, had murals by R. McGill Mackall. Designed by the Philadelphia architect Armand Carroll, the building has a rectangular plan and extends a block north to 20th Street. The facade is dominated by a central block tower. The front face of the tower angles in to form a shallow V that holds a bold finial to which letters that spell "Radio Centre" were once attached. The theater still has a marquee, although it is not original, but the front entrance and windows have been blocked shut.[125]

J. E. Moxley designed the Westway (1939), at 5300 Edmondson Avenue, a small theater in a suburban neighborhood in west Baltimore

right on the line separating the city from the county.[126] Projecting from the southwest corner is a large, nearly circular marquee, behind which is a stepped tower. The one-story entrance pavilion, which has been modified, leads back to a two-story auditorium with enclosed windows on the second story and a side entrance. The theater is now used as a church. Many of Baltimore's Deco-era theaters have been converted into churches. A striking example is the Lord Calvert, at 2444 Washington Boulevard, designed by Oliver B. Wright and built in 1936.[127] In true Baltimore style, the entire facade, including a projecting tower, has been covered by formstone.

David H. Harrison designed the Monroe theater for the Monroe Theater Company. Built at a cost of $30,000 in 1939,[128] this small theater at 1924 West Pratt Street is located in an urban residential neighborhood, and it too has been converted into a church. Harrison also designed the Patapsco theater, at 601–645 East Patapsco Avenue in the south Baltimore neighborhood of Brooklyn. Harrison produced the blueprints for this eight-hundred-seat theater in 1942, but construction was delayed until 1944.[129] The theater has a straightforward rectangular plan. The curved facade is faced with buff brick and horizontal bands of orange brick trim. There is a vertical pavilion with five narrow vertical rows of glass block in the center of the facade. The entrance has been altered.

Following World War II, Hal Miller, the architect of the Samester Parkway Apartments in Pikesville, designed several neighborhood theaters in a restrained Art Deco style. The Paramount (1946), at 6650 Bel Air Road, and the Colgate (1948), at 1718 Dundalk Avenue, are similar. Both have facades clad with orange brick accented with horizontal bands of darker brick and almost no other ornamentation. As with many other theaters in Baltimore, the entrances have been altered and the marquees removed.[130]

A late Baltimore Deco example, the Colony theater (1949), at 8123 Harford Road in Parkville, shows how John Zink's designs

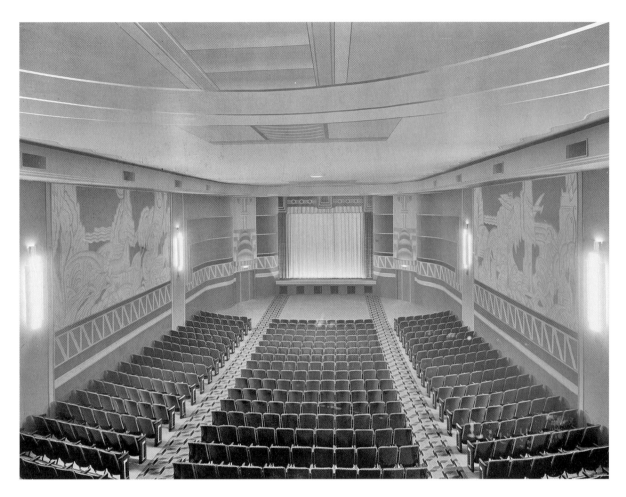

Interior view of the **Brooklyn** theater, date unknown.
The murals shown here now hang in the Club Charles.

Photograph by Consolidated Gas, Electric Light, and Power Company.
From the BGE Collection at the Baltimore Museum of Industry.

drew upon the streamlining of the thirties. The building was a squat, one-story cylinder with glass-block windows, steel canopies, and freestanding, bulb-lit letters spelling "Bar-B-Q" attached to the roof. The building suffered an unfortunate major remodeling and is now a used-auto dealership. Only the cylinder form remains. Other streamlined drive-ins long gone include the Oriole Tower Drive-In, formerly at Broadway and Harford Road; Orye's Drive-In, formerly at 25th Street and Kirk Avenue; and Hobb's Drive-In, formerly on New Edmondson Avenue (Route 40).

Like Washington, Baltimore had White Tower and Little Tavern hamburger stands. A White Tower at Erdman Avenue and Belair Road and one on Howard Street just north of Centre Street, across from the Greyhound Bus Station, have both been demolished. One can glimpse former Little Taverns around the city, but they have been heavily altered. Baltimore retains a wonderful dining car, the Overlea Diner, at 6652 Belair Road.

Baltimore's Mount Vernon neighborhood boasts the Chanticleer Lounge, which is still in operation as the Club Hippo nightclub. William Lillien, of New Jersey, opened the Chanticleer Lounge in 1939. The architect John Poe Tyler designed it, and the Triangle Sign Company provided fluorescent tubular lighting on both the exterior and the interior. The low-slung, brick-clad building with a flat roof occupies the southwest corner of the intersection of Charles and Eager Streets. The club's lower elevation is clad in brick, while the upper part is covered in stucco. At the corner, the sides of the building curve in and a drumlike tower topped with a globe and a weathervane rises up. Extended metal courses and lines give the building horizontal thrust. The main entrance, which has been altered, is set into the building's curved corner. Freestanding porcelain letters were placed upon a ledge that wrapped around the building when the club first opened. Large letters above the entrance spelled out the club's name, with smaller letters

spelling "Cocktail Bar" and "Cocktail Lounge" to either side. Backlighting made the letters stand out in relief at night.

In the Chanticleer's hub was the oval-shaped main lounge, which measured 45 by 100 feet. The center of the room was sunk 18 inches so that patrons on the floor could see the center of the oval-shaped bar, where musicians performed on a revolving stage. The top of the stage was sandblasted plate glass backlit by white fluorescent tubing. Red plastic islands with gold fluorescent tubing, designed to hold glasses and bottles, sat to either side of the stage. More tube lighting, concealed in plaster ceiling troughs, helped create a dramatic atmosphere.[136]

Numerous neighborhood restaurants and bars have kept their Deco storefronts, including Alonso's, at 415 West Cold Spring Lane in Roland Park. Its street-level facade is rendered in polished and banded steel, and there is a large glass-block window in the center. A canopy shelters the plate-glass door of the main entrance. Issac "Poppa" Alonso opened the restaurant and bar bearing his name in 1938. After a stint in the navy during World War I, the Spanish-born Alonso opened a restaurant on Belair Road. He then opened a restaurant in Roland Park—Joe's Place—on the north side of Cold Spring Lane. A builder who was putting up a row of houses across the street asked Alonso if he wanted one for an even bigger restaurant. Alonso bought into the idea with the request for an apartment on the top floor. The builder agreed, and in 1938 the present Alonso's restaurant opened.[137]

Many of Fells Point's ubiquitous neighborhood bars are housed in nineteenth-century structures with Deco-era face-lifts. Two examples are Smedley's and Pearl's. Smedley's, at 600 South Wolfe Street, is on the southwest corner of Wolfe and Fleet Streets. A few blocks away, Pearl's, at 1900 Aliceanna, on the northeast corner of Wolfe and Aliceanna Streets, sits a block from the waterfront. It features a Deco facade at street level.

North of Fell's Point, in Old Town, the Hil-

name. A marble wall extending west from the facade has a portal for cars. Steel letters above the opening read "Drive-Up Service Enter in Rear." The west elevation features three angled drive-up windows with steel surrounds. The bank's interior is completely original. Streamlined classical details and materials such as glass block make the bank a late example of the Deco style, while the drive-up windows speak to the burgeoning car culture of the mid-twentieth century.

Baltimore can also boast of significant Deco-era buildings designed for the transportation industry. A rare Deco-influenced gas station sits on the south side of Frederick Road in the suburban neighborhood of Catonsville. This jewel-box-like building at 585 Frederick Road now houses Ridgeway Automotive. The station is a one-story building with two sections: an office and a garage, or service bay. The office has a parapet with brightly colored details in glazed terra cotta. At the apex, the cornice terminates in scrolls flanking a broochlike detail topped by an elaborate crown design. The front entrance consists of a plate-glass door surrounded by a large display window. There are narrow 1/1 sash windows to either side of the main section, all slightly recessed and topped with arches. The decorative cornice continues on the garage section, which has a simpler design. Remnants of other Deco gas stations are scattered across the city, but most have been heavily altered.

As the United States entered World War II, scores of enlisted men and war workers traveled from their homes to bases on Greyhound buses. To keep pace with the surge in ridership, Greyhound built a new terminal in Baltimore at Howard and Centre Streets in 1942. Wischmeyer, Arrasmith & Elswick, in Louisville, Kentucky, designed the building with the help of Roland Dressler, in Chicago. The local Cummins Construction Company served as general contractor. The building cost $350,000. Its waiting room could accommodate three hundred people, and its canopied platform could accom-

modate twelve buses at once. The second floor housed offices and a reception room.[138]

The Greyhound Bus Terminal at 601 North Howard Street is a two-story building with a rectangular plan and a flat roof. It is clad in cast stone with granite trim. The main entrance was placed in the terminal's southwest corner. On the second story, a horizontal band of paired windows separated by half-cylinders wraps around the facades at the corner of Howard and Centre Streets. A concrete canopy runs in a parallel line below this fenestration and turns upward into a vertical sign on the Howard Street elevation. As the building extends to the north and east, separate bays of fenestration are employed. What was once a service garage east of the terminal has been incorporated into the museum of the Maryland Historical Society. Visitors can view the garage ceiling's large wooden trusses.

The Baltimore City Health Department building, at 1374 North Avenue, originally housed the Brooks-Price Company, a Buick sales-and-service dealership opened in 1938.[139] The facade of this two-story brick rectangular building with buff brick cladding is divided into three bays separated by piers that project above the roofline. The center bay features glass block and brick arranged in a striking geometric design with a vertical thrust. The outer two bays have a horizontal emphasis created by bands of windows, bands of bricks, a metal band between the first and second stories, and blue tile under the first-story windows. A prominent circular marquee projects from the corner of the facade and wraps to the east elevation, where the building's main entrance is located. Glass block surrounds the entrance. The first-story windows on this elevation are also glass block, while the second-story windows are steel awning windows.

Cunliffe Cadillac was a large auto dealership on 25th Street in the 1930s. The building's design was the result of a collaboration between the General Motors Company architect Philip S. Tyre, of Philadelphia, and Howard F. Baldwin, of Baltimore. The three-story building had a granite facade with large, steel casement windows. Each corner of the building featured an eagle of carved stone. The showroom had wrought-iron lighting fixtures, Italian torchères, a Flint Faience tile floor, and a concrete ceiling painted to simulate oak.[140] The building was demolished in the 1990s.

The large vacant building occupying the triangular plot of land at 2300 North Monroe Street was once home to Martin Brothers Auto. The Martin brothers started an auto dealership and repair shop in Baltimore in 1909. This particular building, constructed in 1947, was set back from the street, most likely to make the new cars on display more visible. Martin Brothers is a large, one- and two-story concrete-block building faced with brick. Its massing is an asymmetrical arrangement of boxy forms with horizontal emphasis. The front portion, which probably housed the showroom, and the middle portion, which may have contained sales offices, had curved corners. There are intact expanses of glass block on the second story.[141] The building shows how streamlining continued to be a popular stylistic choice for businesses in the years following World War II.

Schwing Motors, at 3326 Keswick Road, is a two-story rectangular building clad in brick. It was designed by F. J. Heldrich and built in 1948. The northeast corner has a prominent streamlined curve. There are plate-glass door entrances with transoms on the east and north elevations. The first-story windows appear to be replacements, while the second story features horizontal bands of original multipane windows.

### INDUSTRIAL BUILDINGS

Baltimore also has a rich assortment of Deco-era buildings designed for industrial use. These buildings are a testimony to the strength of Baltimore's manufacturing sector in the interwar years despite the challenges of the Great Depression. Their profuse presence on the landscape marks Baltimore as a former industrial powerhouse, and in this respect the city has more in

common with cities like Pittsburgh than it does with Washington, DC.

There is a pocket of industrial buildings from the 1920s and 1930s in northwest Baltimore, off Monroe Street. The Cloverland Farms Dairy plant (1929–43) once occupied a full city block, extending from Monroe to Payson Street on Windsor Avenue. One of the plant's buildings, on the corner of Monroe and Windsor, sported an ornamental milk jug atop a polygonal-bay main entrance. Extant buildings from the complex feature streamlined corners and glass-block panels.[142] Another dairy plant, Green Spring Dairy (1937), which once occupied 1020 West 41st Street, was a broad, low building with a distinctive central tower, large plate-glass windows, speed lines, cantilevered canopies, and Deco signage. Lucius R. White Jr. was the architect.[143]

In the late 1930s and early 1940s north Baltimore developed an industrial section in the vicinity of 25th Street and Kirk Avenue. Access to rail lines and the availability of large parcels of land made this an ideal location for new industrial operations. For the most part, the buildings are simple, large one-story compositions with flat roofs and minimal ornamentation; however, some entrances and office sections have Art Deco detailing. Extant examples of industrial buildings in the area include the Coca-Cola Bottling Company of Baltimore building (1939), at 2525 Kirk Avenue; McCarthy Hicks (1942), at 2728 Loch Raven Boulevard; Hajoca (1944), at 2740 Loch Raven; and Dixie Saw (1945), at 2730 Loch Raven. Of these buildings, the Coca-Cola Bottling Company building is the most architecturally striking.

The Coca-Cola Bottling Company building is a three-story brick building with an irregular (trapezoidal) plan and a flat roof. A three-story square block on the north corner of the building houses offices, while the remainder of the building, comprising the factory area, is two stories high. The building has curved corners and is clad in alternating bands of multicolored brick and limestone. The utilitarian portions of the

The **Coca-Cola Bottling Company** building on Kirk Avenue, November 1939.

Photograph by Consolidated Gas, Electric Light, and Power Company of Baltimore. From the BGE
Collection at the Baltimore Museum of Industry.

building have glass-block windows. The limestone-clad front entrance pavilion has plate-glass double doors with decorative grillwork, a large transom, and fluted door surrounds. The distinctive "Coca-Cola" logo, flanked by medallions featuring glass Coca-Cola bottles, is inscribed above the door in bas-relief.

Following the railroad east from the 25th Street and Kirk Avenue industrial area leads to the five-acre plant that formerly housed Goetze's Meats, in the 2400 block of Sinclair Lane. Following the initial construction in 1923, the company expanded the plant in 1939. The plant is a large, abandoned industrial complex of utilitarian brick buildings. Some Deco-inspired architectural features remain, however, including a massive neon sign on a steel scaffold that reads "Goetze's Meats" and a three-story red brick building with a curved corner that contains two glass-block panels.[144]

The National Can Company plant is on the northeast corner of the intersection of Wolfe and Thames Streets in Fells Point, about half a block from the waterfront. It is a large, four-story brick building with a square plan clad in orange-colored brick in a common bond pattern with black brick accents. Each elevation is divided into three parts, a large central section flanked by large projecting pavilions. These pavilions have a vertical emphasis, achieved by long bands of black brick that break the horizontal line of the windows. The roof line is terraced. The west elevation has "National Can Company" in flush black letters centered above the fourth-story windows of the central section.

The National Can Company building is actually a remodeled building. It originally housed the John Boyle Can Factory. The National Can Company took over the factory in 1921 and undertook a massive renovation in 1939, which resulted in the current Art Deco building. The company's executive offices were in New York City. In addition to its Baltimore branch, the company had factories in Boston, in Hamilton,

Ohio, and in Maspeth, Long Island, with warehouses and sales offices in Chicago and Detroit. In 1939 the Baltimore branch had a production capacity of three million packers' cans per day; it also produced metal home goods such as bread boxes. The company's annual output was about 266 million cans, and the workforce reached nine hundred in the summer during the late 1930s. The plant closed in 1980; it has since been renovated into apartments.[145]

The Cheek Industries building (1945), at 5107 North Point Boulevard, is a massive, two-story industrial building with ribbon windows throughout. Adjacent to the Bethlehem Steel Complex in Sparrows Point, the building is evidence of Baltimore's major role in the defense mobilization of World War II. The office section of the building features streamlined styling, including a bullnose glass-block door surround.

The Salvage Depot (1946), at 2801 Sisson Street, is a two-story red brick building with a rectangular plan. The entrance features a brick bullnose door surround and a plate-glass door with a transom. A glass-block window centered over the entrance is divided into three parts by vertical concrete bands, and there are multiple horizontal brick bands across the facade.

Another interesting Deco industrial building is now, alas, demolished. Hal Miller designed the General Vending Sales Corporation building (1946), once located at 237–245 West Biddle Street. The facade consisted of two roughly equal parts. One part, at 237 West Biddle, was clad in red brick and featured large plate-glass windows flanked by expanses of glass block. The entrance to this portion of the building consisted of a single stainless steel door with a decorative rail pull, a half-round window, and a large transom with the street number, 237, painted in a Deco font. The second part, at 239–245 West Biddle, was also clad in brick, but it had a curved corner with a glass-block inset. The entrance to this section of the building consisted of stainless steel double doors with half-round windows framed

The **National Can Company** building at Wolfe
and Thames Streets, December 1938.

Photograph by Consolidated Gas, Electric Light, and Power
Company of Baltimore. From the BGE Collection at the Baltimore Museum of Industry.

by fluted bullnose concrete surrounds. A wide concrete molding running the entire length of 239–245 West Biddle united the two sections. When it reached 237 West Biddle, the molding jutted upwards and terminated in a large concrete finial sign.

Despite losses, Baltimore retains a wealth of industrial buildings from the interwar years. One sees large expanses of glass block, colored bricks, and remnants of Deco signage in now-quiet sections of town. These structures are too easy to overlook and are usually far down on the list of preservationists' priorities. Nevertheless, they are significant, the true workhorses in the story of how Baltimore became the city we know today.

The city is in the midst of a laudable rejuvenation of its nineteenth-century industrial heritage, as developers convert the great mills of the Jones Falls Valley into homes, businesses, and retail spaces. Some twentieth-century industrial structures have benefitted from this trend, as in the unlikely transformation of a 1923 grain elevator into luxury condominiums in Locust Point. We hope that more buildings from the 1920s and 1930s can find new life in the twenty-first century.

## WASHINGTON

Washington has some excellent examples of Deco buildings built by the federal and District of Columbia governments, including the U.S. Department of Justice building, the Library of Congress Annex, the Bethesda Naval Hospital, Washington National Airport, and the District of Columbia Municipal Center.

### FEDERAL, MUNICIPAL, AND INSTITUTIONAL OFFICE BUILDINGS

Most of the federal architecture in Washington between the world wars partook of classicism. Some of this architecture, such as the works of John Russell Pope and Cass Gilbert, might be called "modern classicism" in the sense that it represented clear twentieth-century salutes to Greco-Roman aesthetics—classicism pure and simple. But other buildings—those designed by Waddy Wood and Paul Philippe Cret, for example—are perhaps better classified as "mod-ern*ized* classicism," thus connoting a pointed *simplification* of the Greco-Roman heritage, the middle range between modernism and tradition-alism that many architects of the period strove for. It was in buildings such as these that the design vocabulary of the 1925 Paris Exposition and the later streamlining fad were often seen.

An important prototypical example in Washington, completed the year before the Paris Exposition, was Bertram Grosvenor Goodhue's design for the National Academy of Sciences Building (1924), at 2101 Constitution Avenue NW.

One of the earliest and most important of the federal buildings to show this fusion was the 1931–35 Department of Justice building, designed by the Philadelphia firm Zantzinger, Borie, & Medary. Treasury Secretary Andrew Mellon, who was initially in charge of the Fed-eral Triangle project, awarded the commission for the Justice Department building to Milton B. Medary, who was already serving as a member of the Board of Architectural Consultants for the Federal Triangle. Each member of this board was given a chance to design one of the build-ings. After Medary's death in 1929, his surviving partners, Clarence Zantzinger and Charles L. Borie Jr., continued the work.

The building occupies a trapezoidal site be-tween 9th and 10th Streets NW (to the east and west, respectively) and Pennsylvania and Con-stitution Avenues (to the north and south). This monumental building contains a very large in-ternal courtyard in the center and three smaller flanking courtyards. Classical in spirit, the build-ing was designed with a rusticated granite base. The middle section and the attic were clad in limestone. The building is crowned with a low hip roof composed of red tile and adorned with polychrome terra-cotta "snow cleats."

Seven stories high, with the top story set back slightly, the building features long Ionic colonnades on the east and south. But on the other two elevations simple, modernized pilasters are used. At the southeast and southwest corners pedimented Ionic pavilions face south toward Constitution Avenue. At the south edges of the 9th and 10th Street elevations, corresponding smaller pavilions with a two-column distyle-in-antis composition extend the treatment. The building's north corners shift from classical to "modernized classical" simplification: they are diagonal planes with distyle-in-antis recesses.[1]

The building's explicitly Deco features consist of elaborate ornamentation. Much of this ornamentation was executed in aluminum and designed by the studio of the sculptor Carl Paul Jennewein. The aluminum ornamentation includes exterior doors and gates, tall, multilevel exterior torchères to the sides of the doors, and a lavish interior ornamental program.

In the auditorium, or Great Hall, on the building's second floor are large aluminum modernistic statues of symbolic figures flanking a small stage—a female figure, the Spirit of Justice, and a male figure symbolizing the Majesty of Law. These figures were cast by the General Bronze Corporation in Long Island. Deco aluminum railings and trim, along with pendant tubular Deco lighting fixtures, grace the Great Hall. All the aluminum lighting fixtures, including the exterior torchères, were the work of the Edward F. Caldwell Company of New York.[2]

The building's Deco ornamentation is extensive: the elevator lobby at the northwest entrance with its large, reeded streamlined columns, beamed polychrome ceiling adornments, aluminum elevator doors with a checkerboard pattern, and pendant lights; the elevator lobby behind the Great Hall, with its silvered ceiling adorned with elaborate Deco floral ornamentation, pendant lights, and a Deco chandelier; the huge aluminum Deco torchères in the law library, each fixture topped with the figure of a rearing Pegasus. Perhaps the most spectacular feature is the polychrome concrete mosaic ceiling that John Joseph Earley was commissioned to design for the 10th Street gateway entrance to the building's central courtyard. The ornamented panels, with colors that range from sandy yellow to cerulean blue, contain rectangular, almost cubistic light fixtures. This ceiling was more than a decorative embellishment; it was a methodological breakthrough in construction methods. To guarantee permanent adhesion—to ensure that the panels would never fall off—the architects directed the Earley studio to fabricate the slabs so that they would form the mold in which cement for the next story of the building would be poured.[3]

At the eastern tip of the Federal Triangle project, where Pennsylvania and Constitution Avenues meet, the Federal Trade Commission building, designed in 1936, was completed in 1938. The building was the work of Edward H. Bennett, the senior partner in the Chicago architectural firm Bennett, Parsons, & Frost. President Roosevelt laid the cornerstone for this "apex building"—the building that completed the Federal Triangle—in 1937. Like the Justice Department building, the wedge-shaped, seven-story Federal Trade Commission building was designed with a granite base, a limestone middle section and attic, and a low hip roof clad in tile. Large recesses in the middle section of each elevation form short pilastered colonnades. The semicircular portico at the eastern tip of the building contains an Ionic colonnade and a saucer dome.

Deco ornamentation in the Federal Trade Commission building includes aluminum gates emblazoned with symbols of trade, such as an ocean liner and a clipper plane, sculpted by William McVey. Bas-relief sculpted panels over the doorways depict kindred themes: scenes of industry and shipping by Chaim Gross and Robert

Laurent and scenes of agriculture by Concetta Scaravaglione and Carl Schmitz. Huge statues of muscular populistic heroes reining in wild horses flank the building. Entitled "Man Controlling Trade," these iconic New Deal images were the work of Michael Lantz.[4]

Two contemporaneous examples of New Deal federal architecture should be mentioned: the 1935–36 Interior Department building, on C Street between 18th and 19th Streets NW, designed by Waddy Wood, and the 1940 Social Security Administration building, in the block between 3rd and 4th Streets SW and Independence Avenue and C Street SW. Both buildings exude New Deal aesthetics but exemplify modernized classicism with little distinctive Art Deco massing or ornamentation.[5] One particular late-blooming specimen of federal architecture deserves to be mentioned as well: the General Accounting Office building, at 441 G Street NW, designed by Gilbert Stanley Underwood and completed in 1949. The principal Deco features of this stripped-down modern building are bands of bas-relief sculpture on the inward-curving stone panels flanking the entrance.

In the decades before home rule arrived (in the 1970s), all District of Columbia municipal buildings were productions of the federal government, since Washington's local administration existed under federal supervision. A large municipal center for the District of Columbia had been envisioned in the McMillan Plan of 1901–2. In the 1930s this concept began to take shape, and the building was constructed to the south of Judiciary Square, at 300 Indiana Avenue NW. Construction began in 1939, and the building was finished in 1941.

The architect of the Municipal Center was Nathan C. Wyeth, who served as the municipal architect for Washington, DC, from 1934 to 1946.[6] This massive rectangular building clad in limestone sits on a slope that contains a terraced court. At its taller, south elevation (at the bottom of the hill) it is six stories high, not counting the

attic. The top two stories and the attic are set back.

This is in most respects a severe, stripped classical building: its elevations are dominated by a colonnaded rhythm of vertical recessed window bays and unadorned three-story piers that read as pilasters. A large portico extends to the west. But this building, like the Justice Department building, has much Deco ornamentation. Above the doors on the Indiana Avenue elevation are aluminum panels with sunray and thunderbolt motifs. Upon the retaining wall for the terrace to the west of the building are two sculpted panels. The first, entitled "Urban Life," was created by John Gregory; it uses classical figures to depict the provision of hospital care, sanitation, prosperity, and justice. Another panel, by Lee Lawrie, bears classical figures representing Light, Water, and Thoroughfare.

On the lobby floor of the C Street entrance is a large terrazzo map of the city. And within the two courtyards of the building are polychrome ceramic sculpted murals. In the west courtyard, a mural by Waylande Gregory, "Democracy in Action," depicts the city's firemen and policemen at work. In the east courtyard, a mural by Hildreth Meière, "Health and Welfare," shows forty-seven people performing or receiving municipal and social services. Northwest of the building, on the Indiana Avenue side, is the octagonal Police Memorial Fountain, created by the Earley studio and completed in 1941.[7]

Very close to the Municipal Center is the Recorder of Deeds Building, designed by Wyeth and built in 1941–42 at 515 D Street NW. President Roosevelt officiated at the ground-breaking ceremony on September 26, 1941. Another modernized classical composition, this building, like the Municipal Center, has Deco ornamentation. And within the building are seven murals produced during World War II—painted by Maxine Seelbinder Merlino, William Edouard Scott, Herschel Levit, Ethel Magafan, Martyl Sweig, Carlos Lopez, and Austin Mecklem—depicting contributions of blacks in American history. The position of the DC recorder of deeds was filled for many years by African Americans. In the building is also a bronze relief portrait of Franklin D. Roosevelt by Selma Burke.[8]

### LIBRARIES, SCHOOLS, AND CHURCHES

One of the most important and influential examples of modernized classicism is the Folger Shakespeare Library, at 201 East Capitol Street SE, on Capitol Hill. Designed by Paul Philippe Cret with the assistance of the consulting architect Alexander Trowbridge, this building has been a prominent landmark since its completion in 1932. Henry Clay Folger (1857–1930), the library's patron, was a wealthy Standard Oil executive who acquired the largest collection of Shakespeariana in the world. The Architect of the Capitol, David Lynn, worked with Cret and Trowbridge to harmonize the library that Folger wished to build with the classicism of the U.S. Capitol enclave.

Originally U-shaped in plan, with a courtyard facing the alley in the rear, the building has become rectangular owing to an infill addition. The original building is clad in white marble. A long horizontal composition on its East Capitol Street facade, the library is symmetrical and maintains the standard classical formula of base, middle, and top. But the orthodox hierarchy is inverted—turned upside down—for the program of bas-relief sculpture (a traditional feature of a classical building's entablature, at the top) is created at the base of this building.

At both ends of the facade are recessed entrance portals flanked by relief depictions of Pegasus and surmounted by relief masks of Comedy and Tragedy. Between the entrance portals is a long colonnaded section of nine recessed window bays separated by fluted pilasters. At the bottom of each window bay is a bas-relief panel. These panels, sculpted by John Gregory, depict scenes from Shakespeare plays selected by Folger. Atop the building is a high attic section inscribed with quotations from Shakespeare plays,

also selected by Folger. On the west elevation, on 2nd Street, two ground-level doors are placed at the edges of a central section with five window bays. At the bottom is a balcony that overlooks a garden and fountain. Atop the fountain is a freestanding statue of Puck, created by Brenda Putnam, with an inscribed quotation of one of his famous lines in *A Midsummer Night's Dream*: "Lord, what fools these mortals be!"

The Deco features of the building are primarily aluminum decorative elements very similar in spirit to those of the Justice Department building. The railings on the balcony on the west elevation, for instance, intersperse the heraldic arms of Shakespeare with Deco floral and geometric motifs. The Alcoa Company produced the aluminum ornamentation to Cret's specifications.

Cret's plan for the building envisioned an archival facility with sufficient stack space to house 75,000 books and with additional space to accommodate another 150,000 volumes. The building contains, in addition to the stacks, an Elizabethan theater, an exhibition gallery, a reading room for scholars, and offices.[9]

Just south of the Folger Library on 2nd Street SE is the Library of Congress Annex (now named the John Adams Building). In 1928 the Librarian of Congress, Herbert Putnam, recommended the construction of an annex to house up to ten million books. A Joint Commission to Acquire a Site and Additional Buildings for the Library of Congress was created. The commission, chaired in the project's early years by Senator Simeon D. Fess of Ohio, included the Architect of the Capitol, David Lynn. In 1930 the Librarian of Congress recommended the retention of the Washington, DC, architectural firm Pierson & Wilson—a partnership of Frank G. Pierson and A. Hamilton Wilson—based on previous work they had done for the Library of Congress.[10] That same year, the firm produced preliminary designs, and they were approved by the Commission of Fine Arts. To ensure that the building would harmonize with the Folger

The facade of the **Folger Shakespeare Library**, late 1970s.

Photograph by Hans Wirz.

The **Library of Congress Annex** from the roof of the main
Library of Congress building, across the street, 1930s.

Library, Pierson & Wilson retained the services of Cret's consulting architect, Alexander Trowbridge.

The Annex was designed to be a state-of-the-art building. It was fireproof, air-conditioned, and equipped with conveyor belts and pneumatic tubes, and a tunnel connected it to the main Library of Congress building, on the other side of 2nd Street. As construction began in the New Deal years, there were pressures to keep down the cost of the building. In an undated memorandum, Trowbridge wrote that "the architects with the constant cooperation of the Library officials produced a solution that I have termed a fine achievement. Am I overstepping the bounds of propriety if I say that it would be a calamity to assume that because of increased building costs and a lower valuation of the dollar we must meet the situation by cutting the volume or cheapening construction?"[11]

The Joint Commission stood firm in defense of the design. An attempt to reduce the building's cost by using limestone instead of marble for cladding was defeated. Senator Alben Barkley of Kentucky, who succeeded Fess as chair of the Joint Commission, observed in 1934 that "if we skimp on this building we will never be satisfied with it. . . . I am therefore in favor of using marble for this building. I guess it is hazardous to proceed on the theory of getting the money but I think we can take a chance on it."[12] Although the building was ready for occupancy in late 1938 and it opened its doors in 1939, its internal adornment would not be completed until 1941.

Five stories high, the Annex is a long, rectangular building with its principal elevations on 2nd and 3rd Streets SE. Each of these long facades features twenty-seven recessed window bays containing vertical metal-frame windows below the attic story, which is set back. Shallow pavilions extend from the center and the ends of these facades. On the south elevation is a porch with symmetrical stairways at the sides. This porch was originally designed as the exterior entrance to the Copyright Office, which occupied the ground-floor space on the south side of the building.

Low-relief ornamentation near the entrances and friezes of geometric patterns near the parapet of the middle section add Deco adornment. So does the bronze and aluminum grillwork atop the inner doors in the vestibules. The same ornamentation was used in the niches to the sides of the vestibules, which contain bronze freestanding torchères, and in a ceiling grille that intersects three pendant diamond-shaped lights. The walls and the floors were clad in tan travertine. Along the center of the floors is a long marble insert with bronze-and-marble plaques. Other superb Deco lighting fixtures—lanternlike, within aluminum frames—were used beside the outer doors of the building, as well as on the balcony and on the railings of the porch. All the metal ornamentation in the Annex was produced by the Flour City Ornamental Iron Company of Minneapolis.

The seven pairs of bronze outer doors—three on the east side, three on the west side, and one at the entrance to the Copyright Office, on the south side—bear figures of legendary alphabet inventors through the ages, figures suggested to the architects by the chief reference librarian, William Adams Slade. These figures, the work of the sculptor Lee Lawrie, were fabricated by the Flour City Ornamental Iron Company.[13]

The interior of the building was largely occupied by stack areas—twelve tiers extending from the basement to the fourth floor—and administrative offices. The chief public spaces were the vestibules, the elevator lobbies on the first and fifth floors, and the two large fifth-floor reading rooms, with a room for card catalogs in between. The vestibules and the elevator lobbies are richly adorned with Deco ornamentation, much of it intricate. The fifth-floor elevator lobbies have terrazzo floors with a checkerboard pattern that expands into radiating diamond shapes. At the edges of the floor are terrazzo borders with an undulating pattern between narrow courses of

The south entrance to the **Library of Congress Annex**,
which originally led to the Copyright Office, ca. 1940.

Photograph by Theodor Horydczak, Theodor Horydczak Collection,
Prints and Photographs Division, Library of Congress.

mosaic. The walls have floor-to-ceiling wainscoting. Crown moldings with denticulated bases feature Deco ornamentation; these moldings step back at the top to accommodate recessed lighting. At the ends of these lobbies are black stone pedestals.

Especially prominent is a floral motif that is repeated on a great many surfaces—on tall bronze doors, where it appears in a central element executed in aluminum; on the etched-glass panels within rectangular ceiling light fixtures; and on the backrests of the seats in the reading rooms. (Most of the furnishings for this building were produced to the architects' specifications by the Stow and Davis Furniture Company.) Portals in the corridors between the reading rooms give access to stairways leading up and down to mezzanine offices. The stairways have railings of bronze and aluminum adorned with zigzag and curvilinear motifs. Even the interiors of the wood-paneled elevator cabs feature bronze Deco ornamentation.

The two reading rooms are more sedate in their overall character than the vestibules and elevator lobbies, but they are extremely modernistic all the same. Colonnaded recesses with rectilinear columns run the length of the side walls, and there is an arched recess behind each of the low circulation desks, which bear the seal of the Library of Congress set off by aluminum trim. The floors are linoleum, and the reading tables are adorned with rows of elegant formal lamps.

An overall assessment of the building appeared in the October 1939 issue of the *Federal Architect*. The critic noted all the special efforts made by the architects to ensure that this massive building would not overwhelm the Folger Library: "Vastly greater in mass the annex carries out the spirit of the lovely Folger Library adjoining. The simplicity of the Folger does not blow up too well to the great expanse of the annex and one cannot but feel that the architects of the annex deliberately sacrificed some of the spectacular they might have achieved had they not chivalrously striven for harmony with the adjoining structure."[14]

The critic was impressed by the library's interior. The entrance lobby, he exulted, was "fully wainscoted with as uniform and harmonious a display of our great American figured marble Saint Genevieve Golden Vein as is ever seen."[15] The reading rooms, in his estimation, were superb:

> The centre catalogue room and the two flanking reading rooms are very fine. They are deliciously and whole-heartedly modern in scheme and accoutrements. . . . [The rooms] have no windows—a heresy in the old days. They are air-conditioned and lighted with diffused and indirect illumination that has the shadowless effect of daylight. The materials for the countertops, catalogue cases, drawer fronts, counter fronts and table tops are most interesting. The counter tops are cork. The catalogue cases are a combination of aluminum and this mysterious phenol-formaldehyde discovery—in this case the product known as Formica."[16]

Formica: produced by "piling a number of sheets of fibre impregnated with a Bakelite or a Urea varnish upon a suitable backing material and subjecting it to heat and pressure." The reading tables looked like "beautiful examples of satiny-finished wood. Actually, they are Formica. The wood effect was obtained by placing a layer of thin veneer walnut in the pile of lamination."[17]

The critic was particularly taken with the murals in the north reading room, painted by Ezra Winter, depicting scenes from Chaucer's *Canterbury Tales*. When the article in the *Federal Architect* was published, the murals in the south reading room were not yet finished. The new Librarian of Congress, Archibald MacLeish, wanted Ezra Winter to produce more elaborate murals of Thomas Jefferson. Winter explained all this to the Joint Commission in 1940: "When Mr. MacLeish took office as Librarian and found

A bronze and aluminum floral motif above the elevator
doors in the lobby of the **Library of Congress Annex**.

Photograph by Hans Wirz.

that mural paintings were being designed for the South Reading Room he immediately suggested that the theme should be of Thomas Jefferson, not only because Jefferson was the founder of the Library of Congress but due to his importance as a man of letters in America and the greatness of his character and influence. I agreed with him of course."[18]

In 1976 this building, with its south reading room so replete with tributes to Jefferson, was named the Library of Congress Thomas Jefferson Building. But only four years later the building was renamed for John Adams. Why? Because some great thinkers on Capitol Hill decided that the original Library of Congress building should be named for Jefferson. So the 1930s Annex, with its Jefferson murals, is now for no particular reason known as the John Adams Building. And this was not to be the last of the misguided actions to affect this building. In the 1980s the Architect of the Capitol commissioned the firm of Arthur Cotton Moore to restore the main Library of Congress Building and the 1930s Annex. Unfortunately, in the name of restoration the firm replaced a number of original interior light fixtures in the Annex with grossly overscale reproductions.

A number of schools built in the Washington area during the 1930s showed the influence of Art Deco, but surely the best of them was Greenbelt Center School, which now serves as the Greenbelt Community Center. The architects were Douglas Ellington and Reginald Wadsworth, the same architects who designed Greenbelt's residential and commercial buildings.

Greenbelt School is an L-shaped building clad in white-painted brick that faces Crescent Road across a wide, majestic lawn. Slightly asymmetrical with an entrance pavilion to the left and a smaller pavilion on the right, this building has an overall feeling of symmetry, and its form is reminiscent of the Folger Shakespeare Library's facade. It is not fanciful to theorize that Ellington and Wadsworth were struck, as so many

others have been, by the understated elegance of Cret's composition for the Folger. Like the Folger facade, the front facade of this principal section of the school has a colonnaded rhythm, with limestone bas-relief sculpted panels at the bottom of window bays. Together with a large companion panel above the front door, these panels illustrate the Preamble to the Constitution, clause by clause. They were sculpted in place on the building by Lenore Thomas Strauss.

The interior of this section of the building contains a combination gymnasium and auditorium. This section is supported by a series of overhead trusses that project from the front and rear of the building like top-heavy fins. These fins are reminiscent of the fluted pilasters on the Folger Library, and the correspondence is established further by fluting on the front-facing surfaces of the fins. Fenestration for the building consists of vertical expanses of metal-frame windows and glass-block expanses over entrances. A classroom wing extends to the rear from the left-hand side of the main section of the building.[19]

In addition to accommodating classrooms for seven grades, this building served as Greenbelt's all-purpose community center when it opened in 1937. After World War II, when the ownership of Greenbelt's buildings was dispersed, this building became the property of the Prince Georges County, Maryland, school system. In the 1980s it was almost destroyed by the county's board of education and replaced by a newer facility, much to the delight of the local PTA, whose members wanted an up-to-date school and were perfectly happy to see an architectural treasure destroyed. But a preservation protest led by the Art Deco Society of Washington, with vigorous support from Greenbelt's mayor and city council, members of the county council, and U.S. Senator Paul Sarbanes, led to cancellation of the demolition plans. The desires of the PTA were met through a land swap in which the school became a city-owned community center and some city land became the site of a brand-

**Greenbelt Center School** soon after its completion in January 1938.

Photograph by Arthur Rothstein, Prints and Photographs Division, Library of Congress.

One of the limestone bas-relief panels sculpted in place on
the facade of **Greenbelt School** by Lenore Thomas Strauss.

Photograph by Herbert Striner.

new county elementary school nearby.[20] Unfortunately, when the building was converted from a school to a community center in the 1990s, the architects used the same sort of oversized Deco Revival lights that now mar certain ceilings of the Library of Congress Annex.

Among the other notable Deco schools in the greater Washington area is the 1935 George Washington High School, at 1005 Mt. Vernon Avenue in Alexandria, Virginia. Designed by Raymond Long, of the Virginia State School Division, the building is clad in red brick with limestone trim. Projecting brick piers with limestone capitals separate the bays, and the entrance features massive, soaring limestone piers that narrow at the center of the section, directly over the doors, where the roofline surges upward in a ziggurat shape.

In the 1930s George Washington University commissioned the architect Waldron Faulkner to design an ensemble of academic buildings and an auditorium for its campus. The central building of this ensemble, Lisner Hall, at 2023 G Street NW, was completed in 1939. Designed as a library, this red brick building with rectilinear setback massing marks the center of the vertical axis of the campus quadrangle.[21] It is flanked by the earlier and smaller Bell Hall (1935), at 2029 G Street NW, and Stuart Hall (1936), at 2013 G Street. Around the corner is the university's Lisner Auditorium, designed by Faulkner and completed in 1942. All of these buildings were chaste in their simplification, but with just enough expressiveness to qualify as "modern*istic.*"

Although church architecture in the 1930s and 1940s was not, as a rule, conducive to Art Deco, several churches in the greater Washington area show unmistakable Deco influence. The earliest of these is the 1934 Lutheran Church of the Reformation, at 212 East Capitol Street NE, designed by Porter & Lockie. Across the street from the Folger Shakespeare Library, this church is yet another handsome example of modernized classicism with Art Deco embellishments. Particularly striking is the low-relief detailing in the limestone pediment above the entrance, where Christ and other figures are depicted in a fanlike pattern. The facade of this church steps back, and some handsome vertical recesses with limestone grilles flush with the facade flank the entrance. Porter & Lockie also designed the large 1939 Scottish Rite Temple, at 2800 16th Street NW, which features an intricate sunburst panel of polychrome concrete mosaic by the Earley studio above the main entrance.

Several churches and synagogues from the 1940s show the influence of streamlining, especially the 1946 B'Nai Israel Synagogue at 4606 16th Street NW, designed by Maurice Courland, and the 1944 Sligo Seventh-Day Adventist Church in Takoma Park, designed by J. Raymond Mims.[22]

## OTHER PUBLIC FACILITIES: HOSPITALS, AIRPORTS, HEATING PLANTS, ARMORIES, AND BRIDGES

Franklin D. Roosevelt's intense interest in the project that became the National Naval Medical Center, popularly known for many years as Bethesda Naval Hospital, had several sources. Like his older fifth cousin Theodore, he served as assistant secretary of the navy and loved to sail. He was also interested in architecture and advocated modernized classicism for federal building projects in or near the nation's capital. He had seen the skyscraper building that Bertram Grosvenor Goodhue designed for the Nebraska State Capitol project, and he also knew of the skyscraper capitol that Huey Long built in Baton Rouge. It occurred to him in 1938, after Congress appropriated funds for the proposed naval hospital, that it ought to be a skyscraper, or at least have a skyscraper component, and he sketched his idea on White House stationery (currently on display in the medical center).

Since FDR's plan for the project exceeded the

height limitations of the District of Columbia, he inspected a number of sites and selected a rolling, wooded hillside just to the north of the Bethesda, Maryland, business district. He said that the tower, to be seen for miles above the trees, might have the soothing effect of a church steeple above an English village. Roosevelt turned over his sketch to the navy's Bureau of Yards and Docks, and the building was designed to his specifications by F. W. Southworth, assisted by Paul Philippe Cret. FDR laid the cornerstone on November 11, 1940, and he presided at the dedication on August 31, 1942.[23]

The hospital was designed with a prominent main building connected to two other buildings that extend in an asymmetrical arrangement to the rear. The main building, clad in cast concrete, is symmetrical; its front and rear facades face west and east, respectively. The tower, which rises more than twenty stories, is flanked by a north and a south wing, which terminate in cross axes extending east and west. In plan, the main building is H-shaped. The hospital exemplifies the modernized classicism that FDR preferred. But thanks to Cret's eclecticism—and his subtlety—it is more than just a modernized classical building. The same traces of streamlining that appeared in his Folger Shakespeare Library can be sensed in many parts of this hospital, especially the summit of the tower. Indeed, the tower itself made it obvious that this building was as much futuristic as traditional. After all, the skyscraper was an icon of modernism.

The sculpted form features setbacks, not only at the top of the tower but also at the tops of the rectangular pavilions that terminate and rise above the north and south wings, where they intersect the cross axes. The massing is articulated further by narrow vertical pavilions on the sides of the tower. Above the seventeenth story these pavilions are surmounted by metal-clad observation porticos, which are also set back. Fenestration consists of sash windows hung vertically in recessed window bays that soar upward. The

doors within the east and west entrance portals are surmounted by high transoms adorned with metal grillwork arranged in concentric vertical rectangles.

The Bethesda Naval Hospital to this day remains a monument to the New Deal. So does the airport that FDR helped to design, though the original facilities are now overwhelmed by the vastly larger complex that constitutes Reagan National Airport today. Only a few years after it opened, the privately owned Washington-Hoover Airport in Virginia was obsolete. But controversy swirled in regard to the possible solutions. In 1937 Congress passed a bill that would have allowed Washington-Hoover to expand, but FDR vetoed the bill. What he wanted instead was a federally owned and operated facility downriver at Gravelly Point, Virginia, which would have to be extended into the Potomac River by a landfill.

In 1938 the president pushed through Congress the new Civil Aeronautics Act, which gave the federal government more authority in matters of air transportation. On September 27, 1938, he authorized the new Civilian Aeronautics Administration (CAA) to build Washington-National Airport at Gravelly Point. Much of the funding would be channeled through the Public Works Administration and the Works Progress Administration.

Colonel Sumpter Smith, who chaired the Washington National Airport Commission (under the aegis of the CAA), directed the Public Buildings Administration to select an architect. Howard Lovewell Cheney, of Chicago, was selected as the consulting architect, but recent scholarship suggests that a great deal of the design work was actually done by his chief designer, Charles M. Goodman.[24] After Goodman produced a preliminary design that was heavily influenced by the International Style, FDR intervened. In 1939 he suggested that the passenger entrance to the airport's terminal should feature a colonnade of rectilinear piers that might create a subliminal association with the portico of

The **National Naval Medical Center**, in Bethesda,
Maryland, soon after its completion in 1942.

Photograph by Theodor Horydczak, Theodor Horydczak Collection,
Prints and Photographs Division, Library of Congress.

The terminal of **Washington National Airport** soon after its completion in 1941.

Photograph by Theodor Horydczak, Theodor Horydczak Collection, Prints and Photographs Division, Library of Congress.

nearby Mount Vernon. Goodman's design was accordingly altered, and FDR laid the cornerstone for Washington-National Airport on September 28, 1940.

The terminal for the airport is a symmetrical four-story building shaped like a crescent. Its central section, which is flanked by lower three-story wings, is capped by a control tower with a glazed octagonal control room—with a faceted shape, like that of a diamond—at the top. Separate entrances were provided for passengers, air mail, and freight, with the passenger entrance placed on the west side. From this entrance canopies with rounded outer edges flare out in both directions and extend along the outward-curving sidewalk. Passengers entered the terminal, ascended to the second-floor lobby and concourse, and then—when their flights were ready for boarding—descended by staircases to one of the fourteen passenger boarding docks on the east side, facing the airfield.

The lobby and concourse on the second floor included a thirty-foot-high glass wall overlooking the field. The exterior of this wall was articulated by a colonnade of narrow, rounded piers. The colonnade on the west side, however—that is, the colonnade at the passenger entrance to the terminal—was visibly smaller and more subdued. This same stylistic dichotomy applied to the fenestration. On the side of the building that faces the runways, long ribbon windows were used in the outer wings. This effect of near-continuous glazing is even more pronounced in the large central section, with its observation wall. But on the landward and side elevations almost all of the windows, with the exception of a ribbon-window sequence on the south wing, are distinct. Stylistically they are more conservative.

The exterior cladding is cast concrete; the interior was done in a rich array of materials. The walls in the concourses, stair halls, and vestibules were finished in exposed concrete aggregate and blue-green terra cotta. The ceilings were adorned with a pattern of circular recesses, and the floors were terrazzo.

The amenities of this airport included an observation deck extending from the second-floor main lobby toward the landing field and a mezzanine dining room reached by a staircase extending upward from the main lobby. The staircase balustrades were composed of non-breakable glass with etched ornamentation. The entrance to the dining room was flanked by Deco relief panels. Overall, the terminal was a thoroughgoing synthesis of radical modernism, modernized classicism, and streamlining. Modern it certainly was, but it was also decidedly *moderne.*

When Washington National Airport opened on June 16, 1941, it was hailed as a spectacular state-of-the-art facility. The critic John Stuart called it "the finest metropolitan air terminal in the world, considered both technically and aesthetically."[25] Decades later, the terminal was swallowed up in a huge expansion of the airport, which ironically was renamed for that dedicated opponent of the New Deal legacy, Ronald Reagan. But the original terminal, so heavily influenced by Franklin D. Roosevelt, has survived as "Historic Terminal A."

Planning for a new National Guard armory dated from the mid-1930s. A site at the eastern terminus of East Capitol Street was approved, and Nathan C. Wyeth created a modernized classical design with Deco embellishments that was approved in September 1939. Construction was completed in 1942. The building is rectangular, with large pavilions extending from the main facades on the north and south and much smaller pavilions on the east and west. Centered atop the building is a massive drum-shaped roof extending upward that people called at the time a "Union Station roof." It sheltered a huge drill hall that could accommodate up to ten thousand people.

Although Wyeth designed the building to be clad in brick, the Commission of Fine Arts insisted on limestone. The horizontal mass of the building is accentuated by the fenestration, consisting for the most part of square sash windows in horizontal bands. Between some of these windows are aluminum spandrels bearing geometric motifs. Some counterbalancing vertical emphasis occurs on the front of the entrance pavilions, each of which contains five vertical bays, and also on the sides of the rooftop drum, which have fourteen vertical window bays apiece.[26]

In addition to his undoubted masterpiece, the Folger Library, and his notable contribution to the Bethesda Naval Hospital, Paul Philippe Cret produced three other designs that contribute to the Art Deco legacy in Washington. One was an industrial facility—a heating plant—and two were bridges. Designed and built in 1933–34, the Central Heating Plant, at 325 13th Street SW, was designed to heat federal buildings near the mall. Cret designed the plant in association with James A. Wetmore, of the Office of the Supervising Architect of the Treasury. A six-story rectangular building, it is clad in blonde, buff, and brown brick. A limestone base is surmounted by a limestone string course.

The main facade, facing 13th Street, has a tripartite entrance pavilion. The central mass, which is framed by columnar piers, extends all the way to the cornice line. Shallow flanking projections, which are also framed by piers, stop well below the cornice, thus creating a ziggurat effect. Between the projecting piers of this pavilion is fenestration, arranged as three vertical panels of metal-frame awning windows. Upon the base of each pier in the entrance pavilion is a terra-cotta relief panel depicting the equipment used and the work performed within the building. The entrance has a limestone frame that contains an aluminum surround with both transom and sidelights. Upon the central upper plane of this pavilion is a larger terra-cotta panel depicting the heating plant's boilers at work. On the side elevations of the plant are tall window bays with projecting brick piers in between.[27] After World War II another heating plant, the 1946–48 West Heating Plant, designed by Gilbert Stanley Underwood and built at the southeastern edge of Georgetown, was constructed

to augment the needs of the steadily expanding federal presence in Washington.

The two Washington bridges designed by Cret are the 1931 Klingle Valley Bridge, on Connecticut Avenue, and the 1935 Calvert Street Bridge. The Klingle Bridge, designed by Cret in association with Frank M. Masters, is harmonious with the adjacent Kennedy-Warren apartment building, directly to the south. The bridge's metal railings feature geometric Deco patterns—thick downward-projecting chevrons superimposed upon diamonds—and fluted glass urns that are familiar landmarks in the Woodley Park and Cleveland Park area. The 1935 Calvert Street Bridge, directly west of Connecticut Avenue where it intersects Calvert—the Shoreham Hotel is on the other side of Connecticut—is a three-arch concrete span faced in stone. At its Calvert Street entrances are pylons with low-relief carvings of symbolic figures produced by Leon Hermont. Perhaps the most memorable of these is a Wagnerian-looking goddess of speed who is racing a streamlined automobile.[28]

## BALTIMORE

In the interwar years, institutions and government agencies based in Baltimore employed modernized classicism on numerous new buildings, looking to updated versions of timeless designs to help promote their various missions. On a handful of buildings, mainly schools and hospitals, architects made a cleaner break with the past.

### FEDERAL AND MUNICIPAL BUILDINGS

The federal government occupied the southeast corner of Lombard and Gay Streets as early as 1839, when the Treasury Department opened the first United States Appraisers' Stores building in Baltimore. Goods brought from abroad were temporarily stored within the four-story building's three-foot-thick walls as federal agents determined the duty to be collected. Although it survived Baltimore's 1904 fire, the original appraisers' building was razed in 1933 to make way for a new, larger building for the same purpose.[29]

Dedicated in April 1935, the new United States Appraisers' Stores building cost nearly $1 million to build. The Baltimore firm Taylor & Fisher and the independent Baltimore architect William F. Stone Jr. worked together to design it under the supervision of the acting supervising architect of the Treasury Department, James A. Wetmore. Wetmore's name is listed first on the building's cornerstone; however, it is unlikely that he had an active role in the design as he was an administrator, not an architect. The basic theme is modernized classicism, as was typical of New Deal–era federal buildings, with Deco-inspired embellishments at the street level and at the level of the uppermost story.

The Appraisers' Stores building is eight stories high, rectangular in plan, with a flat roof. An equipment penthouse, which rises from the center of the roof, has a steeply pitched hip roof with orange ceramic tile. The building's walls are limestone and red brick laid in common bond. The first two stories are faced in limestone; the north, west, and south elevations feature rows of squared limestone pilasters with capitals interspaced with windows. The capitals on the street-front elevations (west and north) are elegantly carved, streamlined versions of Corinthian capitals; those on the south elevation, which faces an alley, are plain. The third through seventh stories are faced in brick. A wide horizontal band of limestone separates the seventh story from the eighth, which is set back at each corner. Large carved stone eagles are integrated into the corners—certainly the most powerful feature of the building's design.

The sculptural rendering is boldly geometric, conveying a sense of power and authority, yet it has an organic quality that almost brings the birds to life. On the eighth story are windows topped with round arches and limestone quoining at each corner. The building's main entrance is located on the west elevation. The door surround, which exhibits lively geometric patterns fashioned in metal, marble, and stone, is topped with a three-dimensional black, spread-winged eagle. "United States Appraisers' Stores" is inscribed above the entrance.

A few blocks due south of the United States Appraisers' Stores building, Baltimore's War Memorial sits at the end of a rectangular plaza opposite City Hall. The architect, Laurence Hall Fowler, employed a Greek-temple form and austere classical styling. The building is an excellent, and early, example of modernized classicism, and the grounds contain Baltimore's finest Art Deco outdoor sculpture.

Planning for a war memorial in Baltimore began shortly after the signing of the armistice that ended World War I. "War mothers" took the lead in calling for an appropriate tribute to Marylanders who had fought in the world conflict. In 1919 the city and the state appointed committees to plan the memorial, and in 1920 a lot east of Gay Street between Fayette and Lexington Streets was selected as the site. On November 11, 1920, civic leaders dedicated the site, which included a plaza stretching west to City Hall. The project broke ground the following day, though actual construction would not begin until December 1922. Mayor William Broening laid the cornerstone on April 29, 1923. The city dedicated the building, at 101 North Gay Street, on April 6, 1925.[30]

Fowler revered architectural tradition, but his winning design for the memorial managed to be both grounded in the past and up to the minute. Here is no rote recitation of Greco-Roman orders, but classical elements stripped to their essence, resulting in a composition that is studied yet effortlessly handled in appearance. It would be a stretch to call Fowler an early modernist; his body of work suggests that he was continuing in the twentieth century the best of American eclecticism. Yet his War Memorial, designed prior to the Paris Exposition, has commonalities with Goodhue's late works, such as the National

The **United States Appraisers' Stores**
building, ornamental detail, 2011.

Photograph by Melissa Blair.

Academy of Sciences, the Los Angeles County Public Library, and the Nebraska State Capitol, which are pivotal buildings in American architecture from the interwar period.

The War Memorial building is rectangular in plan and clad in limestone. The main entrance to the memorial hall is on the west elevation. Wide granite steps lead up to a portico supported by six fluted Tuscan columns. Three large bronze double doors provide access, although these are rarely open except for ceremonial occasions, such as President-elect Barack Obama's address during his inaugural whistle-stop tour on January 17, 2009. A secondary entrance on the north elevation provides day-to-day access.

The names of the counties of Maryland are inscribed on three of the exterior walls. A cornice with elegantly rendered classical details encircles the building. Perhaps the most striking feature is the pair of equestrian sculptures by Edmond R. Amateis, a famous New Deal–era sculptor from New York. Although the horses are slightly different, each holds a carved bird of prey clutching a shield with backswept wings between its front legs. These are not ordinary horses, but fantastical aquatic creatures resting on a base of undulating waves. Their forelegs and tails sprout webbed fins, and their rigid, cropped manes are carved with radial bans of wavy lines evocative of sunbursts.

Because it continues to function as a memorial to veterans, the interior of the War Memorial building is substantially intact. The main hall is devoted to honoring Maryland's fallen soldiers in perpetuity. It consists of a large auditorium with a seating capacity of about two thousand. The hall features an organ loft and walls of imported marble. The walls are inscribed with the names of the battles in which Maryland troops fought and the names of Maryland citizens who gave their lives for their country. The basement floor contains meeting rooms for veterans' and patriotic organizations, a four-hundred-seat Assembly Room, and a Trophy Hall.[31]

Soon after the construction of the War Memorial, city officials began planning a new municipal office building, also to be located on the memorial plaza. As Baltimore's municipal government grew, burgeoning offices choked the floors of George Frederick's 1867 City Hall. Mayor Jackson put the Civic Center Committee of the Department of Efficiency and Economy in charge of creating a new municipal building. They chose the block north of City Hall bounded by Guildford Avenue, Lexington Street, and Holliday Street.

In the first months of 1926 the city previewed the architect William H. Emory Jr.'s plans for an eleven-story building. The *Evening Sun* sent the rendering and all available materials to Lewis Mumford for his opinion. As usual, the nationally known architectural critic did not hold back:

> If the proposed municipal building is the best that the architects can do to improve Baltimore's Civic Center, what hope is there for architecture in the rest of the city? Precious little. If this is architectural inspiration, there is no level to which mere common sense or "efficiency" may not reasonably sink. The Civic Center [Committee members] have doubtless tried to achieve a building which will be in harmony with the existing nucleus of civic buildings on the square, particularly with the severe but impeccable War Memorial. In their effort to achieve "harmony" the architects have used white limestone, have interspaced the windows of the facade with pilasters, and have provided a cornice at the fourth and ninth story. If harmony could be purchased so easily we could all afford a little more of it, but the fact of the matter is that these halfhearted flutings and insertions no more make the municipal building a proper companion of the War Memorial than a Latin quotation in the speech of a Missouri Congressman makes him the rival of Jefferson.[32]

Perhaps Mumford's stinging review prompted the building's planners to go back to the drawing board. The final design was significantly different, most notably in overall form.

**War Memorial** sculpture, with Baltimore's City Hall
in the background, 1943.

Photograph by A. Aubrey Bodine, Baltimore City Life Museum
Collection, courtesy of the Maryland Historical Society.

The Municipal Building, at 200 Holiday Street, is a modernized classical composition named for the famed Baltimore civic leader Abel Wolman. It is a large, fourteen-story steel-frame building clad in limestone with a flat roof. The first five stories form the building's base; the next five floors step back to form a central tower, and the remaining four stories step back even further. This upper portion resembles a Greek temple and evokes Fowler's War Memorial, on the opposite side of the plaza. Exterior decorative detail is used sparingly; it consists of fluted pilasters, plain circular medallions, and a scalloped cornice at the upper reach of the top floor. The building retains its original windows and doors. Its austere lobby is very well preserved. While we do not know whether Mumford considered the final design a success, the Abel Wolman Municipal Building is an important piece of Baltimore's historic civic center, reflecting the ideals of its builders and continuing to serve the function for which it was built.

### LIBRARIES, SCHOOLS, AND CHURCHES

The philanthropist Enoch Pratt (1808–1896) founded the Baltimore public-library system, which still bears his name. Since 1886 the Central Branch of the Enoch Pratt Free Library has occupied the northwest corner of the intersection of Mulberry and Cathedral Streets. Around 1930 the architect Charles L. Carson's Romanesque building (1886) was razed to make way for a much larger library, one that would occupy an entire city block. The old library was not the only building to go; a stately block of mid-nineteenth-century row houses on the west side of the 400 block of Cathedral, directly across from Benjamin Latrobe's Basilica, one of which had been designed by Latrobe himself, gave way as well.[33]

The Baltimore architect Clyde N. Friz designed the library with the help of his son, Nelson Friz, and the New York architects Edward Lippencott Tilton and Alfred Morton Githens, who were specialists in library planning. This team patterned the library after the retail emporiums and libraries of their day. The head librarian, Dr. Joseph L. Wheeler, insisted that the building be as welcoming as possible. No monumental staircase rises to the front of the building; access is provided directly from the street. Large display windows were used to promote books, much as a department store would advertise its wares. The building had a capacity of 1,800,000 volumes. Bernard L. Crozier was the chief engineer, William A. Parr was the buildings engineer, and George A. Fuller was the contractor. The building was completed in 1933.[34]

The Enoch Pratt Free Library, at 400 Cathedral Street, is located on the west side of Cathedral between Franklin and Mulberry. Its main entrance is across the street from Latrobe's Basilica. The library reflects a mingling of streamlining, generalized classicism, and overt Renaissance elements, producing an overall effect that is both modern and traditional. The library's exterior has much in common with the Beaux-Arts classicism of previous decades, yet a closer look reveals detailing that makes the library a clear product of its era.

The three-story limestone building has a rectangular plan. The first story is significantly higher than the second and third stories because of the first floor's twenty-five-foot-high ceilings. The main entrance is centered on the east elevation. It consists of a two-story, round arch portal leading to double doors flanked by single doors. Very elaborate bronze grillwork over the main entrance features Art Deco floral motifs. Fluted pilasters spanning the first and second stories separate the window bays. On the third story, "Enoch Pratt Free Library" is inscribed above the entrance, and the windows on this story have decorative bronze grilles. A cornice with a

(*opposite*) The **Enoch Pratt Free Library** on Cathedral Street, date unknown.

Photograph by A. Aubrey Bodine, Baltimore City Life Museum Collection, courtesy of the Maryland Historical Society.

scalloped classical motif encircles the building. A large 2003 addition is attached to the west elevation.

The interior of the Pratt Library is one of Baltimore's most impressive public spaces. The sumptuous decorative treatments, inspired by the Renaissance and other classical *oeuvres*, were executed with Deco flare, calling to mind the lobby of the Southern California Edison Company Building (1931), a Los Angeles Deco landmark. These interior elements represent the work of numerous artisans. Overall, the interior captures the spirit of the Art Deco movement, albeit at its most traditional.

After passing through a dazzling bronze foyer, visitors enter the central hall, measuring 100 by 40 feet, which is flooded by natural light. The room is dominated by four corner columns and ten freestanding square columns with bases of Pyrenees black-and-white marble and shafts of pale beige Lerado Chiaro marble. The capitals feature ornate carving and painted ornamentation in multiple colors. The columns support a frieze featuring the devices of twenty-three English and American printers and publishers. Above the frieze, a mezzanine level with large casement windows provides a view of the hall below. Between these windows are pilasters with ornate painted capitals and separate rectangular panels. On the north and south ends of the hall, these panels contain murals by George Novikoff depicting William Caxton, the first English printer, presenting his first book to his patroness, Marguerite, Duchess of Burgundy (north end), and a portrait of Johann Gutenberg (south end). The panels on the east and west walls display emblems of European publishers and printers. The central hall also features a terrazzo floor, walnut woodwork, period lighting (freestanding and hung), and six original oil paintings of the first six Lords Baltimore. Various library departments are separated from the central hall by bronze grilles. The Sights and Sounds Department features an ornate ceiling patterned after the ceilings of the Palazzo della Cancelleria and the Church of Santa Maria d'Aracoeli in Rome.[35]

North Baltimore has its own Deco-influenced library in an excellent state of preservation: the Fourier Library at the College of Notre Dame. In 1940 the college built a new library named for Saint Pierre Fourier. Frederick Vernon Murphy, head of the School of Architecture at Catholic University in Washington, DC, designed the building.[36] Reverend John M. McNamara, auxiliary bishop of Baltimore and Washington, dedicated the building in November 1941.

Murphy judiciously employed Deco elements throughout the library's exterior and interior, including nautical and floral-themed bas-relief carvings, metal gates and railings with geometric patterns, and streamlined chandeliers. His restraint seems appropriate for the library of a religious women's college; nonetheless, these period details enliven what might otherwise have been an unremarkable institutional building. The Fourier Library is a two-story brick building with a raised basement and a four-story central tower. The building has a cross-shaped plan. A covered loggia connects it to the college's main building. The hip roof is covered in tile, and the walls are clad in multicolored brick with limestone trim. The main entrance consists of tall, glass double doors with decorative metal grillwork. "Fourier Library" is inscribed above the doors, which are flanked by period lanterns. The windows are hung in pairs, with the first-floor windows topped by round arches. In addition to housing the college's library, the building included a theater, a student lounge, an art studio, meeting rooms, classrooms, and offices.[37]

Several public secondary schools in Baltimore display Art Deco design. Built in 1932, Garrison Junior High School, at 3900 Barrington Road, was designed to serve a large area in west Baltimore. It was designed by Smith & May, with Henry Adams, Inc., serving as consulting engineers.[38] The school is a large red brick building with a complex but symmetrical plan. The front portion forms a truncated H, and the rear portion forms a cross. These two portions are connected to form inner courtyards. Various parts of the building rise one to three stories. The facade (south elevation) features numerous Deco details. Most notable is the large central tower that rises an additional two stories above the roof. It is a square brick tower with multiple piers and setbacks culminating in a crown. Elaborate metalwork, surmounted by four windows contained within a segmental arch, was placed above the doors. This entire ensemble is inset in a cast-stone surround. The school features banded windows—all of which have been replaced—intersected by piers. It is still in use as Garrison Middle School.

At the time of Garrison Junior High's construction, planning was under way across town for a new junior high school for east Baltimore. The school board selected Wyatt & Nolting to design the new Patterson Park Junior High School. Upon its completion in 1934, it was the largest junior high school in the city. Rising seven stories in its highest sections, it was also the tallest school building in the city.[39]

Patterson Park Junior High School, at 101 South Ellwood Avenue, is a five- to seven-story building that occupies an entire city block. It is a complex composition of stepped rectangular forms united by alternating expanses of bright orange-red and dark brown brick. Horizontal bands of large, dark brown metal-frame windows provide a great deal of light to the interior. Its regularity and lack of applied ornamentation make the school an essentially radical modernist composition, yet aspects of the building, such as the brightly colored cladding and strong horizontal lines, reflect the influence of Deco and streamlining. Wyatt & Nolting may have been inspired by Raymond Hood's groundbreaking McGraw-Hill Building in New York City (1930–31), which has a similar aesthetic achieved though horizontal bands of alternating color and large windows. The Paterson Park school has an entrance on every elevation; the most elaborate entrance is on the west elevation. Fluted dark

granite columns flank the door, and a distinctive Deco-style lantern still hangs above it. The building is currently undergoing renovation.

The firm Taylor & Fisher also had an opportunity to design a junior high school during the early 1930s. Like Patterson Park Junior High, the school they designed was to serve east Baltimore. In the Jim Crow era, however, this school was meant exclusively for African Americans. It opened in 1932, the same year as Garrison Junior High School, and it served about the same number of students (1,205). First named the East Baltimore Colored Junior High School, the Dunbar Middle School is a four- to five-story brick building located at Caroline and McElderry Streets. The building's plan is similar to a block letter J, with the longest side running along McElderry Street. Most of the brick is laid in common bond, but expanses between the windows consist of red and dark red bricks of various widths in a decorative pattern. Vertical piers of brick and limestone separate the windows and terminate in finials at the roofline. Upper-story windows are capped with fan-shaped limestone panels. The main entrance is located on the northeast corner of the building. Double metal doors are topped with a large segmental arch transom. The door is flanked by stepped brick pilasters capped with limestone. The most striking feature of the building is an octagonal brick and limestone tower that projects above the roofline over the main entrance. The tower features bas-relief carvings of spread-winged owls perched upon leafy branches.

Clearly, Baltimore's public-school administrators were comfortable with forward-looking design. They approved Lucius White Jr.'s design, resplendent with Deco styling, for their 1931 School Administration Building, at 3 East 25th Street, since demolished. All that remain are two Deco pylons, which mark the entrance to a supermarket that now occupies the site.

Although it was built years after the heyday of Art Deco, Baltimore's Cathedral of Mary Our Queen, at 5200 North Charles Street, may

**Garrison Junior High School**, at Garrison Boulevard
and Barrington Road, July 1948.

Photograph by the Hughes Company, Special Collections,
courtesy of the Maryland Historical Society.

**Dunbar Middle School** (formerly East Baltimore
Colored Junior High), date unknown.

Drawing by Taylor & Fisher. From the BGE Collection at
the Baltimore Museum of Industry.

EAST · BALTIMORE · COLORED · JUNIOR · HIGH · SCHOOL

be one of the city's most interesting Deco-related buildings. Numerous elements, large and small—from the massive angularity of the exterior to the ceremonial candlesticks throughout the interior—express the exuberance of the Deco aesthetic. While its overall monumentality places the cathedral in the context of mid-twentieth-century modernism, Art Deco was clearly the inspiration for the building's extensive decorative program.

The cathedral was the gift of Thomas O'Neill, a native of Ireland who made his fortune as a merchant in Baltimore during the late nineteenth and early twentieth centuries. He willed two-thirds of his estate to the Archiepiscopal See of Baltimore expressly for the building of a new cathedral. Although O'Neill died in 1919, the bequest did not become effective until his wife's death in 1936. In 1952 the Baltimore Archdiocese commissioned the Boston firm Maginnis, Walsh & Kennedy to design the cathedral. The youngest surviving member of the partnership, Eugene F. Kennedy, took on the project.[40]

Archbishop Francis Patrick Keough instructed Kennedy to design a building that would be inspirational and dignified, one that would satisfy the functional needs of the congregation and endure "as the famous Cathedrals of Europe." To that end, they decided to build a true masonry structure using ancient and medieval principles of construction. Keough and Kennedy also agreed that the building would not conform to a traditional architectural style but should be "truly modern in spite of its ageless structural system."[41] The ground-breaking ceremony took place on October 10, 1954, and the cathedral was completed in a breathtaking five years. On the morning of October 13, 1959, a few days beyond the fifth anniversary of the ground-breaking, the archdiocese consecrated the new cathedral.

The exterior iconography develops the theme of redemption by Christ through Mary, while the interior scheme generally follows the church's yearly cycle of feasts from the first Sunday of Advent to the last Sunday after Pentecost. These themes are expressed by the nearly four hundred sculptures and numerous stained-glass windows. Eight pieces of sculpture were produced according to the church's specifications regarding subjects, dimensions, projections, details of costuming, portraiture, emblems, and so on. Nine stained-glass craftsmen, seven American and two French, designed and executed the windows. Many other craftsmen contributed to the interior furnishings, including alters, pews, organs, stalls, screens, and candlesticks. In all, more than one thousand people worked on the building.[42]

The cathedral is 375 feet long and 239 feet wide at its fullest extensions. The plan forms a cross. The front section of the building is dominated by massive square twin towers. To the left of the entrance, a circular baptistery breaks the facade's symmetry. The facade is dominated by a twenty-foot=high statue of Christ, whose image is visible from both inside and outside the church. Carvings of the twelve apostles rise on either side of this statue, which is set in an arched window of imported glass. The sculptor, Theodore Barbarossa, made each ascending figure one inch taller than the preceding one so that all would appear to be the same height when viewed from the ground. Below the statue of Christ, Joseph Coletti's statue of Mary has a prominent place above the front doors; she is flanked by stone panels illustrating the Nativity and Mary's Assumption into Heaven. Above the arch window is a freestanding Crucifixion scene framed by the twin towers. Each tower rises to a height of 134 feet, where it is surmounted by a 29-foot metal spire. A pair of statuary bronze doors open into the Cathedral narthex.

Inside, thirteen massive arches of Indiana limestone span the nave, which is lined on each side with four altars. Forty-six sculptured panels in stone decorate the face of each arch, and twenty-six elaborate light fixtures hang in the nave. The floor is a combination of terrazzo and colorful marble slabs.[43] The sanctu-

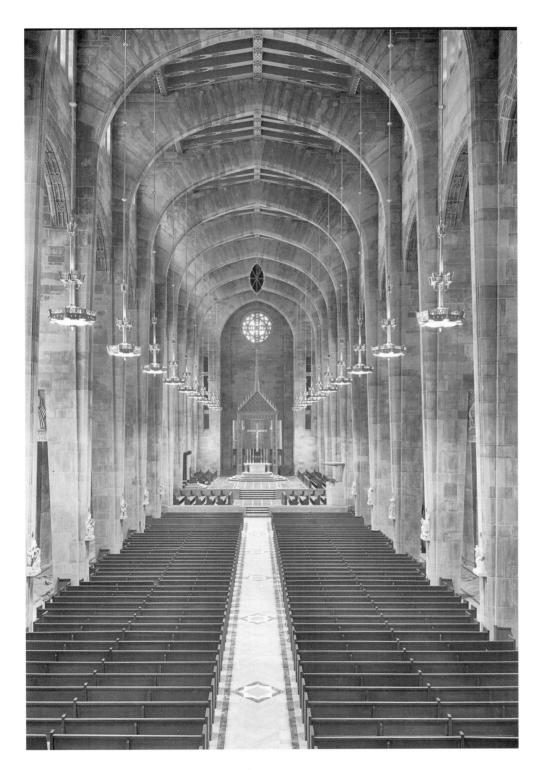

The **Cathedral of Mary Our Queen**, on North
Charles Street, September 1958.

Photograph by A. Aubrey Bodine, Baltimore City Life Museum
Collection, courtesy of the Maryland Historical Society.

ary is separated from the body of the church by a railing of rose marble. The remaining three sides of the sanctuary are enclosed by stained oak screens with undulating geometric patterns. A pendant crucifix of polychrome wood hangs over the main altar, which is sheltered by a huge bronze baldachin supported by four pillars. The foundation structure that supports the altar is completely independent of the rest of the building, an arrangement recalling the concept of a church as built around an altar. A marble pulpit occupies the front right corner of the sanctuary.[44]

The steeple cap of the First Apostolic Faith Church, on South Caroline Street, shows the influence of Art Deco. And the Art Deco designer Hildreth Meière completed commissions for two Baltimore congregations: St. Katherine of Sienna, now Greater Gethsemane Ministries, in east Baltimore, and St. Mark's on the Hill in Pikesville.

## OTHER PUBLIC FACILITIES: HOSPITALS, CHARITIES, WATER TOWERS, AND SEWAGE PLANTS

The College of Medicine of Maryland, the fifth medical school in America, was established in Baltimore in 1807. The first hospital associated with the college opened in 1823. Over the next century the university hospital—the institution merged with the University of Maryland system in 1920—accumulated a conglomeration of buildings. Planning began for a new, four-hundred-bed building in the early 1930s.[45]

Two architects from the offices of Joseph Evans Sperry—Herbert G. Crisp and James R. Edmunds Jr.—designed the new University of Maryland Hospital. Smith & May served as associated architects. In August 1932 Governor Ritchie directed that the construction of the new $1.5 million hospital be expedited as an unemployment-relief measure that would employ several hundred men. The building was completed in the summer of 1934.[46]

The University of Maryland Hospital is located at 22 South Greene Street, between Baltimore and Lombard Streets. The 1934 building has been expanded several times, but much of the original structure is still visible. This twelve-story, steel-frame building clad in brick with limestone trim had a St. George's Cross plan, with four wings radiating north, south, east, and west from a common center. The roof is flat. A central, octagonal tower rises three stories above the twelfth floor, and the top floor of the tower steps back. Windows have been replaced throughout the building.

As originally planned, the hospital was to have its current configuration of twelve stories topped by a three-story central tower. But in 1934, owing to a lack of funds, the building stopped at the tenth floor, with a five-story central tower atop the tenth floor. The two lower levels of the tower were left unfinished. The eleventh and twelfth floors were added in 1938 and 1939. At the time of the building's construction, its style was described as "modified Colonial," an odd description indeed. The multistepped high-rise mass, with a sprinkling of streamlined decorative touches, is characteristic of Art Deco.

The Frank Bressler Research Laboratory, at 29 South Greene Street, sits directly across from the University of Maryland Hospital. It was built as part of the hospital system with funds bequeathed by the Baltimore surgeon Frank Bressler. Herbert Crisp and James Edmunds designed the building, which relates very closely to the larger hospital across the street. Bressler's gift provided $280,000 of the building's cost, and the remainder was provided by the WPA. The builder John McShain completed the building in time for it to be dedicated in May 1940.[47]

The Bressler Building is a six-story, brick-clad rectangular building with a flat roof and limestone trim. The facade (west elevation) is symmetrical. A central recessed entrance consists of a single door with transom and sidelights on a two-story wall of limestone punctuated by wide horizontal bands, also of limestone. The door has bullnose surrounds. Raised steel letters

**University of Maryland Hospital**, at Greene and Redwood Streets, March 1939.

Photograph by Consolidated Gas, Electric Light, and Power Company. From the BGE Collection at the Baltimore Museum of Industry.

spelling "29 S. Greene St." are located above the door, and in the area above the letters the limestone is inscribed with the Maryland shield flanked by the Roman numerals MDCCCVII and MCMXXXIX in Deco typography. There is a single window over the inscription. Two large, round two-story columns set flush with the main facade flank the entrance. The fifth and sixth stories step back by one bay on either side. These upper stories have the appearance of a Greek temple, with scored pilasters separating the windows and a triangular pediment capping the roof.

Another major medical institution with deep roots in Baltimore expanded during the 1930s. In 1861 Baltimore City purchased the site of the Baltimore City Hospitals, now Johns Hopkins Bayview Medical Center, as the location for a new almshouse and hospital for the poor. By late in the second decade of the twentieth century Bay View had gained a reputation for being mismanaged, overcrowded, and unsavory. Beginning in 1923 Bay View underwent a major reorganization, eventually becoming the Baltimore City Hospitals. The reorganization called for a major expansion. The first building to be constructed was a $650,000, nine-story structure built as a home for the hospital's nurses. This building opened in 1932. A general hospital was added in 1935. Edward Palmer designed both buildings, employing a similar architectural style for both. The structures were minimally ornamented, ziggurat-shaped masses of grey-brown brick, with a vertical emphasis achieved by columns of slightly recessed windows.[48]

While the Nurses' Home building is still visible, the 1935 hospital has been consumed by massive additions, to the point that the original form is no longer evident from most vantage points. But portions of the original structure are still visible from the east. Both buildings are faced with grey-brown brick and concrete trim. Doors of stainless steel and glass, as well decorative metal panels separating windows, have been destroyed or replaced, further obscuring

the original aesthetic. Also remaining on the grounds from the 1930s building campaign are the spectacular streamlined limestone entrance gates, although this entrance has been blocked off to cars. The gates, which feature handsome pylons, are inscribed "Baltimore City Hospitals" in a Deco font.

Built in 1939, the Associated Jewish Charities building served as the organization's headquarters from its opening until about 1980. The Associated Jewish Charities was the result of a 1921 merger of the Federation of Jewish Charities, made up of German Jewish organizations, and the United Hebrew Charities, composed of East European Jewish organizations. Throughout the 1920s and 1930s the Associated Jewish Charities served as the sole fund-raising organization of Baltimore's Jewish community. In the early 1940s the Jewish Welfare Fund was created in response to urgent needs overseas, while the Associated Jewish Charities continued to focus on needs at home. The Jewish Welfare Fund and the Associated Jewish Charities merged in 1951.

The headquarters building, at 319 West Monument Street, was a gift of the Baltimore native Max Straus, residing in Los Angeles, and his brother and sister-in-law, Aaron and Lillie Straus. Aaron and Lillie Straus paid for the land, and a bequest from Max Straus's will paid for the building. The architect Benjamin Frank designed the building. When the building was completed in the fall of 1939, the charities' leaders could not have fathomed the full extent of the challenges they would face in the coming decade and a half. By 1955 the Associated Jewish Charities had raised and spent more than $1 million to help to resettle 1,360 refugee families comprising more than 5,000 individuals in Baltimore following the Holocaust. These figures represent only those newcomers who contacted the Associated Jewish Charities, not the total number of Jewish families that settled in Baltimore following World War II.[49]

The Associated Jewish Charities building is a two-story, brick-clad building with a rectangular plan and a flat roof. The brick is laid in Flemish bond. The building has a limestone base and limestone trim throughout. The facade (north elevation) consists of a symmetrical composition with a central entrance. The central bay is faced in limestone on both the first and second stories. The front door is a replacement but retains a transom with a stepped pyramidal upper edge. An inscription east of the door, near the building's base, reads "The Max Straus Aaron Straus and Lillie Straus Memorial" and bears the date 1939 and the number 5699, all in Deco typography. Much smaller letters read "Benj. Frank Arch't." Windows on the facade are separated by green marble panels. Limestone trim adorns the roofline. A second entrance, on the west elevation, is reached by a concert ramp. Windows have been replaced throughout.

Several interesting public-works projects from the thirties survive. In 1937 the city's Bureau of Water Supply used Baltimore's PWA funding to construct a large reservoir on Melvin Avenue in Catonsville. The steel tank, with a capacity of four million gallons, cost $92,000 to construct.[50] The Melvin Avenue Reservoir is a massive, drumlike structure with a domed roof. The tank's orange brick enclosure is decorated with limestone pilasters with ziggurat caps and a cornice carved with a wavelike pattern. Another massive steel water tank, the Curtis Bay Water Tank, on Filbert Street, sits on a hill overlooking the neighborhood of Brooklyn. The Bureau of Water Supply constructed the tank in 1930, and Frank O. Heyder designed an ornamental enclosure for it in 1932.[51] The design is classical in respects, but the creative use of gradually fading multicolored bricks is reminiscent of the Greater Hutzler's building, which was built the same year. Also in the Brooklyn–Curtis Bay vicinity is the Pump and Blower Station of the Patapsco Sewage Plant (1940), also designed by Heyder, which features a Deco entrance and signage.

Baltimore may be insufficiently known for its Art Deco architecture, but Washington clearly has a great deal more, in some cases perhaps more glorious examples. Baltimore taste in the 1930s and 1940s generally and famously followed the traditional, and various eclectic movements of previous decades remained strong in the city well into the period. It should not surprise us that Baltimore architects tended to follow trends more often than they started them, but perhaps they would have designed more Deco buildings if their clientele had asked for them. They were well aware of avant-garde currents elsewhere, and one finds an evolution within the more tried-and-true modes. Palmer & Lamdin, for example, a firm best known for its staid residential architecture, chose radical modernism and streamlining for its own offices. Edward Palmer designed Deco duplexes, which contractors built "on spec." When given an opportunity, local firms could produce admirable Deco compositions. Visitors to Baltimore must see Hildreth Meière's work, along with that of Edmond Amateis.

Washington had and continues to have a larger stock of Deco design than does Baltimore, most likely because of the sheer magnitude of Washington's population growth at the height of the Deco movement. The city provided a proving ground for modernized classical architecture,

both residential and commercial, and also for certain new building types.

Art Deco played out differently in Washington and Baltimore, but the commonalities between them are of interest. Many though by no means all the architects in Washington and Baltimore who employed the idiom of Art Deco had received academic training (Paul Philippe Cret, Douglas Ellington, and James Bosley Noel Wyatt studied at the École des Beaux Arts). For architects in both cities, as elsewhere around the country and around the world, Art Deco appealed strongly in the design of new building types, movie theaters and gas stations being prime examples (though many adopted traditional styles). Most bus stations of the period were streamlined, in part because only three or four firms in the United States specialized in bus-station design, and perhaps they tended to mimic the look Raymond Loewy gave the buses themselves. The legacy of Art Deco in these cities must remain to some extent *sui generis*, a convergence of particular trends, unique personalities, and one-time historical circumstances.

Will Art Deco survive in Washington and Baltimore? The stately modernized classical buildings of the public sector appear for the most part secure. The public may prize the jazziest examples of Art Deco sufficiently to preserve them. Private residential examples face the vagaries of changing ownership and fashion, but most endure. New Deal–era public housing, with few proponents, may not survive much longer in Baltimore, where the public fails to appreciate many of the city's buildings from this vastly understudied period. But the Langston Terrace dwellings in Washington and the residential sections of Greenbelt seem safe for now. Baltimore commercial buildings under threat include Schulte-United, the Ambassador theater, McCrory's, and Read's. If the aforementioned stores survive city plans for the Westside "Superblock," it will probably be as mere facade projects. Werner's Restaurant has happily been rescued in the past year, but the Ambassador theater is in fragile condition after a recent fire. Many more Deco buildings, particularly commercial buildings around the city, hang on in precarious states.

Yet there have been several important preservation successes, such as the adaptive reuse of the Montgomery Ward Warehouse. Several preservation-minded Baltimore developers have an excellent record, among them Struever Brothers (now Cross Street Partners), a prime preservation-minded firm since the 1970s. It has used preservation tax credits as a cornerstone of its business model, converting to mixed-used projects a large number of industrial complexes that would not otherwise have survived. In Washington, Douglas Jemal and a few other developers have established a similar record.

Economics and politics always will be crucial in preserving a city's architectural heritage. Preservation is often the first thing to be sacrificed and the last to be considered in land-use controversies. In a weak economy, development can mean more jobs, while preservation may appear to be only a hindrance. In a strong economy, the power of developers increases, quite often to the detriment of heritage. In the case of the Deco buildings that activists in greater Washington saved, one thing alone saved the day—the capacity to initiate lawsuits and throw politicians out of office. Without a tough and vibrant preservation movement at the grass-roots level, the architectural legacy of Washington and Baltimore will continue to be at the mercy of luck, and that legacy deserves much better.

Perhaps preservationists in Washington and Baltimore will find new ways to collaborate. If for some reason a threat should emerge to the Uptown theater in Washington or the Senator theater in Baltimore, preservationists in both cities could cite the magnitude of destruction that has rendered the theaters John Jacob Zink designed so rare. Regional significance contributes to local significance.

To preservation activists in both Washington and Baltimore we submit this volume as a resource. We hope that it helps, because the threats can emerge quickly, and what preservationists presume safe and secure one day may come tumbling down the day after.

**JOSEPH H. ABEL** *(1905–1985)*: Born in Washington, Abel studied architecture at George Washington University and in the 1920s worked as a draftsman for George T. Santmyers and later for Arthur Heaton. He established the firm Dillon & Abel with Charles Dillon, another Santmyers apprentice, in 1935. In 1941 he formed a partnership with Julian F. Berla, who had studied architecture at MIT, and the firm became Berla & Abel. Abel designed more than one hundred apartment projects in Washington. After Berla retired in 1972, the firm became Abel & Weinstein (with Jessie Weinstein).[1]

**JOHN AHLERS** *(1896–1983)*: Ahlers was born in Germany and moved to Baltimore with his family at the age of nine. After graduating from St. Boniface College in Winnipeg, he returned to Baltimore and worked as a draftsman. He later joined the architectural office of Joseph Evans Sperry. His first major assignment after leaving the firm was the Arts and Crafts row houses along Tuscany Road and Ridgemede Road. His success led to his becoming a company architect for the Roland Park Company, working closely with Edward Palmer. Ahlers is best known for the Original Northwood development, the Roland Park Company's first project aimed at families of moderate means. Built during the Depression, the neighborhood would be one of the company's last projects.[2]

**WILLIAM S. ARRASMITH** *(1898–1965)*: Born in Hillsborough, North Carolina, William Strudwick Arrasmith studied architecture at the College of General Engineering at the University of Illinois. Before graduation, he secured a summer internship with T. Charles Atwood, of Chapel Hill, and served as supervising engineer for the University of North Carolina's building committee. After graduation he worked with McKim, Mead & White in New York, then moved to Louisville, Kentucky, to take a position with the architect Brinton B. Davis. In 1928 he became an associate with the Louisville architect Hermann Wischmeyer. The firm Wischmeyer, Arrasmith & Elswick, created in 1936, designed a variety of building types, but its specialization in bus-terminal design grew steadily. Arrasmith became the preeminent designer of this building type.[3]

**ALVIN L. AUBINOE SR.** *(1903–1974)*: Born in Washington, Aubinoe attended the University of Maryland. In the 1920s he worked as an engineer for the Rust Engineering Company. After working as an engineer for Morris Cafritz starting in 1926, he went into business for himself in 1930 but then rejoined Cafritz as an architect and manager of construction. He left Cafritz again in 1938 to establish his own development business. In addition to apartment buildings, he built office buildings, hotels, and residential subdivisions. Over the years he served as director of the Home Builders Association of Metropolitan Washington, as director of the National Association of Home Builders, and in executive positions with many other construction, real-estate, and civic organizations.[4]

**EDWARD H. BENNETT** *(1874–1954)*: Born in Bristol, England, and trained at the École des Beaux Arts from 1895 to 1902, Bennett worked with Daniel Burnham on his comprehensive plans for San Francisco and Chicago. He founded the firm Bennett, Parsons, & Frost, which served as a consultant on urban-planning issues, and he designed Grant Park for the city of Chicago, along with several structures for the 1933 Chicago Century of Progress Exposition. He chaired the Board of Architects for the Federal Triangle project in Washington, DC.[5]

**ROBERT S. BERESFORD** *(1879–1966)*: Born in Aurenreid, Pennsylvania, Beresford attended Princeton University and worked for the supervising architect of the Treasury and the Architect of the Capitol. From 1909 to 1914 he worked in the architectural office of Jules Henri de Sibour; in 1919 he worked in the office of Appleton P. Clarke. He established his own practice in 1920. In 1922 he was hired to supervise construction of the Mayflower Hotel, designed by Warren & Wetmore. Active on the Washington Board of Trade, Beresford practiced architecture until 1961.[6]

**E. BURTON CORNING** *(1889–1957)*: A native Washingtonian, Edward Burton Corning studied architecture at George Washington University and worked with the firm of Arthur Heaton. In 1932 he left Heaton's firm and practiced under his own name until establishing a partnership, Corning & Moore, with the architect Raymond G. Moore in 1942. After World War II he designed several large apartment buildings, including the Berkshire and the Greenbrier.[7]

**PAUL PHILIPPE CRET** *(1876–1945)*: Born in Lyon, France, Cret attended the École des Beaux Arts and accepted a position as professor of architecture at the University of Pennsylvania. In 1907 he

established a private practice, and by the 1920s he was internationally renowned as a champion of modernized classical architecture.[8]

**HERBERT G. CRISP** *(1865?–1939)*: Born in Anne Arundel County, Maryland, Crisp received his education in Baltimore City schools. At eighteen he began his training as an architect in the office of William Carson. Joseph Evans Sperry worked in the office at the same time; the two would later form a partnership. Crisp's works in the city included the Calvert Building, the Title Guarantee and Trust, Co. building, the Emerson Hotel, and the Provident Savings Bank. Toward the end of his career, he focused on hospitals and other institutional structures, including the University of Maryland Hospital, and buildings for the Johns Hopkins Hospital, Sinai Hospital, Union Memorial Hospital, and Bon Secours Hospital. Crisp died in 1939 at the age of 73.[9]

**JOHN JOSEPH EARLEY** *(1881–1945)*: Earley was the son of an Irish ecclesiastical stone carver, James Earley. The elder Earley came to America with his wife, Mary, in 1881, the year in which John Joseph was born. The Earleys settled in Washington, where James founded a studio devoted to sculpture and architectural stone carving. When his father died in 1906, the younger Earley carried on this tradition. In the 1920s he did important work in the emerging art of exposed aggregate concrete, and he was granted a patent for his own distinctive process. In the 1930s, he and his associate Basil Taylor gained national recognition for prefabricated houses clad in polychrome concrete mosaic. Earley served as president of the American Concrete Institute and received commissions in many different cities. The Earley studio was located in Rosslyn, Virginia.[10]

**JOHN EBERSON** *(1875–1964)*: Born in Romania, Eberson came to the United States as a young man. He moved from St. Louis to Chicago to New York, where he founded an architectural firm in 1926. By the 1930s, with his son, Drew, he built the firm into an international leader in theater design. The Eberson firm designed dozens—according to some accounts, hundreds—of movie theaters over the years.[11]

**JAMES R. EDMUNDS JR.** *(1890–1953)*: Edmunds was born in Baltimore in 1890. After graduating from Boys' Latin in 1908, he attended the University of Pennsylvania, where he received a BS in architecture in 1912. He got his start in Baltimore serving as a draftsman to the firms of Edward L. Palmer Jr. and Wyatt & Nolting. In 1915 Edmunds began his own practice. He lived in Canton, China, from 1918 to 1920, then returned to Baltimore and worked as a senior draftsman for Joseph Evans Sperry. On Sperry's death, Edmunds and Herbert G. Crisp formed the firm Crisp & Edmunds. Following Crisp's death, Edmunds formed a partnership with his son, James Richard Edmunds III. He served as chairman of the Housing Authority of Baltimore City from 1937 to 1941, and he served on the Maryland Board of Examination and Registration of Architects from 1935 to 1944. He was elected an AIA fellow in 1937. From 1945 to 1947 he was president of the AIA. He designed numerous buildings throughout the city, including Western High School, the General Hospital and Psychiatric Institute of the University of Maryland, Hutzler Brothers, and Hochschild, Kohn & Company.[12]

**HARRY L. EDWARDS** *(1902–1958)*: Born in Florida and raised in Alabama, Edwards moved to Washington with his mother at age eighteen and studied architecture at George Washington University. After working as a draftsman for a number of architectural firms, he joined Cafritz in 1930. He was also employed at the time by Monroe Warren to assist in the design of the Kennedy-Warren. After working with Cafritz through 1945, he joined his colleague Alvin Aubinoe in the firm Aubinoe, Edwards & Beery.[13]

**DOUGLAS ELLINGTON** *(1886–1960)*: Born in North Carolina, Ellington studied architecture at Drexel University in Philadelphia, the University of Pennsylvania, and the École de Beaux Arts in Paris. He taught architecture at Columbia University and the Carnegie Institute of Technology.

After establishing a private practice, he designed several buildings in Asheville, North Carolina, including the Art Deco Asheville City Building (1926–28). In the 1930s he and Reginald Wadsworth designed the buildings in the suburb of Greenbelt, Maryland. Ellington lived in Charleston, South Carolina, after his retirement.[14]

**JOHN F. EYRING** *(1896–1963)*: Eyring's father, Erhard Eyring, founded the construction company E. Eyring & Sons in 1887. John Eyring attended Diekman Institute, the Maryland Institute, and the United States Coast Guard Academy before enrolling in the University of Pennsylvania's School of Architecture. In 1927 he started an architectural firm. He concentrated on schools, churches, and commercial and industrial buildings but also designed movie theaters, banks, and civic buildings. A devout Catholic, he received several commissions from the Catholic Church, including the Mount St. Agnes College library and residence hall and the St. Francis of Assisi Church and School. In 1958 Pope Pius XII named him a Papal Knight of the Order of St. Gregory the Great.[15]

**WALDRON FAULKNER** *(1898–1979)*: Born in Paris and educated at Yale, Faulkner won a student medal from the American Institute of Architects while still in college. After moving to Washington, he founded the firm Faulkner, Fryer & Vanderpool (later Faulkner & Kingsbury).

**DAVID KIRKPATRICK ESTE FISHER JR.** *(1892–1978)*: Fisher was the son of a prominent Baltimore attorney, D. K. E. Fisher Sr. Following his graduation from MIT with a degree in architecture in 1916, Fisher joined the army and served as a lieutenant in the first American artillery unit to see action in France during World War I. He served as an instructor at a French artillery school and left the army as a captain. Upon his return to Baltimore, he joined the firm Parker, Thomas & Rice, becoming a partner in 1924. He won the design competition for the Princeton University Theater. In 1927 he established the firm Taylor & Fisher with R. E. Lee Taylor. He served as president of the Baltimore chapter of the AIA in 1937 and

1938. In 1946 he won an AIA national fellowship. In 1978 he died in his home in the Warrington Apartments.[16]

**LAWRENCE FOWLER** *(1877–1971)*: Fowler graduated from the Johns Hopkins University and studied architecture at Columbia University. He worked for Wyatt & Nolting before starting his own practice in 1906. He is best known for his high-end residential architecture; however, he received several major civic commissions, such as the War Memorial in Baltimore and the Maryland Hall of Records in Annapolis. He was chapter president of the Baltimore AIA in 1927 and 1928, and he became an AIA fellow in 1937. Fowler had a passion for historical architecture and willed his extensive collection of drawings and rare architectural books to the Johns Hopkins University.[17]

**BENJAMIN FRANK** *(b. 1885)*: Born in Baltimore, Frank attended public schools and the Marsden School. He earned is BS in architecture at the University of Pennsylvania. During War World I he served in the Bureau of Yards and Docks in Washington, and for fifteen months he was chief of a submarine division. Raised in a Baltimore Jewish family with German roots, Frank was a member of the Baltimore Hebrew congregation.[18]

**CLYDE N. FRIZ** *(1867–1942)*: Friz was born in Chester, Michigan, grew up in Abilene, Kansas, and studied at MIT. After graduating, he worked as an architectural draftsman for a St. Louis firm. In 1900 he moved to Baltimore and took a position with Wyatt & Nolting. After the 1904 fire, he formed a partnership with William Gordon Beecher but later went into business for himself. In addition to the Enoch Pratt Free Library, his major commissions in Baltimore include the Scottish Rite Temple, the Home Friendly Insurance Building, the Central Fire Insurance Building, the Knights of Pythias building, and the Standard Oil Company Building. He drew the design for renovating the Governor's House in Annapolis at the outset of the administration of Governor Harry W. Nice. In 1942 he served as president of the Baltimore chapter of the AIA.[19]

**FRANCIS L. KOENIG** *(1910–1993)*: Born in Chicago and raised in Virginia, Koenig took a correspondence course in architecture offered by the International Correspondence Schools, of Scranton, Pennsylvania. He moved to Washington in 1935 and got work as a draftsman for Harvey Warwick, chief architect for the developer Gustave Ring. Koenig's work impressed Ring so greatly that he was made vice president of the Ring Engineering Company in 1940.[20]

**THOMAS W. LAMB** *(1871–1942)*: Born in Dundee, Scotland, Lamb came to the United States in 1883 and studied at the Cooper Union in New York City. He opened his architectural practice in 1892 and developed a specialty in theater design. Over the course of his career he designed several hundred theaters worldwide. He also designed other building types; among his commissions outside of the theater realm was the 1935 New York City Greyhound Terminal, near Pennsylvania Station.[21]

**WILLIAM LAMDIN** *(1887–1945)*: Lamdin attended high school at Baltimore Polytechnic Institute and studied architecture at Cornell University. He began his career as a developer of the Roland Park–Guilford District. After serving in World War I, Lamdin returned to Baltimore and formed a partnership with Edward Palmer, which lasted until his death in 1945. He joined the AIA in 1920. Lamdin was a member of the Citizens Housing and Planning Commission, the City Planning Commission, and the Board of Registration for Maryland Architects.

**JOSEPH LOCKIE** *(1881–1949)*: Born in Warren, Maine, Lockie moved to Washington, DC, in 1902. He attended evening architecture classes at George Washington University, where he met his future partner, Irwin Stevens Porter. Lockie worked as a draftsman for Frederick B. Pyle, Thomas R. Mullett, and Wood, Donn & Deming. Both he and Porter worked for Waddy Wood after Wood established his own firm. Porter and Lockie founded their own firm in the 1920s, specializing in residential architecture. They turned to commercial and institutional architecture in the 1930s.[22]

**HOWARD MAY** *(1879–1941)*: A Baltimore native, May studied architecture under M. Chequier, a French architect working in Baltimore, before joining Parker, Thomas & Rice. In 1913 he formed the firm Smith & May with Wilson Smith. The firm's works include the North Avenue Market, the Nurses' Home at the University of Maryland School of Medicine, and the School of Law at the University of Maryland. May served as a consulting architect to the Maryland Department of Education.[23]

**MILTON B. MEDARY JR.** *(1874–1929)*: Born in Philadelphia, Medary attended the University of Pennsylvania and then worked with the architectural firms of Frank Miles Day and Richard L. Field. He finally joined the firm of Clarence C. Zantzinger and Charles L. Borie Jr. Specializing in academic and ecclesiastical buildings, he designed the Washington Memorial Chapel at Valley Forge. Before his death in 1929, he served as president of the AIA.[24]

**MIHRAN MESROBIAN** *(1889–1975)*: Born in Turkey of Armenian parents, Mesrobian studied architecture at the Academie des Beaux Arts in Istanbul and was architect to a sultan. Drafted into the Turkish army in World War I, he served as an engineering officer. He emigrated to the United States in 1921. Between 1925 and 1928 he designed the Carleton and Hay-Adams Hotels, receiving an AIA national award for excellence in 1926. In the same year he became chief architect for the developer Harry Wardman. He retired in the early 1950s.[25]

**HAL A. MILLER** *(1903–1953)*: Born in Montreal in 1903 to Polish immigrants, Miller attended McGill University, where he earned a BS in architecture in 1925. A month after graduation, Miller moved to New York City, where he worked as a draftsman for the New York Edison Company and later as an architectural engineer for the New York Central Railroad. Miller took courses in architecture at Columbia University and the College of the City of New York. At Columbia, Miller met his future wife, Minnie Kitt, of Baltimore. The couple moved to Minnie's hometown in 1935, and by 1936 Miller had established his own practice, with offices at 421 St. Paul Place. Miller not only designed the Samester Parkway Apartments but he lived there with his wife, daughter, mother, and father.[26]

**HOWARD M. MOTTU** *(d. 1953)*: Mottu began his career with the firm Baldwin & Pennington. After the Baltimore fire, he established the firm Mottu & White with Henry S. T. White. Together, they designed residences and buildings in Baltimore and its environs as well as in neighboring states. Mottu served on the State Board of Examiners of Architects.[27]

**CHARLES M. NES JR.** *(1907–1989)*: Nes, who started his career in 1930 with Palmer & Lamdin, was a principal in the successor firm Fisher, Nes, Campbell & Partners. Educated at Princeton, Nes served in the Army Air Forces during World War II. He chaired the Baltimore chapter of the AIA in 1951 and 1952 and was made an AIA fellow in 1953. He became president of the AIA in 1966.[28]

**EDWARD L. PALMER JR.** *(1877–1952)*: Palmer graduated from the Johns Hopkins University in 1899 and from the University of Pennsylvania architecture program in 1903. After graduation, he worked as a draftsman for Hornblower & Marshall. Starting in 1907, he spent a decade working with the Roland Park Company, designing a multitude of houses in Roland Park and Guilford, as well as a new community in Dundalk for the Bethlehem Steel Company. He worked independently from 1917 to 1925, then went on to lead one of most enduring Baltimore firms, first named Palmer, Willis & Lamdin, but changing its name multiple times. Palmer kept busy with residential work, but he occasionally took on other types of commissions, such as his 1925 addition to the St. Casimir Church in Canton. He served as president of the Baltimore chapter of the AIA in 1925 and 1926.

**FRANK G. PIERSON** *(1870–1941)*: Archival research has yielded little biographical information on Pierson except that he was born in Philadelphia and admitted to the AIA in 1920.[29]

**IRWIN STEVENS PORTER** *(1888–1957):* Born in Washington, DC, Porter attended George Washington University and studied architecture there while working as a draftsman in the firm Hornblower & Marshall. After receiving his degree, he worked in the firm of Waddy B. Wood, along with his friend Joseph Lockie, with whom he formed a partnership. After Lockie's death in 1949, the firm Porter & Lockie was reorganized as Irwin S. Porter & Sons.[30]

**JOHN STOKES REDDEN** *(1902–1991):* Born in Oakland, Illinois, Redden was educated at Eastern Illinois State College and the University of Florida. He worked with the architectural firms Royer & Danely, in Urbana, Illinois (1924–25), and Holabird & Root, in Chicago (1927–30), before joining the staff of Sears Roebuck, where he was appointed chief architect in 1938.[31]

**HILYARD ROBINSON** *(1899–1986):* One of Washington's most distinguished African American architects, Robinson was born and raised in Washington and studied architecture at the University of Pennsylvania, Columbia University, and the University of Berlin. Over the course of his studies he was heavily influenced by the work of the Bauhaus. He also became an authority on public housing. After teaching at Howard University in 1934, he went to work for the federal government overseeing slum-clearance projects and public housing. He also designed buildings at Howard University.[32]

**GEORGE T. SANTMYERS** *(1889–1960):* Born in Front Royal, Virginia, Santmyers was raised in Baltimore and moved to Washington while he was in high school. From 1908 to 1912 he studied at the Washington Architectural Club Atelier and worked as a draftsman for several Washington architectural firms, including Harding & Upman. He opened his own firm in 1914. During the 1920s he designed large apartment buildings, including 2101 Connecticut Avenue NW (with Joseph Abel) and 4701 Connecticut Avenue NW. In the 1930s he specialized in garden apartments. After World War II, in partnership with James Thomen,

Santmyers designed more large apartments until his death in 1960. Over the course of his career, he designed more than four hundred apartment buildings.[33]

**ROBERT O. SCHOLZ** *(1895–1978):* Born in New Jersey, Scholz moved to Washington in 1918 and worked for the navy designing dockyards. In the 1920s he became a partner in the firm Baer & Scholz. He designed the Alban Towers apartment building in 1928. In 1934 he founded his own firm, the Robert O. Scholz Company. He worked with the developer Monroe Warren, who founded the Meadowbrook Construction Company, to design the Arlington Forest development. He also served as consulting architect to the Perpetual Federal Savings and Loan, building branch offices in Bethesda and Silver Spring, Maryland.[34]

**WILSON L. SMITH** *(d. 1931):* In 1900 Smith graduated from the Johns Hopkins University and studied architecture at Columbia. He traveled to Europe and returned to Baltimore to join the firm Parker, Thomas & Rice. His designs include Gwynn's Falls Junior High School, the McDonogh School, several University of Maryland buildings, and the Canton Company Building. With his partner Howard May, he designed alterations for the Union Trust Company, the Maryland Trust Company, and the Mercantile Trust Company buildings, and they worked with Taylor & Fisher on the Baltimore Trust Company building.[35]

**GILBERT V. STEELE:** Archival sources have yielded no information on Steele, who designed the Hecht Company Warehouse for Abbott, Merkt & Company.

**WILLIAM FUSSELBAUGH STONE JR.** *(b. 1890):* Born in Baltimore, Stone attended public and private schools in Baltimore before going to St. John's College in Annapolis for a year. He then studied at the School of Architecture at the University of Pennsylvania. At age eighteen he took a position in the office of Otto G. Simonson. After Simonson's death in 1923, Stone worked as an independent architect. In addition to numerous residences, Stone designed the Canton National Bank, the parish house for the Church of the Guardian Angel, several churches, Engine Houses 55 and 56, Truck Houses 23 and 24, the WBAL radio and television studios, the Robert E. Lee Apartments, the Park Lynn Apartments, and the bandstand pavilion on Federal Hill. Living into his nineties, Stone designed more than 452 buildings during his long career.[36]

**R. E. LEE TAYLOR JR.** *(1882–1952)*: Born in Norfolk, Virginia, Taylor was the son of Colonel Walter Herron Taylor, adjutant general to General Robert E. Lee. In 1901 Taylor received a BA from the University of Virginia, and in 1904 he received a degree in architecture from MIT. He practiced architecture in Norfolk and then moved to Baltimore to join the firm Parker, Thomas, & Rice. In 1923, this firm became Taylor & Fisher. In addition to the Baltimore Trust Company building, the firm was known for work on the Federal Reserve banks in Richmond and Baltimore, the Baltimore Gas and Electric Company building, the Monumental Life building, and the C&P Telephone building. Taylor served as a member of the University of Virginia's architectural commission and designed many of the university's buildings. He was a member of the PWA Board of Review under Harold Ickes and an adviser in the restoration of Williamsburg.[37]

**REGINALD J. WADSWORTH** *(1885–1981)*: Born in Montreal, Wadsworth studied at the University of Pennsylvania. He was associated with the architectural firm Wadsworth & Henderson and worked as a draftsman with the firms Mellor & Meigs and Bissell & Sinkler in the second and third decades of the twentieth century. He designed a number of residences in Maine and Pennsylvania before relocating to Washington and working for the supervising architect of the Treasury. He assisted Douglas Ellington with the design of the buildings in Greenbelt, Maryland, and continued working on federal projects until 1952.[38]

**RALPH T. WALKER** *(1889–1973)*: Born in Waterbury, Connecticut, Walker attended MIT. In 1919

he joined the New York architectural firm McKenzie, Voorhees & Gmelin, which succeeded the firm of Cyrus Eidlitz. Upon McKenzie's death in 1926, Walker became a partner. He designed several New York skyscrapers, including the Barclay-Vesey Building, the New York Telephone Company Building, and the Irving Trust Company Building. He was active in planning the New York World's Fair of 1939. He served on the U.S. Commission of Fine Arts from 1959 to 1961 and received numerous honors, including the AIA Centennial Medal, the Gold Medal of the Architectural League of New York, the Gold Medal of the National Institute of Arts and Letters, and the Gold Medal of the New York chapter of the AIA.[39]

**HARVEY H. WARWICK SR.** *(1893–1972)*: Born in Kansas City, Missouri, Warwick worked in the offices of Midwestern architects and moved to Washington after World War I. He opened an architectural office in 1922 and worked in partnership with Louis Justement from 1927 to 1930. Warwick designed the Westchester Apartment complex in association with Morris Cafritz and Gustave Ring. He designed other buildings for the Cafritz Company, as well as the Colonial Village project in Arlington, Virginia.[40]

**HENRY S. TAYLOR WHITE SR.** *(1879–1946)*: White was educated in Baltimore schools and began his career at Baldwin & Pennington. With his partner Howard Mottu he designed the Baltimore Life Insurance Company building, the Hagerstown Post Office, Trinity College in Ilchester, Maryland, and numerous residences in Baltimore and on the Eastern Shore. He served as president of the Baltimore AIA chapter in 1931 and 1932. He partnered with his son Henry S. Taylor White Jr. before moving to France to work on the American Church in Paris. White Jr. is also credited as working on the Baltimore Life Insurance Company building.[41]

**LUCIUS WHITE** *(1887–1970)*: A native Baltimorean, White graduated from Baltimore City College in 1905 and received a BS in architecture from the University of Pennsylvania in 1909. His first architectural job was as a draftsman for Otto G.

Simonson, with whom he worked for thirteen years, becoming a partner. White continued the firm after Simonson's death, establishing an independent practice. In 1940 he joined the Maryland Board of Examiners and Registration of Architects, becoming its chairman in 1952. In 1941 and 1942 he served as president of the Baltimore chapter of the AIA, and he was made a fellow in 1952. His works in Baltimore include the Court Square Building, Bachrach Studios, the Crown Cork & Seal Company building, the new Baltimore City Jail, the Ashburton Filtration Plant, and buildings for Loyola College.[42]

**A. HAMILTON WILSON** *(1892–1956)*: Born in Washington, DC, Wilson entered the design field in 1914, designing hangars and airfields, and was subsequently admitted to the AIA. During his partnership with Frank G. Pierson he helped design the Library of Congress Annex, and after Pierson's death he did classified design work during World War II and then formed the firm Wilson & Denton. Among his other Washington commissions were the headquarters building for the International Association of Machinists and Our Lady of Victory School.[43]

**JAMES BOSLEY NOEL WYATT** *(1847–1926)*: Educated at Harvard University, MIT, and at the École de Beaux Arts, Wyatt came from a family with deep Baltimore roots. When he was eighteen, his family moved to Massachusetts, staying there while Wyatt studied at Harvard and MIT. After studying in Paris for three years, he returned to Baltimore in 1874 and began working for Francis Baldwin. At Baldwin's firm he met Joseph Evans Sperry, with whom he partnered from 1877 to 1887. In 1889 he would partner with William G. Nolting. Their firm, Wyatt & Nolting, designed major buildings throughout the city. The firm trained many of Baltimore's major early twentieth-century architects, including Clyde Friz, William Lamdin, John Zink, and Lawrence Hall Fowler. Wyatt served as president of the Baltimore chapter of the AIA from 1902 to 1911.[44]

**NATHAN C. WYETH** *(1870–1963)*: Born in Chicago, Wyeth was trained at the school of the Metropolitan Museum of Art in New York City and later at the École des Beaux Arts. After working for a year with the firm Carrere & Hastings, he joined the Office of the Supervising Architect of the Treasury. He then became chief designer for the Architect of the Capitol and served as the District of Columbia municipal architect from 1934 to 1946. During his long career he designed a diverse range of buildings and structures, including school buildings, hospitals, memorials, bridges, governmental office buildings, and private residences.[45]

**JOSEPH YOUNGER** *(1892–1932)*: A prominent Washington architect who opened his own practice in 1922, Joseph Younger won praise for his designs for the Wardman Saddle Club in Rock Creek Park, the Sixth Presbyterian Church, and the Kennedy-Warren. In 1932, at the age of forty, he died of a self-inflicted gunshot wound in his apartment in Tilden Gardens as his horrified wife looked on. Joseph Abel revealed in an interview during the 1980s that Younger had suffered shell shock during World War I and had subsequently experienced periods of depression.[46]

**JOHN JACOB ZINK** *(1886–1952)*: A Baltimore native, Zink attended the Maryland Institute and worked for the Baltimore architectural firm Wyatt & Nolting. He subsequently studied architecture at Columbia University and worked for the architect Thomas Lamb. By the 1920s he had returned to Baltimore and established an independent practice. He designed his own family's home, which contained his office, in Montebello Park. Late in his career he established the firm Zink, Atkins & Craycroft. Zink designed dozens of movie theaters in the Mid-Atlantic region.[47]

**CHAPTER 1. THE SPIRIT OF ART DECO**

1. Bevis Hillier, *Art Deco* (London: Studio Vista / Dutton Pictureback, 1968).

2. David Gebhard, "The Moderne in the U.S., 1920–1941," *Architectural Association Quarterly* 2, no. 3 (July 1970): 4–20.

3. Bevis Hillier, *The World of Art Deco* (New York: E. P. Dutton, 1971), 23.

4. The scholarly literature on Art Deco is considerable. In addition to the previously cited works by Hillier and Gebhard, see Martin Battersby, *The Decorative Twenties* (New York: Collier Books, 1969); idem, *The Decorative Thirties* (New York: Collier Books, 1969); Donald J. Bush, *The Streamline Decade* (New York: George Braziller, 1975); Martin Greif, *Depression Modern* (New York: Universe Books, 1975); Elayne H. Varian, *American Art Deco Architecture* (New York: Finch College Museum of Art, 1975); Eva Weber, *Art Deco in America* (New York: Exeter Books, 1985); Richard Guy Wilson, Dianne H. Pilgrim, and Dickran Tashjian, *The Machine Age in America* (New York: Harry N. Abrams, 1986); Alastair Duncan, "Art Deco Lighting," *Journal of Decorative and Propaganda Arts* 1 (Spring 1986): 20–31; Isabelle Gournay, "Architecture at the Fontainebleau School of Fine Arts, 1923–1939," *Journal of the Society of Architectural Historians* 45, no. 3 (September 1986): 270–85; Alastair Duncan, *American Art Deco* (London: Thames & Hudson, 1986); Carol Willis, "Zoning and 'Zeitgeist': The Skyscraper City in the 1920s," *Journal of the Society of Architectural Historians* 45, no. 1 (March 1986): 47–59; Dan Klein, Nancy McCleeland, and Malcolm Haslam, *In the Art Deco Style* (London: Thames & Hudson, 1987); Alastair Duncan, *Art Deco* (London: Thames & Hudson, 1988); Jean Paul Bouillon, *Art Deco, 1903–1940* (New York: Rizzoli, 1989); Patricia Bayer, *Art Deco Interiors: Decoration and Design Classics of the 1920s and 1930s* (Boston: Little, Brown, 1990); Richard Striner, "Art Deco: Polemics and Synthesis," *Winterthur Portfolio* 25, no. 1 (Spring 1990): 21–34; Robert Heide and John Gilman, *Popular Art Deco: Depression Era Style and Design* (New York: Abbeville, 1991); Patricia Bayer, *Art Deco Architecture: Design, Decoration and Detail from the Twenties and Thirties* (New York: Harry N. Abrams, 1992); Barbara Capitman, Michael D. Kinerk, and Dennis Wilhelm, *Rediscovering Art Deco U.S.A.* (New York: Viking, 1994); David Gebhard, *The National Trust Guide to Art Deco in America* (New York: John Wiley & Sons, 1996); Giovanna Franci, Rosella Mangaroni, and Esther Zago, *A Journey through American Art Deco: Architecture, Design, and Cinema in the Twenties and Thirties* (Seattle: University of Washington Press, 1997); Bevis Hillier and Stephen Escritte, *Art Deco Style* (London: Phaidon, 1997); Simon Dell, "The Consumer and the Making of the 'Exposition Internationale des Arts Décoratifs et Industriels Modernes,' 1907–1925," *Journal of Design History* 12, no. 4 (1999): 311–25; J. Stewart

Johnson, *American Modern, 1925–1940: Design for a New Age* (New York: Harry N. Abrams, 2000); Ingrid Cranfield, *Art Deco House Style* (Newton Abbot, UK: David & Charles, 2001); Adrian Tinniswood, *The Art Deco House* (New York: Watson-Guptill, 2002); Iain Zaczek, *Essential Art Deco* (New York: Paragon, 2002); Charlotte Benton, Tim Benton, Ghislaine Wood, and Oriana Baddeley, *Art Deco: 1910–1939* (London: V&A Publications, 2003); Carla Breeze, *American Art Deco: Modernistic Architecture and Regionalism* (New York: W. W. Norton, 2003); Gabrielle M. Esperdy, *Modernizing Main Street: Architecture and Consumer Culture in the New Deal* (Chicago: University of Chicago Press, 2008); Alastair Duncan, *Art Deco Complete: The Definitive Guide to the Decorative Arts of the 1920s and 1930s* (New York: Harry N. Abrams, 2009); and Michael Windover, *Art Deco: A Mode of Mobility* (Quebec: Presses de l'Université du Quebec, 2012). For local studies, see Dan Vlack, *Art Deco Architecture in New York* (New York: Harper & Row, 1974); David Gebhard and Harriette Von Bretton, *LA in the Thirties* (Santa Barbara: Art Galleries of the University of California, 1975); Cervin Robinson and Rosemarie Haag Bletter, *Skyscraper Style: Art Deco in New York* (New York: Oxford University Press, 1975); Ave Pildas, *Art Deco Los Angeles* (New York: Harper & Row, 1977); Lawrence Kreisman, *Art Deco Seattle: Walking Tour* (Seattle: Allied Arts of Seattle, 1979); Carol Newton Gambino, *Tulsa Art Deco* (Tulsa: Tulsa Foundation for Architecture, 1980); Laura Cerwinske and David Kaminsky, *Tropical Deco: The Architecture and Design of Old Miami Beach* (New York: Rizzoli, 1981); Norbert Messler, *The Art Deco Skyscraper in New York* (Frankfurt am Main: Peter Lang, 1983); Hans Wirz and Richard Striner, *Washington Deco: Art Deco in the Nation's Capital* (Washington, DC: Smithsonian Institution Press, 1984); Sherry Cucchiella, *Baltimore Deco: An Architectural Survey of Art Deco in Baltimore* (Baltimore: Maclay & Associates, 1984); Keith Root, *Miami Beach Art Deco Guide* (Miami Beach, FL: Miami Design Preservation League, 1987); Barbara Capitman, *Deco Delights: Preserving the Beauty and Joy of Miami Beach* (New York: E. P. Dutton, 1988); Judith Singer Cohen, *Cowtown Moderne: Art Deco Architecture in Fort Worth, Texas* (College Station: Texas A&M University Press, 1988); Carla

Breeze, *LA Deco* (New York: Rizzoli, 1991); idem, *New York Deco* (New York: Rizzoli, 1993); Marcus Whiffen and Carla Breeze, *Pueblo Deco: The Art Deco Architecture of the Southwest* (Albuquerque: University of New Mexico Press, 1994); Michael F. Crowe, *Deco by the Bay: Art Deco Architecture in the San Francisco Bay Area* (New York: Viking Studio Books, 1995); Paul Clemence, *South Beach Architectural Photographs* (Atglen, PA: Schiffer Books, 2004); David Garrard Lowe, *Art Deco New York* (New York: Watson-Guptill, 2004); Elizabeth McMillian, *Deco and Streamline Architecture in LA: A Moderne City Survey* (Atglen, PA: Schiffer Books, 2004); Rebecca Binno Savage and Greg Kowalski, *Art Deco in Detroit* (Charleston, SC: Arcadia, 2004); Richard Berenholz, *New York Deco* (New York: Welcome Books, 2005); Susanne Tarbell Cooper, J. Christopher Launi, and John W. Thomas, *Long Beach Art Deco* (Charleston, SC: Arcadia, 2005); Susanne Tarbell Cooper, Amy Ronnebeck Hall, and Frank Cooper Jr., *Los Angeles Art Deco* (Charleston, SC: Arcadia, 2005); Michael F. Crowe and Robert W. Bowen, *San Francisco Art Deco* (Charleston, SC: Arcadia, 2007); Beth Dunlop, *Miami: Mediterranean Splendor and Deco Dreams* (New York: Rizzoli, 2007); Sharon Koskoff, *Art Deco of the Palm Beaches* (Charleston, SC: Arcadia, 2007); Jim Parsons, David Bush, and Madeleine McDermott Hamm, *Houston Deco: Modernistic Architecture of the Texas Coast* (Houston: Bright Sky, 2008); Theresa Poletti, *Art Deco San Francisco: The Architecture of Timothy Pflueger* (Princeton, NJ: Princeton Architectural Press, 2008); David Bush and Jim Parsons, *Hill Country Deco: Modernistic Architecture of Central Texas* (Fort Worth: Texas Christian University Press, 2010); and Steven Brooke, *Miami Beach Deco* (New York: Universe Books, 2011).

5. Roland N. Stromberg, *European Intellectual History since 1789* (Englewood Cliffs, NJ: Prentice-Hall, 1975), 229.

6. Fritz Schumacher, "Trends in Architectural Thought," *Architectural Forum* 54, no. 4 (April 1931): 402.

7. Le Corbusier, *Towards a New Architecture*, trans. Frederick Etchells (London: Architectural Press,

1948), 268–69, 12. Originally published as *Vers une architecture* (Paris: Les Editions G. Cres et Cie, 1923).

8. Waldo Frank, *The Re-Discovery of America* (New York: Charles Scribner's Sons, 1929), 90–91.

9. Milton B. Medary, "President Medary's Address, the 1927 Convention, American Institute of Architects," *Architectural Forum* 46, no. 6 (June 1927): 2.

10. C. Howard Walker, quoted in "Modernist and Traditionalist," *Architectural Forum* 53, no. 1 (July 1930): 49–50.

11. See Striner, "Art Deco: Polemics and Synthesis."

12. Henry-Russell Hitchcock Jr., "Modern Architecture," pt. 1, "The Traditionalists and the New Tradition," and pt. 2, "The New Pioneers," *Architectural Record* 63, no. 4 (April 1928): 337–49 and no. 5 (May 1928): 453–57.

13. "Can Modern Architecture Be Good?" *Federal Architect* 1, no. 2 (October 1930): 6–9.

14. Charles R. Richards, "A Present-Day Outlook on Applied Art," *Architectural Record* 77, no. 4 (April 1935): 228–30.

15. "Editor's Note," *Architectural Forum* 48, no. 2 (February 1928): 156.

16. For excellent cultural commentary on the sources of the Meso-American influence, see Hillier, *Art Deco*, 40–51, and *World of Art Deco*, 26–32.

17. John Dos Passos, *Manhattan Transfer* (1925; reprint, Boston: Houghton Mifflin, 1963), 12.

18. Rebecca West, quoted in Herbert Croly, "A New Dimension in Architectural Effects," *Architectural Record* 57, no. 1 (January 1925): 93.

19. Ralph T. Walker, "A New Architecture," *Architectural Forum* 48, no. 1 (January 1928): 1.

20. Anne Morrow Lindbergh, *The Wave of the Future: A Confession of Faith* (New York: Harcourt, Brace, 1940).

21. Walter Dorwin Teague, *Design This Day: The Technique of Order in the Machine Age* (New York: Harcourt, Brace, 1940).

22. Frank Lloyd Wright, *Modern Architecture, Being the Kahn Lectures for 1930* (Princeton, NJ: Princeton University Press, 1931), 35.

23. See David W. Look and Carole L. Perrault, *The Interior Building: Its Architecture and Its Art* (Washington, DC: National Park Service, Preservation Assistance, 1986), 11–17.

24. See Henry-Russell Hitchcock Jr. and Philip Johnson, *The International Style: Architecture since 1922* (1932; reprint, New York: W. W. Norton, 1966).

25. Helen Appleton Read, "The Exposition in Paris," *International Studio* 82, no. 342 (November 1925): 93.

26. Hildreth Meière, "The Question of Decoration," *Architectural Forum* 57, no. 1 (July 1932): 1, 2.

27. Walker, "New Architecture," 1.

28. Alfred H. Barr Jr. and Philip Johnson, introduction to *Machine Art: March 6–April 20, 1934*, by Philip Johnson (1934; reprint, New York: Museum of Modern Art, 1969), 9.

29. Michael Dugdale, "Safety First," *Architectural Review* 71, no. 424 (March 1932): 122.

30. Ellow H. Hostache, "Reflections on the Exposition des Arts Décoratifs," *Architectural Forum* 44, no. 1 (January 1926): 11, 15.

31. Le Corbusier, "Architecture, the Expression of the Materials and Methods of Our Times," *Architectural Record* 66, no. 2 (August 1929): 126, 128.

32. Philip Johnson, *Machine Art*, 10.

33. John McAndrew, "'Modernistic' and 'Stream-lined,'" *Bulletin of the Museum of Modern Art*, no. 5 (December 1938): 2.

34. Sheldon Cheney and Martha Cheney, *Art and the Machine: An Account of Industrial Design in Twentieth-Century America* (New York: Whittlesey House / McGraw-Hill, 1936), 98, 294, 102.

35. Sheldon Cheney, *The New World Architecture* (New York: Longmans, Green, 1930), 29, 175.

36. Talbot Faulkner Hamlin, "A Contemporary American Style: Some Notes on Its Qualities and Dangers," *Pencil Points* 19, no. 2 (February 1938): 100.

37. Talbot Faulkner Hamlin, "The International Style Lacks the Essence of Great Architecture," *American Architect* 143, no. 2615 (January 1933): 12.

38. See Richard Guy Wilson, "High Noon on the Mall: Modernism versus Traditionalism, 1910–1970," in *The Mall in Washington, 1791–1991*, ed. Richard Longstreth (Hanover, NH: National Gallery of Art and University Press of New England, 1991).

39. David Gebhard, "About Style, Not Ideology," *Architecture* 73, no. 12 (December 1983): 35.

40. Wright, *Modern Architecture*, 39–40.

## CHAPTER 2. WASHINGTON AND BALTIMORE IN THE AGE OF ART DECO

1. On the McMillan Plan, see Sue Kohler and Pamela Scott, eds., *Designing the Nation's Capital: The 1901 Plan for Washington, D.C.* (Amherst: University of Massachusetts Press, 2007); Jon A. Peterson, *The Birth of City Planning in the United States, 1840–1917* (Baltimore: Johns Hopkins University Press, 2003); Thomas S. Hines, "The Imperial Mall: The City Beautiful Movement and the Washington Plan of 1901–1902," in *The Mall in Washington, 1791–1991*, ed. Richard Longstreth (Hanover, NH: National Gallery of Art and University Press of New England, 1991); Jon A. Peterson, "The Mall, the McMillan Plan, and the Origins of American City Planning," in ibid.; and Mel Scott, *American City Planning since 1890* (Berkeley and Los Angeles: University of California Press, 1971).

2. See Richard Striner, *The Committee of 100 on the Federal City: Its History and Its Service to the Nation's Capital* (Washington, DC: Committee of 100, 1995), 2–3.

3. For background on the Federal Triangle project, see Constance McLaughlin Green, *Washington: Capital City*, vol. 2, *1879–1950* (Princeton, NJ: Princeton University Press, 1962), 279; Frederick Gutheim, *Worthy of the Nation: The History of Planning for the National Capital* (Washington, DC: Smithsonian Institution Press, 1977), 174–75; Lois Craig et al., *The Federal Presence: Architecture, Politics, and Symbols in United States Government Buildings* (Cambridge, MA: MIT Press, 1977), 310–17; and Sally Kress Tompkins, *A Quest for Grandeur: Charles Moore and the Federal Triangle* (Washington, DC: Smithsonian Institution Press, 1992).

4. David Burner, *Herbert Hoover: A Public Life* (New York: Alfred A. Knopf, 1979), 143, 229–30.

5. Though economic historians differ as to whether there was a cause-and-effect relationship between the Wall Street Crash and the Depression, the evidence and analysis presented by John Kenneth Galbraith a half-century ago remain compelling. Galbraith showed the extent to which money from banks and corporations was diverted into stock speculation by 1928 and 1929. When the value of the stocks collapsed, those banks and corporations had to compensate for the losses by calling in loans and contracting operations. See John Kenneth Galbraith, *The Great Crash, 1929* (Boston: Houghton Mifflin, 1954).

6. The other members of the board were Milton B. Medary (responsible for the Justice Department building), succeeded after his death by his partner,

Clarence C. Zantzinger; Louis Ayres (Commerce Department building); Arthur Brown Jr. (Interstate Commerce Commission and Labor Department buildings); William Adams Delano (Post Office building, which should not be confused with the older Romanesque Victorian Post Office building nearby); John Russell Pope (National Archives building); and Louis Simon (Internal Revenue Service building). Bennett was given responsibility for the apex building at the eastern point of the triangle, which would house the Federal Trade Commission. See Lois Craig, "Hidden Treasures of a Walled City," *AIA Journal* 67 (June 1978): 21. See also Steven McLeod Bedford, *John Russell Pope: Architect of Empire* (New York: Rizzoli, 1998).

7. "Can Modern Architecture Be Good?" *Federal Architect* 1, no. 2 (October 1930): 6, 8–9.

8. See James M. Goode, "Flying High: The Origin and Design of National Airport," *Washington History* 1, no. 2 (Fall 1989): 4–25.

9. The action of Theodore Roosevelt in 1907 might well be regarded as a precedent. At J. P. Morgan's behest, Roosevelt deposited some federal funds in New York banks to reverse a financial panic.

10. The historian William Leuchtenburg gave this account: "In the spring of 1933, Washington quickened to the feverish pace of the new mobilization. From state agricultural colleges and university campuses, from law faculties and social work schools, the young men flocked to Washington to take part in the new mobilization. Wholly apart from their beliefs or special competences, they imparted an enormous energy to the business of governing and impressed almost everyone with their contagious high spirits." William Leuchtenburg, *Franklin D. Roosevelt and the New Deal* (New York: Harper Torchbooks, 1963), 63.

11. George Peek, *Why Quit Our Own*, with Samuel Crowther (New York: D. Van Nostrand, 1936), 20.

12. Franklin Delano Roosevelt, address delivered

in Syracuse, NY, 29 September 1936, in *The Public Papers and Addresses of Franklin D. Roosevelt*, ed. Samuel I. Rosenman (New York: Random House, 1938), 5:389–90.

13. See Green, *Washington: Capital City*, 2:393.

14. Edwin Rosskam, *Washington: Nerve Center* (New York: Alliance Book Corporation and Longmans, Green, 1939), 17–19.

15. The historian Richard Longstreth has observed in a seminal study that "the Washington, D.C., metropolitan area ranked among the major proving grounds for the neighborhood [shopping] center at [a] pivotal stage of its development. A national paradigm for the shopping center, independent of a planned residential enclave and configured as a drive-in facility, was built there in 1930. During the second half of the decade, examples proliferated in the Washington area to a degree unmatched by any other city before the war." "The Neighborhood Shopping Center in Washington, D.C., 1930–1941," *Journal of the Society of Architectural Historians* 51, no. 1 (March 1992): 7.

16. Robert Sellers, "The Art Deco Era in Washington Lives!" *Georgetowner*, 10–23 January 1985. As to the Silver Fox, the local historian William Offut named Fred Johannsen as the owner: "And just across the District Line Fred Johannsen was putting the finishing touches on his new cocktail lounge–supper club, the Silver Fox." William Offutt, *Bethesda: A Social History of the Area through World War II* (Bethesda, MD: Innovation Game, 1996), 454.

17. See Constance McLaughlin Green, *The Secret City: A History of Race Relations in the Nation's Capital* (Princeton, NJ: Princeton University Press, 1967); and Jacqueline M. Moore, *Leading the Race: The Transformation of the Black Elite in the Nation's Capital, 1880–1920* (Charlottesville: University of Virginia Press, 1999).

18. The Annex, with its Thomas Jefferson Reading Room and its murals of Jefferson, was later re-

named for John Adams so that the original nine-teenth-century Library of Congress building could be called the Thomas Jefferson Building. But this quintessential example of Washington foolishness pales in comparison with the renaming of Washington National Airport—an FDR project—for Ronald Reagan, who sought to undo FDR's legacy.

19. See Albert Mayer, "Green-Belt Towns for the Machine Age," *New York Times Magazine*, 2 February 1936, 8–9; Henry Churchill, "America's Town Planning Begins," *New Republic*, 3 June 1936, 96–98; Rexford Guy Tugwell, "The Meaning of the Greenbelt Towns," ibid., 17 February 1937, 42–43; Felix Belair, "Greenbelt—an Experimental Town—Starts Off," *New York Times Magazine*, 10 October 1937, 3, 21; Francis Fink, "First Resettlers," *Literary Digest*, November 1937, 13–15; George A. Warner, *Greenbelt, the Cooperative Community: An Experience in Democratic Living* (New York: Exposition Press, 1954); Leslie Gene Hunter, "Greenbelt, Maryland: A City on a Hill," *Maryland Historical Magazine* 63 (Summer 1968): 105–36; Joseph L. Arnold, *New Deal in the Suburbs: A History of the Greenbelt Town Program, 1935–1954* (Columbus: Ohio State University Press, 1971); Mary Lou Williamson, ed., *Greenbelt: History of a New Town, 1937–1987* (Norfolk VA: Donning, 1987); Susan L. Klaus, *Links in the Chain: Greenbelt, Maryland and the New Town Movement in America; An Annotated Bibliography on the Occasion of the Fiftieth Anniversary of Greenbelt, Maryland* (Washington, DC: Center for Washington Area Studies, George Washington University, 1987); and Cathy D. Knepper, *Greenbelt, Maryland: A Living Legacy of the New Deal* (Baltimore: Johns Hopkins University Press, 2001).

20. Mary E. Van Cleave, "We Pioneers," *Greenbelt Cooperator* 1, no. 1 (24 November 1937): 4.

21. Linda Lyons, "National Naval Medical Center Honors F.D.R.'s Design Role," *Trans-Lux* 13, no. 4 (January 1997): 1–2.

22. As the historian James M. Goode has observed, the runways of National Airport were "state-of-the-art, unobstructed, and designed to provide the opti-mum safe gliding angle for takeoff and landing. The enormous quantities of concrete used, produced on the site, made this the largest paving project ever attempted in the nation at the time." Goode, "Flying High," 17. See also John Zukowsky, ed., *Building for Air Travel: Architecture and Design for Commercial Aviation* (Chicago: Prestel-Verlag / Art Institute of Chicago, 1996); and Geza Szurovy, *The American Airport* (Osceola, WI: Zenith, 2003).

23. See "New Greyhound Terminal Here Will Be Opened Today," special section, *Washington Post*, 25 March 1940.

24. See "Jitney Into Giant," *Fortune*, August 1934, 42–43. Richard Longstreth has summarized the factors that led to the firm's success: "Greyhound was in the forefront of making bus transportation not just acceptable but appealing to a large clientele. At a time when long-distance travel by automobile often could be arduous, the bus provided a desirable alternative. Before and after World War II, Grey-hound introduced a steady succession of new mod-els that not only seemed the *ne plus ultra* in mod-ern, streamlined styling, but offered amenities that could be substantially greater than the family car, even for people lucky enough to have a new model. Bus passengers could recline; take in the view from a lofty position, read, sleep, or chat; forget about traffic, narrow and winding roads, poor roadside facilities, and they could do so in a then all-too-rare air-conditioned environment." Richard Longstreth, foreword to *The Streamline Era Greyhound Termi-nal: The Architecture of W. S. Arrasmith*, by Frank E. Wrenick (Jefferson, NC: McFarland, 2007), 1–2. See also idem, *History On The Line: Testimony in the Cause of Historic Preservation* (Ithaca, NY: Historic Urban Plans and National Council for Preservation Education, 1998), 3–13; Albert E. Meier and John P. Hoschek, *Over the Road: A History of Inter-City Bus Transportation in the United States* (Upper Montclair, NJ: Motor Bus Society, 1975); and Oscar Schisgall, *The Greyhound Story: From Hibbing to Everywhere* (Chicago: J. G. Ferguson, 1985).

25. See "Streets as Bus Terminals," *Washington Star*, 7 February 1932; "Bus Terminal Postponement

is Denied Line," *Washington Herald*, 19 July 1932; and "New Site Selected for Bus Terminal After Lost Fight," ibid., 8 August 1932.

26. See Richard Guy Wilson, "High Noon on the Mall: Modernism versus Traditionalism, 1910–1970," in *The Mall in Washington, 1791–1991*, ed. Richard Longstreth (Hanover, NH: National Gallery of Art and University Press of New England, 1991), 158–59.

27. See "Wright Designs 'Crystal City' for Temple Heights," *Evening Star*, 24 September 1940, B-1; Gerald G. Gross, "Architect Visions $15,000,000 City Of Future on Temple Heights," *Washington Post*, 25 September 1940, 12; "$15,000,000 'Crystal Palace' to Rise on Connecticut Avenue," *Washington Times Herald*, 25 September 1940; "Crystal City May Require Special Act of Congress," *Evening Star*, 9 October 1940, B-1; "Crystal City Plan Rejected by Zoning Unit," *Washington Times Herald*, 17 January 1941; Bruce Brooks Pfeiffer, "Oh, What We Missed," *Washington Post Magazine*, 5 January 1986, 16–19; William F. Powers, "Frank Lloyd Wright's Dream Deferred in District: Famed Architect's Crystal Heights Design Failed to Impress the City's Conservative Establishment," *Washington Post*, 4 July 1992, E-1, E-4; Donald Leslie Johnson, *Frank Lloyd Wright versus America: The 1930s* (Cambridge: MIT Press, 1994); Bruce Brooks Pfeiffer, *Treasures of Taliesin: Seventy-six Unbuilt Designs of Frank Lloyd Wright* (Carbondale: Southern Illinois University Press, 1985); and Arthur Drexler, *The Drawings of Frank Lloyd Wright* (New York: Horizon, 1962).

28. Harry Hopkins, quoted in Leuchtenburg, *Franklin D. Roosevelt and the New Deal*, 263.

29. Craig et al., *Federal Presence*, 416–19. See also Alfred Goldberg, *The Pentagon: The First Fifty Years* (Washington, DC: US Government Printing Office, 1992); and Steve Vogel, *The Pentagon: A History* (New York: Random House, 2007).

30. William K. Klingaman, *APL, Fifty Years of Service to the Nation: A History of the Johns Hopkins Applied Physics Laboratory* (Laurel, MD: Johns Hopkins University Applied Physics Laboratory, 1993), 9–10.

31. On FDR in wartime, see James MacGregor Burns, *Roosevelt: The Soldier of Freedom, 1940–1945* (New York: Harcourt, Brace, Jovanovich, 1970).

32. H. L. Mencken, "The Baltimore of the Eighties," in *The Vintage H. L. Mencken*, ed. Alistair Cooke (New York: Vintage Books, 1955), 4–5.

33. Robert J. Brugger, *Maryland: A Middle Temperament, 1634–1980* (Baltimore: Johns Hopkins University Press and Maryland Historical Society, 1988), 457.

34. Sherry H. Olson, *Baltimore: The Building of an American City* (Baltimore: Johns Hopkins University Press, 1980), 302.

35. Sherry Olson has written of the buoyant mood among the city's local visionaries during this period: "Baltimore's self-image took a new turn. . . . What Mencken called 'the boosters, boomers, go-getters and other such ballyhoo men' were hard at work promoting new product lines in manufacturing and new speculations in fresh land . . . Industry would be set in a park; workers and neighbors would enjoy 'daylight houses' and clean air. The whole city, well planned and well ordered, would be spacious, healthy, and productive. Skyscrapers and smokeless stacks would reach up to where sunshine burst through the clouds. Dirigibles would hang in its skies. European flights would land at a municipal airport built out of the harbor mud off Dundalk. Seaplanes, built in Baltimore, would land in the harbor itself." Ibid.

36. Ibid., 303–5.

37. Andrea Bakewell Lowery, "Glenn L. Martin Airport and Plant," Maryland Inventory of Historic Properties Form, Maryland Historical Trust, August 1997, sec. 7, p. 4.

38. Mary Ellen Hayward and Charles Belfoure, *The*

*Baltimore Rowhouse* (1999; New York: Princeton Architectural Press, 2001), 138–49.

39. H. L. Mencken, *Evening Sun*, 10 September 1923, quoted in Olson, *Baltimore*, 331.

40. H. L. Mencken, 11 June 1934, quoted in ibid., 315.

41. See Olson, *Baltimore*, 331–32; and Brugger, *Maryland*, 468.

42. Olson, *Baltimore*, 325.

43. Brugger, *Maryland*, 475–76.

44. Christopher Weeks, "Modernisms, Modernists, and Modernity, 1904–1955," in *The Architecture of Baltimore: An Illustrated History*, ed. Mary Ellen Hayward and Frank R. Shivers (Baltimore: Johns Hopkins University Press, 2004), 237, 244.

45. Brugger, *Maryland*, 495, 501–2.

46. Olson, *Baltimore*, 345.

47. Ibid., 340–41; "Local Projects Comprise 59% of PWA Jobs," *Evening Sun*, 15 June 1937.

48. Jo Ann E. Argersinger, *Toward a New Deal in Baltimore: People and Government in the Great Depression* (Chapel Hill: University of North Carolina Press, 1988), 92.

49. Paul R. Lusignan, "Public Housing in the United States, 1933–1949," Multiple Property Documentation Form, National Register of Historic Places, December 2004.

50. Brugger, *Maryland*, 525.

51. Ibid., 533.

52. Lowery, "Glenn L. Martin Airport and Plant," sec. 7, p. 2.

53. Olson, *Baltimore*, 349.

54. Brugger, *Maryland*, 532.

55. "Armistead Gardens Project Sold To U.S.," *Baltimore Sun*, 19 March 1941.

56. Brugger, *Maryland*, 541.

**CHAPTER 3. RESIDENTIAL ARCHITECTURE**

1. "A 'Nautical' Apartment Building," *Architectural Record* 63, no. 3 (March 1928): 223–25.

2. James M. Goode, *Best Addresses: A Century of Washington's Distinguished Apartment Houses* (Washington, DC: Smithsonian Institution Press, 1988), 253–55.

3. Clear Deco influence can be seen in Harvard Hall (1928), designed by Louis Justement (1650 Harvard Street NW); Park Central (1928), designed by Harvey Warwick Sr. (1900 F Street NW); Parklane (1928), also designed by Warwick (2025 I Street NW, demolished); Senate Courts (1928), designed by George T. Santmyers (120 C Street NE, demolished); Park Tower (1928), designed by William Harris (2440 16th Street NW); Woodley Park Towers (1929), designed by Louis T. Rouleau Sr. (2737 Devonshire Place NW), and Capitol Towers (1929), designed by Warwick (208 Massachusetts Avenue NE, altered). On Harvard Hall and Woodley Park Towers, see ibid., 280–83, 293–96. Capitol Towers has become a facade project.

4. Carolyn Mesrobian Hickman, "Mihran Mesrobian (1889–1975): Washington Architect," *Design Action* 2, no. 3 (May–June 1983): 3–4.

5. Goode, *Best Addresses*, 297–99. See also "Apartment Hotel to be Constructed on Calvert Street," *Evening Star*, 30 December 1929, 17; "Ultra-Modern Apt. Hotel Soon to Rise," ibid., 25 January 1930, B-1; "Shoreham Hotel to Open Thursday," *Washington Post*, 26 October 1930; and "New Shoreham Hotel Opens Tomorrow," *Washington Herald*, 30 October 1930, 1.

6. For excellent coverage of the Kennedy-Warren, see Goode, *Best Addresses*, 307–13. See also "Huge Apartment Hotel to Start Soon," *Evening Star*, 11 October 1930; "Large Apartment Nears Completion," ibid., 20 June 1931; "Art Stone Is Used in Hotel Entrance" and "Bird's Eye View of the Kennedy-Warren," *Washington Post*, 13 September 1931; "Dining Room Will Open October 15," ibid., 11 October 1931; and "Kennedy-Warren To Be Enlarged," *Evening Star*, 12 May 1935.

7. Linda Lyons, "Kennedy-Warren to Expand by Preserving its Art Deco Past," *Trans-Lux* 13, no. 3 (November 1996): 1–2.

8. *The Kennedy-Warren: Washington's First Completely Air Cooled Apartment*, ca. 1932, Collection of the Historical Society of Washington, DC.

9. For a detailed description of the Kennedy-Warren interior, see Marilyn M. Harper, "Kennedy-Warren Apartment Building, Interior Designation," application for Historic Landmark or Historic District designation, DC Historic Preservation Review Board (Art Deco Society of Washington, applicant), 2008, 18 pp.

10. Hickman, "Mihran Mesrobian," 4. See also Goode, *Best Addresses*, 314–17.

11. On the Majestic, see Goode, *Best Addresses*, 343–46.

12. For more on the General Scott, see ibid., 364–67.

13. Paul Shoemaker, interview by Richard Striner, 10 January 2012. The conceptual drawings of William Henry Shoemaker, on tracing paper, are at this writing in the collection of his son, Paul Shoemaker, of Easton, Maryland. Many of these drawings bear the stamp of the Dillon & Abel firm. Some surviving promotional brochures of the firm in this collection contain renderings that bear the initials W.H.S.

14. Joseph Abel and Fred N. Severud, *Apartment Houses* (New York: Reinhold, 1947), 80.

15. On 2929 Connecticut Avenue, see Goode, *Best Addresses*, 340–42. Elizabeth M. Davis, a student of Richard Longstreth's, discovered in researching this building that the use of red brick was dictated by the Commission of Fine Arts, which oversees new construction on the major avenues of Washington's L'Enfant Plan. Abel had originally planned to use blonde brick. See minutes from meetings of the Commission of Fine Arts, 16 September and 23 October 1936, cited in Davis, "2929 Connecticut Avenue, A Paper for Historic Preservation 271," 28 October 1985, in Richard Striner Historic Preservation Papers, Historical Society of Washington, DC, series 6, folder 123 (hereafter cited as Striner Papers).

16. Joseph Abel and Jesse Weinstein, interviews by Richard Striner, 1983.

17. John McAndrew, ed., *Guide to Modern Architecture—Northeast States* (New York: Museum of Modern Art, 1940), 26.

18. Abel and Severud, *Apartment Houses*. See also Goode, *Best Addresses*, 347–50. For preconstruction publicity, see "A $400,000 Apartment in Black, Buff, and Blue," *Washington Daily News*, 3 September 1938, 23.

19. For records pertaining to the Governor Shepherd preservation campaign, see "Governor Shepherd Case, 1984–1985," Striner Papers, series 1, folder 8.

20. On the Marlyn, see Goode, *Best Addresses*, 354–59; and "119 Rental Units, Marlyn Apartments, Washington, DC, Harvey Warwick, Architect," *Architectural Record* 84, no. 3 (September 1938): 127–29.

21. On Dorchester House, see Goode, *Best Addresses*, 379–81.

22. On the Delano, see ibid., 375–78.

23. Oscar A. de Lima to Richard Striner, 1 November 1973, in Striner's possession.

24. Howard's book, first published in 1898, was

originally entitled *To-Morrow: A Peaceful Path to Real Reform*. The book was republished in 1902 as *Garden Cities of To-Morrow* (London: S. Sonnenschein).

25. Richard Longstreth, ed., *Housing Washington: Two Centuries of Residential Development and Planning in the National Capital Area* (Chicago: Center for American Places at Columbia College Chicago and University of Chicago Press, 2010), chaps. 8–10. On Stein, see Kermit Carlyle Parsons, *The Writings of Clarence S. Stein, Architect of the Planned Community* (Baltimore: Johns Hopkins University Press, 1998).

26. Parsons, *Writings of Clarence S. Stein*, 325, 332–36; Longstreth, *Housing Washington*, chap. 8, pp. 13–21.

27. Other Art Deco garden-apartment buildings in this district include 4031 Davis Place NW (1938), designed by Dana B. Johannes; Monte Vista (1938), at 3901–3905 Davis Place NW, designed by Santmyers; and 3806–3822 Davis Place NW (1940), designed by Santmyers and including the buildings at 2514–2518 Tunlaw Road and 2517–2519 39th Street NW. All of these buildings were clad in red brick, and a period fixture in many of them is a large incinerator chimney.

28. Jerry A. McCoy and the Silver Spring Historical Society, *Historic Silver Spring* (Charleston, SC: Arcadia, 2005), 49.

29. On Lee Gardens, see Stephen A. Morris, "Lee Gardens: Historic Preservation, George Washington University, Professor Richard Longstreth, Spring Term 1986," and "Lee Gardens," Historic Resources Survey Form, Arlington County, Historic Affairs and Landmark Review Board, 24 November 1986, both in Striner Papers, series 4, folder 32.

30. Goode, *Best Addresses*, 337–39. For more on Langston Terrace Dwellings, see McAndrew, *Guide to Modern Architecture—Northeast States*, 26; Glen B. Leiner, "The Langston Terrace Dwellings," *Trans-Lux* 2, no. 3 (August 1984): 1, 9; "First Low-Cost Housing Project for D.C.," *Washington Times*, 17 December 1935; "Langston Terrace," *Washington Post*, 24 July 1936; "Frieze Shows Progress of Race," *Evening Star*, 11 October 1936; Anne Simpson, "Langston Wins Historic Status," *Washington Post*, 27 August 1987, DC-1, DC-2; and Benjamin Forgey, "The Enduring Ideals of Langston Terrace," ibid., 4 June 1988, C-1, C-7.

31. On this and other aspects of Robinson's design, see Kelly Anne Quinn, "Making Modern Homes: A History of Langston Terrace Dwellings, A New Deal Housing Program in Washington, D.C." (PhD diss., University of Maryland, 2007).

32. Cathy D. Knepper, *Greenbelt, Maryland: A Living Legacy of the New Deal* (Baltimore: Johns Hopkins University Press, 2001), 14.

33. David P. Fogle, "The Development of Greenbelt," in *Greenbelt: History of a New Town, 1937–1987*, ed. Mary Lou Williamson (Norfolk, VA: Donning, 1987), 26.

34. Knepper, *Greenbelt, Maryland*, 19, 35.

35. Leta Mach, "Constructing the Town of Greenbelt," in Williamson, *Greenbelt*, 31.

36. Clarence S. Stein, *Toward New Towns for America*, 3d ed. (Cambridge, MA: MIT Press, 1966), 150. For Stein's role in advising the planners of Greenbelt, see Knepper, *Greenbelt, Maryland*, 15; and Richard Longstreth, *City Center to Regional Mall: Architecture, the Automobile, and Retailing in Los Angeles, 1920–1950* (Cambridge, MA: MIT Press, 1997), 287, 289.

37. Stein, *Toward New Towns for America*, 150.

38. Mach, "Constructing the Town of Greenbelt," 31.

39. Barbara Likowski and Jay McCarl, "Social Construction," in Williamson, *Greenbelt*, 71; Knepper, *Greenbelt, Maryland*, 32–33.

40. Knepper, *Greenbelt, Maryland*, 23–29.

41. Wallace Richards to Eleanor Roosevelt, 28 October 1937, and memos of Eleanor Roosevelt and Franklin D. Roosevelt, 6 November 1937, quoted in ibid., 30–31.

42. Mach, "Constructing the Town of Greenbelt," 33.

43. Ibid., 31, 34.

44. Eric Kohler, untitled essay in *Eugene Schoen: Furniture from the Morris and Gwendolyn Cafritz Estate* (New York: Donzella, 2000), 9; K. Larsen, *Cafritz House Description* (Washington, DC: The Field School, 2001), 1.

45. Larsen, *Cafritz House Description*.

46. See Frederick W. Cron, *The Man Who Made Concrete Beautiful: A Biography of John Joseph Earley* (Fort Collins, CO: Centennial, 1977). See also "John J. Earley Develops Shop-Cast Panel House," *American Builder*, November 1934, 32–33; "Prefabrication for Architects," *Architectural Forum* 62, no. 2 (February 1935): 187–89; "Earley System," ibid. 63, no. 6 (December 1935): 553; "Products and Practice: Architectural Concrete Slabs," ibid. 72, no. 2 (February 1940): 101–6; and William M. Avery, "Earley's Mosaic Concrete Opens Limitless Vistas in Products Field," *Concrete Manufacturer*, special section of *Pit and Quarry*, September 1944, 131–34. On 31 March and 1 April 2001 the Latrobe chapter of the Society of Architectural Historians, in partnership with the School of Architecture at the University of Maryland, College Park, sponsored the symposium "John Joseph Earley: Expanding the Art and Science of Concrete." Isabelle Gournay chaired the symposium. Among the papers presented were "John Joseph Earley: Toward A Catalogue Raisonné," by Nancy Witherell and Judith Robinson, and "The Polychrome Houses: Precursor to Precast Concrete Curtain Wall Construction," by John A. Burns. Unfortunately, the proceedings of this symposium have never been published.

47. John Joseph Earley, "Architectural Concrete Makes Prefabricated Houses Possible," *Journal of the American Concrete Institute* 31 (1935): 513–14.

48. Ibid., 517, 524–25.

49. See Terry B. Morton, *The Pope-Leighey House* (Washington, DC: National Trust for Historic Preservation, 1969).

50. Judith H. Lanius, "Palisades," in *Washington at Home: An Illustrated History of Neighborhoods in the Nation's Capital*, ed. Kathryn Schneider Smith (Baltimore: Johns Hopkins University Press, 2010), 152–53; Alice Fales Stewart, *Images of America: The Palisades of Washington, D.C.* (Charleston, SC: Arcadia, 2005), 121. The name Ethel Nixon-Mounsey appears on the building permit.

51. Robert Reed, "By Design: A Wrightian Villa On Seminary Hill," *Alexandria Port Packet*, 18–24 April 1985.

52. *Architectural Forum* 75, no. 5 (November 1941): 120–21.

53. Some examples are the houses at the following addresses: 3210 Reservoir Street NW, in Georgetown, built in 1937 and designed for Alexander Hawes by Theodore Dominick; 3415 36th Street NW, built in 1937 and designed by Waldron Faulkner; 3718 Calvert Street NW, built in 1938 for M. J. Kossow and designed by Dillon & Abel; 3125 Chain Bridge Road NW, designed by Alfred Kastner; 4012 25th Road, in Arlington, Virginia, built in 1940 and designed by John Kennedy Sullivan; 1732 Portal Drive NW, built in 1946–47 and designed by Bernard Lyon Frishman; 1249 Irving Street NE, built in 1948 for Joseph Hopkinson and designed by H. H. Mackey; and 2248 North Quebec Street, in Arlington, designed by Joseph Abel (year of construction unknown). Windshield surveys have found many other houses such as these in the greater Washington area, houses whose designer and year of construction remain unknown. Among these are houses at the following addresses: 1204 Q Street NW; 1509 28th Street NW; 6306 Wisconsin Avenue, in Chevy Chase, Maryland; 9013 Flower Avenue and 206 East Wayne Avenue, both in Silver Spring, Maryland; 5542 North 11th Road, in Arlington, Virginia; 3301 Cameron Mills Road in

Alexandria, Virginia; and Argyle Drive (a group of 20 houses), also in Alexandria. No doubt there are many others.

54. "Two Impressive New Apartment Developments," *Power Pictorial*, no. 24 (December 1932): 16, 21.

55. For an excellent overview of Colonial Revival architecture in the thirties, see David Gebhard, "The American Colonial Revival in the 1930s," *Winterthur Portfolio* 22, nos. 2–3 (Summer–Autumn 1987): 109–48. Carol Willis reveals the connections between zoning legislation and the emergence of a new aesthetic for large-scale buildings in "Zoning and 'Zeitgeist': The Skyscraper City in the 1920s," *Journal of the Society of Architectural Historians* 45, no. 1 (March 1986): 47–59.

56. *Power Pictorial*, no. 13 (November 1928): 20.

57. Mary Ellen Hayward and Frank R. Shivers, eds., *The Architecture of Baltimore: An Illustrated History* (Baltimore: Johns Hopkins University Press, 2004), 138.

58. Betty Bird, "Samester Parkway Apartments," nomination form, National Register of Historic Places, 1998, sec. 8, pp. 1 and 8; Charles Belfoure, "Fallstaff Nice and Convenient for Walking to Synagogue," *Baltimore Sun*, 7 January 2001, 1L–2L.

59. Jo Ann E. Argersinger, *Toward a New Deal in Baltimore: People and Government in the Great Depression* (Chapel Hill: University of North Carolina Press, 1988), 92. Argersinger elaborates: "Baltimore's municipal leadership never fully supported the New Deal and often actively undermined its programs and openly criticized its purposes. City officials followed the inconsistent but expedient course of simultaneously disavowing local responsibility for unemployment relief and challenging federal encroachments on municipal obligations. Only when New Deal programs provided federal money without requiring matching funds or policy initiatives did state and local officials respond enthusiastically.

What they wanted from the New Deal was a federally financed old deal that catered to their traditional constituencies and enhanced political loyalties" (92).

60. Melissa Hess, "'Where People Learn to Live Better': The Prescriptive Nature of Early Federal Public Housing" (MA thesis, University of South Carolina, 2002), vi, 5.

61. Peter Henry Henderson, "Local Deals and the New Deal State: Implementing Federal Public Housing in Baltimore, 1933–1968" (PhD diss., Johns Hopkins University, 1994), 10. Henderson observes: "Conservative, anti-New Deal Democrats, who grounded their policies in fiscal conservatism, racial segregation, and support of the business community, dominated the city in the 1930s. The city was not only absent from the list of locales in the vanguard on public housing, it was also generally unreceptive to public housing as originally configured" (10). See also Argersinger, *Toward a New Deal in Baltimore*, 92–97.

62. Argersinger, *Toward a New Deal in Baltimore*, 98–101.

63. Ibid., 106–7.

64. "Plan Up Today in Removal of Negro School," *Baltimore Sun*, 1 August 1939.

65. On Latrobe Homes, see the following in the *Baltimore Sun*: "Housing Authority Takes New Options," 21 March 1939; "Plan Up Today in Removal of Negro School," 1 August 1939; "Third Housing Job Will Start Soon," 4 February 1940; "New Housing Project Ready for Occupancy," 17 August 1941; and "Latrobe Unit Occupied," 19 August 1941.

66. Spiro Kostof, *A History of Architecture: Settings and Rituals* (New York: Oxford University Press, 1985), 699. Kostoff elaborates: "The blocks are single files of apartments, never more than two rooms deep, stacked up on three to five stories. They turn their narrow ends towards a main traffic street, while between the blocks all cross-traffic is

barred. In effect, this arrangement rejects both the traditional city block and the street-defining role of buildings" (699).

67. See Richard W. Longstreth, "Academic Eclecticism in American Architecture," *Winterthur Portfolio* 17, no. 1 (Spring 1982): 55–82.

68. Deed, Roland Park Company to George and Julia Streeter, 29 October, 1937, Maryland Land Records, Baltimore City, book SCL 5669, folio 462; "Exhibition of The House of Tomorrow," *Gardens, Houses and People* 12, no. 3 (March 1937): 23–27; "Guilford Offers Beauty within the City," ibid. 12, no. 4 (April 1937): 31–36.

69. "New Homes Built by Kelly & Sadtler," *Gardens, Houses and People* 14, no. 5 (May 1939): 32–33.

70. Examples, most from the 1940s, include the Soderstrom residence at 300 Northfield Place, built in 1947 and designed by S. Shackelford; 304 Kerneway Avenue, built in 1945; 311 Southway, built in 1947; 106 Castlewood Road, designed by John Ahlers and built in 1938; 107 Castlewood Road, designed by the architect Lawrence A. Menefee and built in 1940 by William H. Sands; and the house at the southeast corner of Paddington Road and Broadmoor Road in Homeland, built in 1940 and based on a design for *Life* magazine by Perry, Shaw & Hepburn of Boston but adapted by the architect Kenneth C. Miller. For 106 Castlewood Road, see Mary Stoy Vaughan, "Modern Simplicity and Grace," *Gardens, Houses and People* 13, no. 6 (June 1938): 44–45; and Douglas H. Gordon, "The Orchards Maintains the Best Tradition of its Past," ibid. 13, no. 4 (April 1938): 26–31. For 107 Castlewood Road, see "Strictly in the District," ibid. 15, no. 12 (December 1940): 18–19. For the house at Paddington and Broadmoor, see "The 1940 Life House in Homeland," ibid. 15, no. 5 (May 1940): 28–29.

## CHAPTER 4. COMMERCIAL ARCHITECTURE

1. On the C&P Telephone Company building, see "C & P Erects New Office Building," *Evening Star*, 21 July 1928; and "Chesapeake and Potomac Telephone Company Buildings," application for Historic Landmark designation, Joint Committee on Landmarks of the National Capital (Don't Tear It Down, applicant), 5 July 1981, 14 pp.

2. On the Tower Building, see "Browning-Warren Bank and Office Building, Washington, D.C.; Robert F. Beresford, Architect," *American Architect* 134, no. 2556 (5 November 1928): 610–11; Cleland McDevitt, *The Book of Washington* (Washington, DC: Washington Board of Trade, 1930); "New Refinements Presented by Tower Building: Lofty K Street Structure Has Innovations in Many Features," *Washington Daily News*, 29 June 1929, 12; "Washington's First Pyramid Building," *Washington Times*, 4 November 1928; "Washington's Tallest Office Building Now Completed," *Evening Star*, 3 August 1929, 14; and Eve Lydia Barsoum, "The Tower Building," registration form, National Register of Historic Places, 7 August 1995, 13 pp.

3. Glen B. Leiner, "Small Comeback at Dupont Circle," *Trans-Lux* 4, no. 2 (Spring 1986): 8–9. In the course of his research on this building, which was partially restored in the 1980s, Mr. Leiner interviewed the architect.

4. On the Walker Building, see "A 12-Story General Purpose Office Building, Rentable Area 60,000 Square Feet," *Architectural Record* 82, no. 6 (December 1937): 96–97.

5. Traces of the facade of Ginn's stationary store remain at 915 E Street NW (the address was changed during redevelopment of the block). Long, rounded panels of red-and-tan concrete mosaic were retained for some reason when the property was converted into a condominium apartment building. On Herzog Men's Wear, see "Downtown Building Being Remodeled," *Evening Star*, 13 April 1948. For an overhead view of Wilson Boulevard and North

Highland Street in Arlington, Virginia, showing the now-demolished Hahn Shoe Store, Quality Shop, and Yeatman's Hardware, see Arlington Historical Society, *Arlington* (Charleston, SC: Arcadia, 2000), 79.

6. For local coverage of the Hahn shoe stores, see "Modernistic Structure for Shoe Store," *Washington Post*, 25 December 1938; and "New Store in Silver Spring," *Evening Star*, 20 August 1949, B-2.

7. See "Brownley Building Plans Under Way," *Evening Star*, 6 February 1932; "Brownley Building Will Be Supplanted," *Washington Post*, 6 February 1932; "New Building Activities Begun on F Street: Four-Story Structure Being Erected at 1309 for Brownley's," *Washington Star*, 4 June 1932; "New Brownley Store Modern," *Washington Times*, 22 October 1932; and Stephen Calcott, "Brownley Confectionary Building," nomination form, National Register of Historic Places, 19 July 1994, 16 pp.

8. Jim Byers, "East Washington Heights," in *Washington At Home: An Illustrated History of Neighborhoods in the Nation's Capital*, ed. Kathryn Schneider Smith (Baltimore: Johns Hopkins University Press, 2010), 407.

9. "Remington Rand Building, Washington, D.C., Holabird & Root, Architects," *Architectural Forum* 64, no. 1 (January 1936): 57–60.

10. "Lansburgh & Bro. Will Remodel Store," *Washington Post*, 30 April 1940.

11. See, e.g., Edward M. Stanton, *Branch Stores* (New York: National Retail Dry Goods Association, 1955), 105.

12. "Hechts Dedicate New Warehouse," *Washington Star*, 23 November 1936, B-1.

13. "Hecht Company Warehouse One of East's Best," *Washington Herald*, 30 June 1937. For further local press coverage of the Hecht Company Warehouse, see "Plans Drawn For Hecht Company's New Warehouse," *Washington Post*, 12 January 1936, R-5; "Hecht Company's New Warehouse," *Washington Times*, 10 March 1936; "Hecht Ceremony Speakers Chosen," *Washington Star*, 22 November 1936, A-6; "Hecht Company Set to Dedicate New Warehouse," *Washington Post*, 23 November 1936; and "Hecht Officiates at Dedication of Warehouse," ibid., 24 November 1936, X-12.

14. From the date of its completion, the design of the Hecht Company Warehouse was attributed simply to the engineering firm Abbott, Merkt & Company. Only an interview conducted in November 1990 by Richard Longstreth with a former owner of the firm, Colonel Richard Tatlow III, of Scarsdale, New York, together with research in the company's surviving documents, suggested that the warehouse design was assigned to the staff member Gilbert V. Steele. No information on Steele has emerged from archival sources.

15. This information was obtained by Richard Longstreth in interviews with Warren O. Simonds, a retired senior vice president of Hecht's, in the 1990s. See Richard Longstreth, "Hecht Company Warehouse: Going Beyond the Obvious," in *History On The Line: Testimony in the Cause of Historic Preservation* (Ithaca, NY: Historic Urban Plans and National Council for Preservation Education, 1998), 14–24, 33, 104n2. For more excellent coverage of the Hecht Company Warehouse, see "The Hecht Company Warehouse," application for Historic Landmark designation, DC Historic Preservation Review Board (Art Deco Society of Washington, Committee of 100 on the Federal City, and DC Preservation League, applicants), 3 July 1991, 20 pp.

16. See Raymond McGrath and A. C. Frost, *Glass in Architecture and Decoration* (London: Architectural Press, 1937), 48; "Products and Practice: Glass Block," *Architectural Forum* 72, no. 5 (May 1940): 327; Owens-Illinois Insulux Glass Block advertisement, *Architectural Record* 82, no. 2 (August 1937): 150; and "Glass Block," in *Twentieth Century Building Materials: History and Conservation*, ed. Thomas C. Jester (New York: McGraw-Hill, 1995), 194–99.

17. *Washington Herald*, 30 June 1937.

18. Richard Kent, "Two Glass Buildings: Washington and Columbus Again Make History," *Pencil Points* 17, no. 12 (December 1936): 679–82.

19. "A Department Store Builds a New Warehouse," *Architectural Record* 81, no. 6 (June 1937); "Pittsburgh Glass Institute Announces Winners in its 1937 Competition for Executed Examples of the Use of Glass in Architecture," *Architectural Forum* 67, no. 2 (August 1937): 47–142.

20. An excellent source on the Silver Spring Hecht Company building and the retailing trends that form its context, see Richard Longstreth, "The Mixed Blessings of Success: The Hecht Company and Department Store Branch Development After World War II," Center for Washington Area Studies, Occasional Paper No. 14, January 1995. For trade journal and press coverage of the building, see "Hecht's Silver Spring, Maryland," *Retail Management*, 1 November 1947, 18, 43; M. O. Waugh, "Hecht's, Silver Spring," *Display World*, December 1947, 30–31; Annette C. Ward, "Washington— Problem of Logistics," *Women's Wear Daily / Retail Executive*, 27 April 1949, F-4; "Silver Spring Hecht Store Deal Closed," *Washington Post*, 25 November 1945, 4-R, 6-R; "$2,500,000 Hecht Store to Open Doors in Silver Spring Saturday," ibid., 26 October 1947, 1-R; and "Snip, Snip—And Thousands Swarm Into Hecht's Silver Spring Store," *Washington Daily News*, 1 November 1947. For examples of advertising publicity in trade journals, see "Almost Time to Pass the Cigars: The Hecht Company, The Great Store Serving Greater Washington," *Women's Wear Daily*, 24 October 1947, 44; "Now! First in Sales in the Washington Retail Area: The Hecht Company, Washington and Silver Spring," ibid., 25 October 1948, 9; and "Your Suburban Store: Abbott, Merkt & Company, Designers of Department Store Structures," *Stores*, February 1949, 94.

21. See "New Neisner Store to Open Tomorrow," *Evening Star*, 28 July 1948.

22. For advertising publicity regarding this building, see "Frick Installation Cools Sears, Roebuck's Washington Store," *Federal Architect* 8, no. 1 (June 1937): 41.

23. For analysis of these trends in Sears merchandising and design, see Richard Longstreth, "Sears, Roebuck and the Remaking of the Department Store, 1924–42," *Journal of the Society of Architectural Historians* 65, no. 2 (June 2006): 238–79.

24. For trade journal and press coverage of the Sears building, see "Sears Opens," *Women's Wear Daily*, 1 October 1941, 1, 20; "Shopping Conveniences Feature Big Sears Store," *Chain Store Age*, administrative ed., no. 18 (June 1942): 8–9; John Stokes Redden, "Sears Store for Washington," *Architectural Concrete* 8, no. 4 (December 1942): 10–13; "Selecting the Surface Texture for Sears Architectural Concrete Building," *Concrete* 51 (February 1943): 5–6; and "New Sears, Roebuck," *Evening Star*, 1 October 1941, A-13. See also Judith Beck Helm and Kathryn Collison Ray, "Tenleytown," in Smith, *Washington At Home*, 117, 120.

25. On this building type in its formative stage of development in Washington, see Richard Longstreth, "The Neighborhood Shopping Center in Washington, D.C., 1930–1941," *Journal of the Society of Architectural Historians* 51, no. 1 (March 1992): 5–34.

26. On the Greenbelt commercial center, see Richard Longstreth, *City Center to Regional Mall: Architecture, the Automobile, and Retailing in Los Angeles, 1920–1950* (Cambridge, MA: MIT Press, 1997), 286–88.

27. See Cathy D. Knepper, *Greenbelt, Maryland: A Living Legacy of the New Deal* (Baltimore: Johns Hopkins University Press, 2001), 41.

28. See "Kass Realty Plans Shopping, Parking Center," *Washington Post*, 11 July 1937, V-4; "Chevy Chase Ice Palace, Bowling Alleys, Shopping Center Opens Wednesday," ibid., 20 November 1938, V-11; and "Park-and-Shop Building Also Includes Sport

Facilities," *Architectural Record* 87, no. 6 (June 1940): 119–20.

29. On the Silver Spring Shopping Center, see "Business Center for Silver Spring," *Evening Star*, 12 June 1937, C-2; "Silver Spring Shop Center is Proposed," *Washington Post*, 13 June 1937, V-7; "Projected Community Shopping Center for Silver Spring, Md.," ibid., 26 September 1937, V-15; "New Yorker Engaged for Silver Spring Job," *Evening Star*, 27 November 1937, B-2; "Expert to Plan Center at Silver Spring," *Washington Post*, 28 November 1937, V-4; "Large Shopping Center Nearing Completion at Silver Spring, Md.," ibid., 14 August 1938, V-6; "Shops Adjoin Theatre in Silver Spring," ibid., 18 September 1938, V-3; "Silver Spring Center to Open on Thursday," ibid., 23 October 1938, V-1, V-6; "Silver Spring Shopping Center Opens Today," special section, ibid., 27 October 1938; "6,000 Attend Trade Center Gala Opening," *Washington Herald*, 28 October 1938, 17; "Trade Center Opening Draws Crowd of 6,000," *Washington Times*, 28 October 1938, 10; Alfred Reeves, "Increasingly More People Want Automobiles," *Toledo Business*, March 1940, 9 (photograph of the Silver Spring Shopping Center); and Stephen A. Morris, "Silver Theatre and Silver Spring Shopping Center," Historic Sites Inventory Form, Maryland Historical Trust, National Register nomination (Art Deco Society of Washington, applicant), 1 May 1987, 38 pp. For discussion of the role of the Silver Spring Shopping Center in the Silver Spring central business district, see Mark Walston, "The Commercial Rise and Fall of Silver Spring," *Maryland Historical Magazine* 81 (Winter 1986): 330–39; and Richard Longstreth, "Silver Spring: Georgia Avenue, Colesville Road, and the Creation of an Alternative 'Downtown' for Metropolitan Washington," in *Streets: Critical Perspective on Public Space*, ed. Zeynep Celik, Diane Favro, and Richard Ingersoll (Berkeley and Los Angeles: University of California Press, 1994), 247–58.

30. For excellent coverage of these issues, see Robert K. Headley, *Motion Picture Exhibition in Washington, D.C.: An Illustrated History of Parlors, Palaces and Multiplexes in the Metropolitan Area, 1894–1997* (Jef-

ferson, NC: McFarland, 1999); and Douglas Gomery, "A Movie-Going Capital: Washington, D.C., in the History of Movie Presentation," *Washington History* 9, no. 1 (Spring–Summer 1997): 4–23.

31. See Jane Preddy, *Glamour, Glitz, and Sparkle: The Deco Theatres of John Eberson*, annual of the Theatre Historical Society of America, no. 16 (Chicago: Theatre Historical Society of America, 1989), 16–19.

32. On the Penn Theatre, see Headley, *Motion Picture Exhibition in Washington, D.C.*, 140–41, 146, 148, 304, 361; *Better Theatres*, 4 April 1936; and "Penn Theater, House of Streamlined Beauty, Opened with Brilliant Audience," *Washington Times*, 28 December 1935.

33. "Penn Theater, House of Streamlined Beauty, Opened with Brilliant Audience." See also "Warner Theater Formally Opens," *Washington Star*, 28 December 1935.

34. On the Circle theater, see Headley, *Motion Picture Exhibition in Washington, D.C.*, 247–48. See also "Circle Theater, 1986," Richard Striner Historic Preservation Papers, Historical Society of Washington, DC, series 4, folder 31 (hereinafter cited as Striner Papers).

35. On the Uptown theater, see Headley, *Motion Picture Exhibition in Washington, D.C.*, 132–33, 138, 142–43, 146, 148, 336–38; "Streamlining Features New Theater," *Evening Star*, 24 May 1935; "Work Will Begin on New Theater," ibid., 11 April 1936; Vesta Cummings, "Uptown Theatre Opens Tomorrow," ibid., 28 October 1936, A-12; "New Uptown Theater Opened," ibid., 29 October 1936; "Uptown Theater Part of $4,000,000 Program," *Washington Herald*, 29 October 1936; and "New Theater, 'Uptown,' Has Gala Opening," ibid., 30 October 1936. See also Kathleen Sinclair Wood, "Cleveland Park," in Smith, *Washington At Home*, 324, 327.

36. "Gala Festivities to Usher in Washington's New Screen Palace," *Washington Herald*, 29 October 1936, 10.

37. Headley, *Motion Picture Exhibition in Washington, D.C.*, 132.

38. The case can be made that the PADC should not have been given jurisdiction over the 1300 block of F Street. The buildings it demolished there were in no way symptomatic of so-called urban blight. A full retrospective assessment of the work of PADC from the standpoints of historic preservation and urbanism has yet to be written. The preservation assessment would in all probability be scathing.

39. "New Theater, Trans-Lux, Opens, Trans-Lux Theater to Open Tonight, Newest in Lighting in Trans-Lux House, Projection Device Novel, Air Control in Trans-Lux Latest," *Washington Times*, 12 March 1937, 20.

40. Jay Carmody, "Translux Makes Its Bow at an Unofficial Preview: Real Opening Set for Tonight, Will Introduce Public to Strikingly Modern Theater Serving Special Field," *Evening Star*, 12 March 1937, C-2. For additional coverage of the Trans-Lux at the time, see "New Trans-Lux Theater Plans Many Innovations for Patrons," *Washington Post*, 18 October 1936; Mabelle Jennings, "Trans-Lux Makes Bow as Capital's Newest Theater: Outer Glass Tower World's Largest, New System of Air Control in Trans-Lux, Lighting Features Newsreel House," *Washington Herald*, 12 March 1937; Nelson B. Bell, "New Trans-Lux Given Notable Opening Night," *Washington Post*, 12 March 1937, 18; and Carter Heslep, "Trans-Lux Policy Lauded by Audience at 'Preview,'" *Washington Daily News*, 12 March 1937, 36. For coverage in trade journals at the time, see "Trans-Lux Plans Large Theater in Washington, D.C.," *Motion Picture Herald*, 9 December 1936, 38; and "Trans-Lux Increasing Total of Theaters," ibid., 5 June 1937, 40. See also Headley, *Motion Picture Exhibition in Washington, D.C.*, 140, 143, 332–33; Christine Grenz, *Trans-Lux: Biography of a Corporation* (Norwalk, CT: Trans-Lux, 1982), 3–11, 28–32; and Ray Gingell, "Trans-Lux," *Marquee* 7, no. 3 (1975): 20–21.

41. Gomery, "Movie-Going Capital," 14.

42. See Gary Wolf, letter to the editor, *Washington Post*, 4 July 1975, A-27; and James M. Goode, *Capital Losses: A Cultural History of Washington's Destroyed Buildings* (Washington, DC: Smithsonian Institution Press, 1979), 378–81.

43. On the Sheridan theater, see Headley, *Motion Picture Exhibition in Washington, D.C.*, 138, 146, 148, 319; "Warner Bros. New Sheridan Theater: Gala Festivities Usher in Amusement Center on Upper Georgia Avenue," *Washington Times*, 14 January 1937; and "Sheridan Theater Dedicated Here," *Evening Star*, 15 January 1937.

44. On the Calvert theater, see Headley, *Motion Picture Exhibition in Washington, D.C.*, 135, 138, 142–43, 146, 148, 238; "Warners Will Build 16TH Local Theater," *Washington Daily News*, 30 July 1936; "Warners Plan Picture House in Georgetown," *Washington Post*, 30 July 1936; "Calvert Theater Plans Announced," *Evening Star*, 30 July 1936; and "New House is Opened by Warners," ibid., 7 May 1937.

45. See Headley, *Motion Picture Exhibition in Washington, D.C.*, 135.

46. On the Beverly theater, see ibid., 136, 142, 146, 148, 235; "New Motion Picture Theater for Northeast Section," *Washington Post*, 29 May 1938, V-7; and "Warners to Have New Movie House: 'Beverly' Will Be Located on Fifteenth Street Northeast," *Evening Star*, 28 May 1938.

47. Headley, *Motion Picture Exhibition in Washington, D.C.*, 136.

48. On the Boro/Bethesda theater, see ibid., 150, 236; and "Boro Theater Opens Thursday," *Bethesda–Chevy Chase Tribune*, 17 May 1938, B-1, B-6. See also Linda Lyons, "Bethesda Theatre," registration form, National Register of Historic Places (Art Deco Society of Washington, applicant), 19 August 1998, 19 pp.; and William Offutt, *Bethesda: A Social History of the Area through World War II* (Bethesda, MD: Innovation Game, 1996), 406.

49. For complete documentation of the Bethesda theater case, see "Bethesda Theatre Case, 1984–2005," Striner Papers, series 3, folders 21–28. The chairman of Maryland's National Register review board—the Governor's Consulting Committee on the National Register, or GCC—recused himself because he had testified on an earlier occasion in opposition to the Bethesda theater scheme. He might otherwise have broken the deadlock. The Art Deco Society appealed this case all the way to the National Park Service, which administers the National Register program. The protest might have succeeded at the federal level had not the administration of George W. Bush transferred the Keeper of the National Register, Carol Shull, to another post and replaced her with a political appointee. Bush's interior secretary, Gale Norton, was ideologically averse to "interference" in private property rights.

50. See Headley, *Motion Picture Exhibition in Washington, D.C.*, 146, 148, 320. For contemporaneous publicity on the Silver Theater, see "Suburb Gets New House Next Fall," *Washington Star*, 8 March 1938; "Work on New Silver Theatre Project Started This Week," *Maryland News*, 11 March 1938, 1; "Modern Silver Theatre for Silver Spring," ibid., 8 April 1938, 3; "A Salute to Silver Spring: Warner Bros. Silver Theatre" (advertisement), ibid., 16 September 1938, 4; and "Theatre and Colesville Pike Stores," in "Silver Spring Shopping Center Opens Today," special section, *Washington Post*, 27 October 1938, 12.

51. For trade-journal coverage, see "Warner Silver Theatre in Silver Springs [*sic*], Md.," *Better Theatres*, 12 November 1938, 12, 26; and *The 1939 Film Daily Year Book of Motion Pictures* (New York: Film Daily, 1939), 1063. See also the following advertisements in ibid.: "John Eberson Specifies and Uses 'Fabrics by Dazian's, Inc.': View of Silver Springs [*sic*], Md. Theatre, a John Eberson show place with stage and wall draperies by Dazian's," 1058; and "Adler 'Streamline' Slotted Silhouette Letters, Warner Bros. Silver Theatre, Silver Springs [*sic*], Md., John Eberson, Architect; Adler Silhouette Letters and Equipment Almost Exclusively Mentioned in Architect Eberson's Specifications," 1060. For a complete chronology of the Silver Spring preservation case, containing public documents, private memoranda, correspondence, and press coverage, see "Silver Spring, 1984–2004," Striner Papers, series 5, folders 43–104.

52. The Art Deco Society of Washington purchased most of these original foyer doors from an Alexandria, Virginia, antique shop.

53. On the Hyattsville theater, see Headley, *Motion Picture Exhibition in Washington, D.C.*, 273; "Hyattsville Theater Opens Thursday Night," *Washington Star*, 19 November 1939; and "The New Hyattsville," *Theatre Catalog, 1941* (Philadelphia: Emanuel, 1941), 29–31.

54. On the Reed theater, see Headley, *Motion Picture Exhibition in Washington, D.C.*, 142, 308–9.

55. On the Newton theater, see ibid., 141, 298; and "New Newton Theater is Dedicated," *Evening Star*, 30 July 1937.

56. On the Atlas theater, see Headley, *Motion Picture Exhibition in Washington, D.C.*, 142, 172, 175, 209, 221, 235, 298. See also the full-page advertisement in the *Washington Daily News*, 31 August 1938, 15; "Atlas Theater and Shops," application for Historic Landmark designation (DC Preservation League, applicant), undated, 25 pp., designation date 24 October 2002; and Denise Liebowitz, "Atlas Rising: A Refurbished Landmark Brings Back the Buzz on H Street, N.E.," *Architecture DC*, Spring 2008, 20–22.

57. On the Apex theater, see Headley, *Motion Picture Exhibition in Washington, D.C.*, 142–43, 148, 161, 177, 180, 208, 212, 255, 297, 298, 361. For trade-journal coverage, see "Apex, Washington, D.C.," *Theatre Catalog, 1942* (Philadelphia: Emanuel, 1942), 21–23.

58. For commentary on this demolition, see Goode, *Capital Losses*, 381–82; and Charles Paul Freund, "Another Silent Screen," *Washington Post*, 23 October 1976, A-19.

59. On the Senator theater, see Headley, *Motion Picture Exhibition in Washington, D.C.*, 161, 318. See also "Senator Theater," application for Historic Landmark designation (Art Deco Society of Washington, applicant), 16 November 1989, 11 pp.; and "Senator Theater, 1990–1991," Striner Papers, series 4, folders 35–36,.

60. On the Savoy theater, see Headley, *Motion Picture Exhibition in Washington, D.C.*, 149, 314–15.

61. On the Home theater, see ibid., 271–72.

62. Headley provides coverage of these theaters as follows in ibid.: Atlantic, 161, 169, 232; Kaywood, 154, 169, 278; Naylor, 169, 297–98; Langston, 153, 169–70, 282; MacArthur, 143, 168, 170, 174, 176, 290; Anacostia, 157, 227; Virginia, 158, 339–40; Carver, 240–41; Cheverly, 159, 172, 246; Coral, 160, 251; Flower, 170, 176, 262.

63. Offutt, *Bethesda*, 504.

64. Mark K. Miller, "Kalorama Roller Rink: It Ought to be in Pictures," *Trans-Lux* 4, no. 3 (Summer 1986): 3–4.

65. On Glen Echo, see Gary Scott, "Glen Echo Park Historic District," nomination form, National Register of Historic Places, 23 April 1984, 13 pp.; Benjamin Levy, *Glen Echo on the Potomac* (Washington, DC: National Park Service, Division of History, 1980); and Ray Burkett and Randee Berstein, "Deco 'Echoes' in Former Washington Amusement Park," *Trans-Lux* 1, no. 2 (February 1983): 6–8. See also Gary Kyriaxi, *The Great American Amusement Parks: A Pictorial History* (Secaucus, NJ: Citadel, 1976); and Tim Onosko, *Funland U.S.A.* (New York: Ballantine Books, 1978).

66. In addition, the overall form and shape of the bar might have been inspired by the Green Room bar in New York City's Edison Hotel, which opened in 1931.

67. *Washington Herald*, 10 July 1934.

68. *Fortune*, December 1934, 63.

69. Kay Ware, "Vacation Time Finds Capital With Abundance of Gay Spots," *Washington Post*, 31 August 1934.

70. On the Carlton Club, see Sue A. Kohler and Jeffrey R. Carson, *Sixteenth Street Architecture*, vol. 2 (Washington, DC: Commission of Fine Arts, 1988), 126–27, 132.

71. "Mayfair Restaurant: Café of All Nations, Washington, D.C.," *Architectural Record* 78, no. 1 (July 1935): 13–14.

72. Richard Striner, "Deco Restaurants, Part Two: Crisfield's," *Trans-Lux* 1, no. 4 (November 1983): 7.

73. Anne Groer, "Washington's Art Deco Restaurants: The Seven Seas," ibid. 1, no. 3 (July 1983): 6.

74. Bill Ivory, "Deco Restaurants, Part 2: Arbaugh's," ibid. 1, no. 4 (November 1983): 6.

75. Avis Black, "Thai Taste: A Deco Tradition Continues," ibid. 2, no. 3 (August 1984): 5.

76. The developer who destroyed Whitlow's was Oliver Carr, and his project architect was Shalom Baranes.

77. For reminiscences of the Blue Mirror Grill, see John Kelly, "D.C.'s 2 Blue Mirror Joints," *Washington Post*, 4 July 2010, accessible online at www.washingtonpost.com/wp-dyn/content/article/2010/07/03/AR2010070302708.html.

78. See Paul Hirshorn and Steven Izenour, *White Towers* (Cambridge, MA: MIT Press, 1979).

79. Ibid., 123, 128–33.

80. See "Harry F. Duncan Dies; Founded Little Tavern," *Washington Post*, 21 April 1992.

81. Lynne Heneson and Larry Kanter, "Little Tav-

erns: Renovating a Commercial Landmark," *Trans-Lux* 1, no. 2 (February 1983): 1, 3–4.

82. See Chester H. Liebs, *Main Street to Miracle Mile: American Roadside Architecture* (Boston: Little, Brown, 1985), 70–71; and "The Howard Johnson Restaurants," *Fortune*, September 1940, 82.

83. One Howard Johnson restaurant building from the 1930s survives in Alexandria, Virginia. The protection of this building, which no longer houses a Howard Johnson restaurant, may be credited to the efforts of the preservation staffer April Eberly Luber, who worked in the 1980s to reverse the previously terrible record of Alexandria in protecting important early twentieth-century buildings within its historic district.

84. See Richard J. S. Gutman and Elliott Kaufman, *American Diner* (New York: Harper & Row, 1979); and Liebs, *Main Street to Miracle Mile*, 216–24.

85. See "In Suburban Washington the Spotlight's on Warner's Tastee Diners," *Diner*, May 1947, 8–11.

86. J. Gordon Carr, "Bus Stations," in *Forms and Functions of Twentieth-Century Architecture*, ed. Talbot Faulkner Hamlin (New York: Columbia University Press, 1952), 597. For more on the Washington Greyhound Terminal, see "New Greyhound Terminal Preview Draws Thousands," *Washington Star*, 26 March 1940; "New Greyhound Terminal Here Will Be Opened Today," special section, *Washington Post*, 25 March 1940; "Super Terminal," *Bus Transportation*, April 1940, 166–68; "Large Terminal With Paying Concessions," *Architectural Record* 90, no. 4 (October 1941): 85–87; Manfred Burleigh and Charles F. Adams, eds., *Modern Bus Terminals and Post Houses* (Ypsilanti, MI: University Lithoprinters, 1941), 141; "A Modern Bus Terminal with Formica," advertisement for Formica Insulation Company, *Federal Architect* 12, no. 2 (January–March 1942): 3; "Greyhound Terminal of Washington," in *Railroad and Bus Terminal and Station Layout* (Boston: American Locker, 1945), 89; "Greyhound Bus Terminal," application for Historic Landmark designation, Joint Committee on Landmarks of the National

Capital (Art Deco Society of Washington and Don't Tear It Down, applicants), 21 February 1984, 13 pp.; Longstreth, *History On the Line*, 3–13; and Frank E. Wrenick, *The Streamline Era Greyhound Terminal: The Architecture of W. S. Arrasmith* (Jefferson, NC: McFarland, 2007), 110, 136–39, 180.

87. "Super Terminal," 168.

88. See assorted advertisements in "New Greyhound Terminal Here Will Be Opened Today," special section, *Washington Post*, 25 March 1940.

89. Wilson L. Scott, "Bus Terminal is Busy Wartime Mecca," *Washington Times Herald*, 2 May 1943, D-3.

90. For a complete chronology of the Greyhound Terminal preservation case, containing public documents, private memoranda, correspondence, and press coverage, see "Greyhound Terminal Case, 1984–1994," Striner Papers, series 2, folders 9–20.

91. See "Star Parking Plaza, Unique in Design, Opened to Public," *Evening Star*, 15 March 1940; and "Garage Has 2-In. Concrete Walls," *Architectural Record* 88, no. 1 (July 1940): 44–46.

92. "In the Shadow of the Nation's Capitol," *Orange Disc*, May–June 1937, 16–17; "America's Great Merchandisers Build With Architectural Terra Cotta," *Federal Architect* 8, no. 1 (July 1937). For general background on gas-station design in the 1930s, see Liebs, *Main Street to Miracle Mile*, 102–10; and Daniel Vieyra, *"Fill 'Er Up": An Architectural History of America's Gas Stations* (New York: Collier Books, 1979).

93. See Glen B. Leiner, "Miracle on 14TH Street: Doomed Laundry Saved," *Trans-Lux* 4, no. 3 (Summer 1986): 2–3.

94. On the Coca-Cola and Canada Dry bottling plants, see Jerry A. McCoy and the Silver Spring Historical Society, *Historic Silver Spring* (Charleston, SC: Arcadia, 2005), 50–54.

95. Alice G. Bickerstaff, "Farmers Banking and

Trust Company," Historic Sites Inventory Form, Maryland Historical Trust, December 1980.

96. *The New Baltimore Trust Building* and *The Best Known Business Address in Baltimore, With Illustrations of Its Many Desirable Features,* undated promotional brochures, Vertical Files, Maryland Department, Enoch Pratt Free Library, Baltimore.

97. Ibid.

98. Baltimore Trust Company, promotional newsletter, 6 December 1929, Vertical Files, Maryland Department, Enoch Pratt Free Library, Baltimore.

99. "Baltimore Trust Building Wins Architectural Medal for 1929," *Evening Sun,* 2 January 1930.

100. "Federal Agencies Crowd Into 'Little Washington,'" ibid., 30 September 1942.

101. "Baltimore Life enters its Second Century by looking over the past," *What's Happening* [Baltimore Life Insurance Company newsletter], 27 March 1982, 10; Janet Davis, "Baltimore Life Insurance Company Headquarters Building," Historic Sites Inventory Form, Maryland Historical Trust, 1984.

102. John Dorsey and James D. Dilts, *A Guide to Baltimore Architecture,* 3d ed. (Centreville, MD: Tidewater, 1997), 274.

103. "Monumental Life Insurance Company Moves into New Building," *Baltimore,* January 1940, 31.

104. "Monumental Life Erects Office Building," *Power Pictorial,* no. 44 (February 1940): 16.

105. "New Telephone Headquarters Will Be Served by Purchased Power and Steam," ibid., no. 45 (August 1940): 10; "New Business Office of C.&P. Telephone Company Opened on April 28," *Baltimore,* May 1941.

106. Fred B. Shoken, "Montgomery Ward Warehouse & Retail Store," nomination form, National Register of Historic Places, 2000, sec. 8.

107. Peter Kurtze and Edward Perlman, "Hutzler Brothers Palace Building," nomination form, National Register of Historic Places, 1984, sec. 7, p. 1.

108. Ibid., sec. 8, p. 4.

109. Russell Wright, "Greater Hutzlers," nomination form, National Register of Historic Places, 1978, sec. 7.

110. "Hutzler Brothers Co. Starts Large Addition," *Power Pictorial,* no. 47 (June 1941): 15.

111. "Hutzler Brothers' New Store," *Baltimore Magazine,* October 1932. Recently, Michael J. Lisicky produced a wonderful book-length treatment of the company, *Hutzler's: Where Baltimore Shops* (Charleston, SC: History Press, 2009).

112. Jennifer Goold, "Hochschild, Kohn Belvedere and Hess Shoes," nomination form, National Register of Historic Places, 2003, sec. 8.

113. *Power Pictorial,* no. 30 (December 1934): 25–26.

114. Jacques Kelly, "You Can't Run Right to Read's," *Baltimore News American,* 7 August 1977.

115. "Read's Opens Wonder Store to Public," *Baltimore News and Post,* 21 September 1934, Vertical Files, Maryland Department, Enoch Pratt Free Library, Baltimore.

116. Janet Davis, "S. S. Kresge Store No. 20," Historic Sites Inventory Form, Maryland Historical Trust, 1985, sec. 8.

117. "McCrory Stores Return to Lexington Street," *Power Pictorial,* no. 18 (December 1930): 60.

118. "A New Department Store for Baltimore," ibid., no. 16 (June 1930): 61.

119. See the advertisement for Carl, Inc., in *Gardens, Houses and People* 12, no. 12 (December 1937): 19.

120. Janet L. Davis and Fred B. Shoken, "The Sena-

tor Theater," nomination form, National Register of Historic Places, 26 April 1989, sec. 7.

121. Robert K. Headley, *Motion Picture Exhibition in Baltimore: An Illustrated History and Directory of Theaters, 1895–2004* (Jefferson, NC: McFarland, 2006), 194–98 (Ambassador), 221–22 (Bridge), 259–60 (Edgewood).

122. Ibid., 355.

123. Ibid., 257.

124. Ibid., 370.

125. "Modern Note in Entertainment," *Power Pictorial*, no. 43 (September 1939): 7; Headley, *Motion Picture Exhibition in Baltimore*, 230–31.

126. Headley, *Motion Picture Exhibition in Baltimore*, 438.

127. Ibid., 328.

128. Ibid., 340.

129. Ibid., 366.

130. Ibid., 240, 361–62.

131. Patricia Altman and Andrea Schoenfeld, "Colony Theater," Maryland Inventory of Historic Properties Form, Maryland Historical Trust, May 2006.

132. Headley, *Motion Picture Exhibition in Baltimore*, 224–25; Vince Peraino, personal communication, 13 December 2012. The Club Charles, a Baltimore institution, contains original Deco elements, such as the back bar. In the late seventies the owners hired Peraino to redesign the club's interior. When he purchased the murals from the Apex Ladder Company, they were heavily faded and soiled. He used one of the two murals for the club's front room, cleaning and repainting it according to the original color scheme and slightly modifying the original composition by adding wings to a horse. Portions of the second mural were added to the club's back room during a later renovation.

133. "Comfort Cooling an Essential Feature of New Construction," *Power Pictorial*, no. 40 (July 1938): 31.

134. Gilbert Sandler, "One From Column A, One From Column B," *Baltimore Magazine*, February 1989, 70; "War Interest in China Booms Baltimore Restaurant Trade," *Baltimore Sun*, 17 August 1942.

135. Baltimore City directories, 1930, 1936, 1937, 1940, and 1942. In 1930 the space at 227–231 Redwood was vacant, but the city directories of 1936, 1937, 1940, and 1942 list Edward A. Belaga as the owner of a restaurant in the current Werner's location.

136. M. Roseman, "Fluorescent Lighting . . . A 1940 Sales Outlet," *Signs of the Time: The National Journal of Display Advertising*, January 1940, 22–23.

137. Carol Jean Keiser, "Hanging Out at Alonso's," *Baltimore Messenger*, 10 August 1979, 4–5.

138. "Bus Terminal Rises on North Howard Street," *Power Pictorial*, no. 49 (August 1942): 11.

139. "Brooks-Price Company," *Baltimore Sun*, 1 October 1938.

140. *Power Pictorial*, no. 17 (September 1930): 64–65.

141. "Martin Brothers in Business 25 Years," newspaper clipping, 30 June 1934, Vertical Files, Maryland Department, Enoch Pratt Free Library, Baltimore.

142. "Cloverland Farms Dairy," *Power Pictorial*, no. 15 (December 1929): 55; "Cloverland Buzzings," ibid., no. 18 (December 1930): 68–69; "Cloverland Dairy Acquires Stark Ice Plant," ibid., no. 51 (August 1943): 17–18.

143. "The Milky Way from Farm to Table," *Gardens,*

*Houses and People* 12, no. 12 (December 1937): 21; "... and now Green Spring Dairy presents," *Evening Sun*, 13 December 1937.

144. "Albert F. Goetze, Inc. Expands Again!," *Grocer's Skirmisher*, May 1939; "City Among Top 10 Meat Producers," *Baltimore Sun*, 15 January 1961; "Goetze Gives Up Plan to Reorganize," *News American*, 10 June 1975.

145. "National Can Corp. Modernizes on Large Scale," *Power Pictorial*, no. 42 (April 1939).

## CHAPTER 5. PUBLIC AND INSTITUTIONAL ARCHITECTURE

1. On the Justice Department building, see Judith H. Robinson, Sophie Cantrell, and Tim Kerr, "Pennsylvania Avenue National Historic Site," nomination form, National Register of Historic Places, 29 May 2007, sec. 7, p. 74, and sec. 8, p. 163; and Antonio Vasaio, *The Fiftieth Anniversary of the U.S. Department of Justice Building, 1934–1984* (Washington, DC: US Government Printing Office, 1984).

2. Vasaio, *Fiftieth Anniversary*, 41, 43. See also Shirley Reiff Howarth, *C. Paul Jennewein, Sculptor* (Tampa, FL: Tampa Museum, 1980); George Gurney, *Sculpture and the Federal Triangle* (Washington, DC: Smithsonian Institution Press, 1985); and Lois Craig, "Hidden Treasures of a Walled City," *AIA Journal* 67 (June 1978): 21.

3. John Joseph Earley, "Mosaic Ceilings, U.S. Department of Justice Building," *Journal of the American Concrete Institute* 31 (1935): 559; Frederick W. Cron, *The Man Who Made Concrete Beautiful: A Biography of John Joseph Earley* (Fort Collins, CO: Centennial, 1977), 49–51.

4. On the Federal Trade Commission building, see Robinson, Cantrell, and Kerr, "Pennsylvania Avenue National Historic Site," sec. 7, p. 76, and sec. 8, p. 164.

5. On the Interior Department building, see David W. Look and Carole L. Perrault, *The Interior Building: Its Architecture and Its Art* (Washington, DC: National Park Service, Preservation Assistance Division, 1986).

6. Nathan C. Wyeth should not be confused with the illustrator N. C. Wyeth, father of the studio artist Andrew Wyeth.

7. On the District of Columbia Municipal Center, see Robinson, Cantrell, and Kerr, "Pennsylvania Avenue National Historic Site," sec. 7, p. 58, and sec. 8, pp. 167–68; and Linda Lyons, "Nathan C. Wyeth and the 'Greco Deco' Style, Part Two: The Municipal Center," *Trans-Lux* 19, no. 2 (June 2001): 5–8. On the Police Memorial Fountain, see Robinson, Cantrell, and Kerr, "Pennsylvania Avenue National Historic Site," sec. 7, pp. 58–59.

8. On the Recorder of Deeds Building, see Robinson, Cantrell, and Kerr, "Pennsylvania Avenue National Historic Site," sec. 8, pp. 168–69; and Linda Lyons, "Nathan C. Wyeth and the 'Greco Deco' Style," *Trans-Lux* 19, no. 1 (March 2001): 5–10. See also "7 Winners Chosen in Mural Contest for Deeds Building," *Washington Star*, 7 April 1943.

9. See "The Folger Shakespeare Library, Washington, D.C.," *Architectural Forum* 56, no. 6 (June 1932): 74; Ernest Allen Connally, "Folger Shakespeare Library," nomination form, National Register of Historic Places, 23 June 1969; Paul Philippe Cret, "Ten Years of Modernism," *Federal Architect* 4, no. 1 (July 1933): 7–12; and Theophilus White, ed., *Paul Philippe Cret: Architect and Teacher* (Cranbury, NJ: Associated University Presses, 1973).

10. Minutes of the Meeting of the Joint Commission to Acquire a Site and Additional Buildings for the Library of Congress, 19 June 1930, Record Group 40, series 40.3, box 6, Archives of the Architect of the Capitol.

11. Record Group 40, series 40.3, box 6, Archives of the Architect of the Capitol.

12. "Minutes of the Meeting of the Joint Commission to Acquire a Site and Additional Buildings for the Library of Congress," 20 June 1934, ibid.

13. James Waldo Fawcett, "Legends Traced On Bronze Doors: Library of Congress Annex Portals Depict Story of Written Word," *Washington Star*, 20 June 1938.

14. "Annex to the Congressional Library," *Federal Architect* 10, no. 2 (October 1939): 15.

15. Ibid.

16. Ibid., 16–17.

17. Ibid., 17.

18. Minutes of the Meeting of the Joint Commission to Acquire a Site and Additional Buildings for the Library of Congress, 10 January 1940, 10, Record Group 40, series 40.3, box 6, Archives of the Architect of the Capitol.

19. See "Elementary School and Community Building, Greenbelt, Md.," *Architectural Forum* 68, no. 3 (March 1938): 234–36; and Cathy D. Knepper, *Greenbelt, Maryland: A Living Legacy of the New Deal* (Baltimore: Johns Hopkins University Press, 2001), 21, 34, 48, 54, 56, 150, 215.

20. On the Greenbelt School preservation case, see "Greenbelt School Case, 1983–1996," Richard Striner Historic Preservation Papers, Historical Society of Washington, DC, series 1, folders 4–5.

21. John Russell Mason, "George Washington University's New Library," *Library Journal*, 1 November 1940, 908–9.

22. A subtle Art Deco influence can also be seen in some terra-cotta ornamentation of the 1930 monastery of the Franciscan Friars of the Holy Name Province at 14th and Shepherd Streets NE. This building, affiliated with Holy Name College, was designed by Chester Oakley.

23. Linda Lyons, "National Naval Medical Center Honors F.D.R.'s Design Role," *Trans-Lux* 13, no. 4 (January 1997): 1–2; William Offutt, *Bethesda: A Social History of the Area through World War II* (Bethesda, MD: Innovation Game, 1996), 454, 456–57.

24. See James M. Goode, "Flying High: The Origin and Design of National Airport," *Washington History* 1, no. 2 (Fall 1989): 4–25. See also "Washington Airport," special issue, *Federal Architect* 11, no. 4 (April–June 1941); and "Washington National Airport," *Architectural Record* 90, no. 4 (October 1941): 48–57.

25. John Stuart, "The Washington National Airport," *Federal Architect* 11, no. 4 (April–June 1941): 15.

26. See Linda Lyons, "Nathan C. Wyeth and the 'Greco Deco' Style," pt. 3, *Trans-Lux* 18, no. 4 (September 2001): 9–10.

27. Erin E. Brasell, "Central Heating Plant," nomination form, National Register of Historic Places, 12 May 2006.

28. "Calvert Street Bridge, Paul Philippe Cret, Architect, Modjeski, Masters and Case, Engineers," *Architectural Forum* 65, no. 4 (October 1936): 378–79; Donald Beekman Myer, *Bridges and the City of Washington* (Washington, DC: US Commission of Fine Arts, 1974), 70–71.

29. For an image of the original United States Appraisers' Stores building, see Carleton Jones, *Lost Baltimore: A Portfolio of Vanished Buildings* (Baltimore: Johns Hopkins University Press, 1993), 124–25.

30. "War Memorial Building Nearing Completion," *Baltimore Municipal Journal* 7, no. 6 (25 March 1924): 1, 3; "Report Submitted on War Memorial," ibid. 8, no. 14 (25 July 1925): 4.

31. Col. Harry C. Jones, "Many Patriotic Bodies Meet in War Memorial," ibid. 8, no. 14 (25 July 1925): 1, 3–4.

32. Lewis Mumford, "The New Municipal Building," *Evening Sun*, 11 February 1926, sec. 2, p. 23.

33. Jones, *Lost Baltimore*, 92–93, 224–25.

34. "Cornerstone of New Pratt Library is Laid by Mayor," *Baltimore Sun*, 13 January 1932; Stirling Graham, "The New Enoch Pratt Free Library," ibid., 23 October 1932; "Jackson Calls New Library Credit to City," ibid., 12 January 1933.

35. *Architectural Features at the Central Library* and *Art at the Central Library*, undated pamphlets prepared by the Central Branch, Enoch Pratt Free Library, Baltimore.

36. "Notre Dame Completes New Library Building," *Power Pictorial*, no. 58 (December 1941): 27.

37. "Notre Dame Takes Pride in Library," *Catholic Review*, 21 November 1941.

38. *Power Pictorial*, no. 22 (May 1932): 63.

39. *Power Pictorial*, no. 25 (May 1933): 36; "New Junior High School is Accepted," *Baltimore Sun*, 10 July 1934; "200,000-Foot Gym Area in New City High School," ibid., 11 July 1934.

40. Rev. J. Joseph Gallagher, *The Cathedral of Mary Our Queen: The Story of Baltimore's New Cathedral* (Baltimore: Welch, Mirabile, 1960), 2–4, 8.

41. Eugene F. Kennedy Jr., "The New Catholic Cathedral," *Baltimore Engineer* 25, no. 4 (April 1960): 8, 14–15.

42. Ibid., 15.

43. Kathryn Geraghty, "5 Years, 1,000 Men, $8,500,000 Fulfill a Dream," *Baltimore Sun*, 15 November 1959.

44. Gallagher, *Cathedral of Mary Our Queen*, 55.

45. "New Home For an Old Hospital," *Baltimore Sun*, 13 May 1934.

46. *Power Pictorial*, no. 26 (September 1933): 15–16.

47. Ibid., no. 42 (April 1939): 17; *Baltimore Sun*, 31 May 1940.

48. "Baltimore City Hospitals—A New Institution for the Care of a City's Suffering Wards," *Power Pictorial*, no. 21 (January 1932): 88–92; "Luxury is Keynote of New City Hospitals' Nurses Homes," *Baltimore Sun*, 8 February 1932; "Hospital Building Here is Dedicated," *Evening Sun*, 29 April 1935; "Hospital Plans Being Completed," *Baltimore Sun*, 26 October 1932.

49. "Finishing Jewish Charities Building," *Evening Sun*, 1 August 1939; "Jewish Charities Home Dedicated," *Baltimore Sun*, 30 October 1939; Henry W. Levy, "Associated Jewish Charities Agencies Have Spent Over a Million Dollars in Local Refugee Relief in Past Decade," typewritten report, April 1955, in Vertical Files, Maryland Department, Enoch Pratt Free Library, Baltimore; *Baltimore Shalom: A Guide to Baltimore*, printed report, Associated Jewish Charities and Welfare Fund, n.d., in ibid.

50. "Local Projects Comprise 59% of PWA Jobs," *Evening Sun*, 15 June 1937.

51. Brooklyn–Curtis Bay Historical Committee, *A History of Brooklyn–Curtis Bay* (Baltimore: J. C. O'Donovan, 1976), 124–25.

**PRINCIPAL ARCHITECTS**

1. James M. Goode, *Best Addresses: A Century of Washington's Distinguished Apartment Houses* (Washington, DC: Smithsonian Institution Press, 1988), 350; "Joseph H. Abel," *Washington Post*, 30 November 1985, F-4.

2. "John Ahlers Dies; Won Architects' Award," *Baltimore Sun*, 25 July 1983.

3. Frank E. Wrenick, *The Streamline Era Greyhound Terminal: The Architecture of W. S. Arrasmith* (Jefferson, NC: McFarland, 2007).

4. Ibid., 345–46; "Alvin Aubinoe, Builder, Architect, Dies at 71," *Washington Post*, 21 June 1974, B-12; "Alvin L. Aubinoe Dies, Area Builder, Architect," *Washington Star-News*, 21 June 1974.

5. Edward H. Bennett Collection, Ryerson & Burnham Libraries, Art Institute of Chicago, available online at digital-libraries.saic.edu.

6. "R. S. Beresford, Was Architect for Notable Buildings," *Evening Star*, 20 December 1966.

7. "Architect Corning Dead at Sixty Eight," *Washington Post*, 10 December 1957, B-2; "Edward Corning Dies, Architect for Fifty Years," *Evening Star*, 9 December 1957, B-14.

8. See Theophilus White, ed., *Paul Philippe Cret: Architect and Teacher* (Cranbury, NJ: Associated University Presses, 1973); Elizabeth Grossman, "Paul Philippe Cret: Rationalism and Imagery in American Architecture" (PhD diss., Brown University, 1980); Travis McDonald, *Modernized Classicism: The Architecture of Paul Philippe Cret in Washington, D.C.* (MA thesis, University of Virginia, 1980); and Elizabeth Grossman, *The Civic Architecture of Paul Philippe Cret* (Cambridge: Cambridge University Press, 1996).

9. Obituary, *Evening Sun*, 19 July 1939.

10. Frederick W. Cron, *The Man Who Made Concrete Beautiful: A Biography of John Joseph Earley* (Fort Collins, CO: Centennial, 1977).

11. "The Works of John and Drew Eberson, Architects," *Theatre Catalog, 1948–49* (Philadelphia: Emanuel, 1949), 1–32; Jane Preddy, *Glamour, Glitz, and Sparkle: The Deco Theatres of John Eberson*, annual of the Theatre Historical Society of America, no. 16 (Chicago: Theatre Historical Society of America, 1989).

12. Morris Radoff, *The Old Line State: A History of Maryland*, vol. 3 (Baltimore: Historical Record Association, 1956), 1672–74.

13. Goode, *Best Addresses*, 345–46; "Harry Edwards, Architect, Dead," *Washington Post*, 17 January 1958, B-2.

14. Douglas Swaim, ed., *Cabins and Castles: The History & Architecture of Buncombe County, North Carolina* (Asheville: Historic Resources Commission of Asheville and Buncombe County, 1981), 52, 93–94, 171–72. See also toto.lib.unca.edu/WNC _architecture/architects/ellington/ellington_bio.htm.

15. Obituary, *Evening Sun*, 7 January 1963.

16. "Architects' Fellowship Given D. K. E. Fisher, Jr.," *Baltimore Sun*, 12 May 1946; obituary, ibid., 28 January 1978.

17. John Dorsey and James D. Dilts, *A Guide to Baltimore Architecture*, 3d ed. (Centreville, MD: Tidewater, 1997), 399; Charles Belfoure, *AIA Baltimore: A Chapter History from 1870 to 2005* (Baltimore: AIA Baltimore, 2004), 92.

18. Matthew Page Andrews, *Tercentenary History of Maryland* (Chicago: S. J. Clarke, 1925), 3:713–14.

19. "Friz, Architect, Dies in Hospital," *Baltimore Sun*, 23 November 1942; Belfoure, *AIA Baltimore*, 93.

20. Goode, *Best Addresses*, 358–59.

21. Christopher Gray, "An Architect for Stage and Screen," *New York Times*, 10 October 2008; Richard Longstreth, *History On The Line: Testimony in the Cause of Historic Preservation* (Ithaca, NY: Historic Urban Plans and National Council for Preservation Education, 1998), 11.

22. Carolyn Brown, "The Local Architectural Practice During the Interwar Period: An Examination of Porter & Lockie, Architects," 30 November 1989, unpublished study in the files of DC Preservation League; and Stephen Calcott, "Brownley Confectionary Building," nomination form, National Register of Historic Places, 19 July 1994, 16 pp.

23. Obituary, *Baltimore Sun*, 29 January 1941.

24. See www.archives.upenn.edu/people/1800s/medary_milton.html.

25. Carolyn Mesrobian Hickman, "Mihran Mesrobian (1889–1975): Washington Architect," *Design Action 2*, no. 3 (May–June 1983): 1–4; idem, "A Selection of the Architectural Oeuvre of Mihran Mesrobian: Beaux Arts Architect, Washington, D.C." (MA thesis, Tulane University, 1978); "Mihran Mesrobian, 86, Designed Carleton Hotel," *Washington Post*, 26 September 1975; "Mihran Mesrobian, 86, Award-Winning Architect," *Washington Star-News*, 25 September 1975.

26. Frederic Arnold Kummer, *The Free State of Maryland: A History of the State and Its People, 1634–1941* (Baltimore: Historical Record Association, 1941), 966–68.

27. Obituary, *Baltimore Sun*, 8 October 1953.

28. Belfoure, *AIA Baltimore*, 94; Dorsey and Dilts, *Guide to Baltimore Architecture*, 410; "Spokesman for America's Architects," *Baltimore*, June 1966.

29. "Frank G. Pierson, D.C. Architect, Dies," *Evening Star*, 13 October 1941.

30. "Irwin Stevens Porter, District Architect, Dies," *Washington Post*, 4 January 1957; "I. S. Porter, Architect in District," *Washington Star*, 3 January 1957.

31. George S. Koyl, ed., *American Architects Directory* (New York: R. R. Bowker, 1955), 453.

32. See Goode, *Best Addresses*, 339.

33. Ibid., 378; Pamela Scott, "Expansion Architectural Survey Report," Historic Takoma, Inc., for the DC Office of Historic Preservation, 31 October 2002.

34. "Robert O. Scholz, Architect, Builder, In Area 50 Years," *Washington Post*, 8 June 1978, C-16; "Arlington Forest," nomination form, National Register of Historic Places, 2004, sec. 7, pp. 3–4.

35. Obituary, *Baltimore Sun*, 10 September 1931.

36. Matthew Page Andrews, *Tercentenary History of Maryland* (Chicago: S. J. Clarke, 1925), 4:450–53; Natalie Webb Oles, "A Blueprint for Longevity," *Baltimore Messenger*, 19 March 1980, 6–7.

37. "R. E. Lee Taylor, '01," *University of Virginia Alumni News*, September–October 1935; "R. E. Lee Taylor, Architect, Dies," *Evening Sun*, 23 June 1952; "R. E. L. Taylor Services Set," *Baltimore Sun*, 24 June 1952.

38. Koyl, *American Architects Directory*, 580.

39. Ralph T. Walker, *Ralph Walker, Architect* (New York: Henahan House, 1957); Wolf Von Eckardt, "Ralph Walker, 'Architect of Century,'" *Washington Post*, 19 January 1973.

40. "Harvey Warwick, Architect for Colonial Village," *Evening Star*, 18 July 1972, B-4; Richard Longstreth, ed., *Housing Washington: Two Centuries of Residential Development and Planning in the National Capital Area* (Chicago: Center for American Places at Columbia College Chicago and University of Chicago Press, 2010), chap. 8, p. 14; Dennis Domer, "Escaping the City: New Deal Housing and Gustave Ring's Garden Apartment Villages," in *Urban Forms, Suburban Dreams*, ed. Malcolm Quantrill and Bruce Webb (College Station: Texas A&M University Press, 1993), 77.

41. Obituary, *Baltimore Sun*, 25 October 1946; obituary (White Jr.), *Evening Sun*, 15 August 1944.

42. Radoff, *Old Line State*, 1425–28.

43. "A. H. Wilson, Designer of D.C. Buildings, Dies," *Washington Star*, 20 January 1956.

44. Dorsey and Dilts, *Guide to Baltimore Architecture*, 419.

45. Harry Gabbett, "Nathan C. Wyeth, Architect for D.C., Is Dead Here at 93," *Washington Post*, 31 August 1963; M. M. Flatley, "Architect's Widow Recalls

the Past," *Washington Star*, 13 December 1970, F-1, F-3.

46. "Architect Is Found Shot To Death Here: Joseph Younger, Designer of Kennedy-Warren Is Gun Victim," *Washington Post*, 16 May 1932; "Architect Tests Gun And Then Ends Life In Apartment: Wife Looks On Helplessly as Joseph Younger Fires Bullet Into Heart," *Washington Star*, 16 May 1932.

47. Albert Zink to Robert K. Headley Jr., 21 August 1971, in Richard Striner's possession; Sherry Cucchiella, *Baltimore Deco: An Architectural Survey of Art Deco in Baltimore* (Baltimore: Maclay & Associates, 1984), 59.

The literatures pertaining to this study are vast. Since any effort to provide a truly comprehensive bibliographical coverage here would be impractical, this essay is deliberately brief. Full publication information is given here only for works not cited in the notes; for those works that are cited in the notes, short citations are given here.

On the subject of Art Deco, endnote 4 to chapter 1 presents an extended chronological list of the major works. The earliest and most influential works were *Art Deco*, by Bevis Hillier (1968), and "The Moderne in the U.S., 1920–1941," by David Gebhard (1970) (chap. 1, nn. 1 and 2). Amid the controversies surrounding the definition of *Art Deco*, this study is grounded in the interpretation of Richard Striner in his essay "Art Deco: Polemics and Synthesis" (1990). For a useful critique of "style" as an interpretive construct in architectural history, see Richard Longstreth, "The Problem with 'Style,'" in *The Forum: Bulletin of the Committee on Preservation, Society of Architectural Historians* 6 (December 1984): 1–4.

The scholarship of James Goode on particular buildings and building types has enriched the study of Art Deco design in greater Washington tremendously. In particular, his book *Best Addresses: A Century of Washington's Distinguished Apartment Houses* (1988) is invaluable, and his article "Flying High: The Origin and Design of National Airport" (1989) is also extremely useful.

On movie-theater design in Washington and Baltimore, the work of Robert K. Headley is basic and comprehensive, especially his *Motion Picture Exhibition in Washington, D.C.: An Illustrated History of Parlors, Palaces and Multiplexes in the Metropolitan Area, 1894–1997* (1999) and *Motion Picture Exhibition in Baltimore: An Illustrated History of Theaters, 1895–2004* (2006). Douglas Gomery's "A Movie-Going Capital: Washington, D.C., in the History of Movie Presentation" (1997) provides a wealth of additional information on the Washington scene.

Certain buildings and architects covered in this book have been the subjects of monographic study. On the Greyhound bus terminals of Washington and Baltimore, Frank Wrenick's *Streamline Era Greyhound Terminal: The Architecture of W. S. Arrasmith* (2007) is extremely helpful. On the Department of Justice building, see Antonio Vasaio's *The Fiftieth Anniversary of the U.S. Department of Justice Building, 1934–1984* (1984). On the architect Paul Philippe Cret, the book to read is still Theophilus White, *Paul Philippe Cret, Architect and Teacher* (1973). On John Joseph Earley, the maverick master of concrete mosaic, the standard work is still Frederick W. Cron's *The Man Who Made Concrete Beautiful: A Biography of John Joseph Earley* (1977). On Mihran Mesrobian, see Carolyn Mesrobian Hickman, "Mihran Mesrobian (1889–1975): Washington Architect" (1983). On Hilyard Robinson, there is Kelly Anne Quinn's doctoral dissertation, "Making Modern Homes: A History of Langston Terrace Dwellings, A New Deal Housing Program in Washington, D.C." (2007). Michael Lisicky's well-illustrated *Hutzler's: Where Baltimore Shops* (2009) chronicles the Hutzler Brothers Company.

Various multiauthored books on local history contain useful information on Art Deco buildings in Washington, especially *Washington at Home: An Illustrated History of Neighborhoods in the Nation's Capital*, edited by Kathryn Schneider Smith (2010).

Richard Longstreth, past president of the Society of Architectural Historians, has set an exemplary standard in his interdisciplinary approach to architectural history, encompassing wide-ranging studies of building types and locales, as well as business and industrial trends, demographics, and cultural patterns as they affected architecture. Several of his studies have contributed not only to a greater understanding of particular Art Deco buildings in Washington but to their preservation as well. Among his key works cited in the notes are *History On The Line: Testimony in the Cause of Historic Preservation* (1998); "The Neighborhood Shopping Center in Washington, D.C., 1930–1941" (1992); "Silver Spring: Georgia Avenue, Colesville Road, and the Creation of an Alternative 'Downtown' for Metropolitan Washington" (1994); and "Sears, Roebuck and the Remaking of the Department Store, 1924–42" (2006).

Useful sources on the history of Greenbelt, Maryland, are Cathy D. Knepper, *Greenbelt, Maryland: A Living Legacy of the New Deal* (2001); and Mary Lou Williamson, ed., *Greenbelt: History of a New Town, 1937–1987* (1987).

*Trans-Lux*, the quarterly newsletter of the Art Deco Society of Washington, has featured useful articles on a number of Art Deco buildings and architects, especially those by Glen Leiner, who has written on the architect Gertrude Sawyer as well as on the Langston Terrace project of Hilyard Robinson, and Linda Lyons, who has written on the National Naval Medical Center and the District of Columbia municipal buildings of Nathan C. Wyeth.

District of Columbia building permits for many of the Washington Art Deco buildings are preserved on microfilm at the National Archives. The Washingtoniana Division of the Martin Luther King Library, in Washington, DC, has useful newspaper clippings in its vertical files.

Christopher Weeks's chapter "Modernisms, Modernists, and Modernity, 1904–1955" in Mary Ellen Hayward and Frank R. Shivers's *Architecture of Baltimore: An Illustrated History* (2004) provides a context for Baltimore architecture in the first half of the twentieth century, with coverage of some of Baltimore's better-known Art Deco buildings. John Dorsey and James Dilts's *Guide to Baltimore Architecture* (1997) covers specific buildings from the interwar years as well and provides biographical information on Baltimore architects. Charles Belfoure's *AIA Baltimore: A Chapter History from 1870 to 2005* (2004) is another excellent source on Baltimore architects and their buildings.

Mary Ellen Hayward's unparalleled scholarship in *The Baltimore Rowhouse* (Princeton Architectural Press, 1999), with Charles Belfoure, and *Baltimore's Alley Houses: Homes for Working People since the 1780s* (Baltimore: Johns Hopkins University Press, 2008) brings to life Baltimore's ubiquitous and most enduring residential forms. Without her work, we could not properly understand the less common residential architectural trends.

At the Maryland Department of the Enoch Pratt Free Library, both the vertical files and the photographic collection are particularly rich sources of information on Baltimore in the 1930s. The convergence of a new library facility; the visionary leadership of Dr. Joseph Wheeler, director of the Pratt from 1926 to 1945; and researchers working at the Pratt under the WPA's Federal Writers' Project during the New Deal help account for the deep coverage of the thirties.

For research on Art Deco buildings in both Washington and Baltimore, we used newspaper coverage on microfilm as well as the national architecture periodicals—*Architectural Forum, Architectural Record, Pencil Points, Federal Architect*—and trade journals of various industries, including *Bus Transportation, Theatre Catalog, Better Theatres, Film Daily Year Book of Motion Pictures*, and *Women's Wear Daily*, among others.

George Washington University campus, 172

glass block, 31, 32, 34, 43, 51, 55, 72, 80–82, 122

Glen Echo amusement park (Glen Echo, Maryland), 108

Glenn L. Martin Company administration building (Baltimore), 19

Glover Park (Washington), 39–41

Goetze's Meats plant (Baltimore), 156

Gomery, Douglas, 233

Goode, James, 233

Goodhue, Bertram Grosvenor, 1, 10–11, 15, 159, 172, 178, 180

Goodman, Charles M., 16, 173, 176

Governor Shepherd apartment building (Washington), 32, 34–35, 213n19

Great Depression, 4, 5, 11–17, 20–21, 53, 90

Greater Hutzler's building (Baltimore), 20, 133–35

Greenbelt Center School (Greenbelt, Maryland), 15, 169–72, 228n20

Greenbelt, Maryland, 15, 46–48, 84–85, 90, 169–72

Greenbelt Shopping Center (Greenbelt, Maryland), 84–85

Greenbelt Theater (Greenbelt, Maryland), 85, 90

Green Spring dairy building (Baltimore), 154

Gregory, John, 161, 162

Gregory, Waylande, 161

Greyhound Bus Terminal (Baltimore), 21, 153

Greyhound Bus Terminal (Washington), 16, 116–20, 224n90

Greyhound Lines, 16, 116–19, 210n24

Gross, Chaim, 160

Gwenwood apartment building (Washington), 31

Hahn shoe stores (Washington), 76–77

Hajoca building (Baltimore), 154

hamburger stands, 114–15, 150

Hamlin, Talbot, 7, 8

Harrison, David H., 146

Harvard Hall apartment building (Washington), 212n3

Headley, Robert K., 233

Heaton, Arthur, 84

Hecht Company, 80–83

Hecht Company branch store (Silver Spring, Maryland), 82–83, 219n20

Hecht Company Warehouse (Washington), 34, 80–82, 218n15

Heidelbach Company building (Baltimore), 140

Hermant, Leon, 177

Herzog Men's Wear (Washington), 76

Heurich Building (Washington), 74–75

Heyder, Frank O., 193

Highland theater (Baltimore), 101

High Towers apartment building (Washington), 31

Hillegeist, C. H., 86

Hillen Lounge (Baltimore), 150, 152

Hillier, Bevis, 1, 233

Hitchcock, Henry-Russell, 3, 6

Hitler, Adolf, 5, 17

Hochschild, Kohn & Company store building (Baltimore), 135–36

Hoffmann, Josef, 1

Holabird & Root, 79

Home theater (Washington), 104–6

Hoover, Herbert, 5, 10, 11–12

Hopkins, Harry, 13, 18, 29

Hostache, Ellow H., 6

Hot Shoppe restaurants, 14, 116

House of Tomorrow (Baltimore), 65, 67

Howard, Ebenezer, 37

Howard Johnson restaurants, 115–16, 224n83

Hudiakoff, Andres, 93

Hutzler Brothers department store building (Baltimore), 20, 133–35

Hyattsville theater (Hyattsville, Maryland), 101

Ickes, Harold, 5, 13, 15, 45

Imperial Bowling Alleys (Baltimore), 148

Interior Department Building (Washington), 5, 161

International Style, 6, 8, 35, 43, 45, 47, 48, 64, 68, 173

Jackson, Howard, 20–21, 62, 135, 180

J. C. Penney store (Silver Spring, Maryland), 87

Jefferson Memorial, 8

Jennewein, Carl Paul, 160

Johns Hopkins Applied Physics Laboratory (Silver Spring, Maryland), 18, 42

Johnson, Philip, 6

Joseph Urban Associates, 110

Julian, William Alexander, 86

Justement, Louis, 39

Justice Department building (Washington), 14, 159–60